W9-BSL-548

DISCARD

BLOOMINGTON
PUBLIC LIBRARY

MAY   2011

BULLPEN
DIARIES

ALSO BY CHARLEY ROSEN

NONFICTION

The First Tip-Off: The Incredible Story of the Birth of the NBA (2008)
The Pivotal Season (2005)
Chocolate Thunder (with Darryl Dawkins, 2003)
More Than a Game (with Phil Jackson, 2002)
The Wizard of Odds (2001)
Players and Pretenders (1981)
God, Man, and Basketball Jones (1979)
Scandals of '51 (1978)
Maverick (with Phil Jackson, 1976)

FICTION

No Blood, No Foul (2008)
Barney Polan's Game (1998)
The House of Moses All-Stars (1996)
The Cockroach Basketball League (1992)
A Mile Above the Rim (1976)
Have Jump Shot Will Travel (1975)

BULLPEN DIARIES

Mariano Rivera, Bronx Dreams,
Pinstripe Legends, and the Future of
THE NEW YORK YANKEES

CHARLEY ROSEN

HARPER
An Imprint of HarperCollins*Publishers*
www.harpercollins.com

BULLPEN DIARIES. Copyright © 2011 by Charley Rosen. All rights reserved. Printed in the United States of America. No part of this book may be used or reproduced in any manner whatsoever without written permission except in the case of brief quotations embodied in critical articles and reviews. For information, address HarperCollins Publishers, 10 East 53rd Street, New York, NY 10022.

HarperCollins books may be purchased for educational, business, or sales promotional use. For information, please write: Special Markets Department, HarperCollins Publishers, 10 East 53rd Street, New York, NY 10022.

FIRST EDITION

Designed by Renato Stanisic

Library of Congress Cataloging-in-Publication Data has been applied for.

ISBN: 978-0-06-200598-4

11   12   13   14   15   OV/RRD   10   9   8   7   6   5   4   3   2   1

To the late Bob Feller,
A great man and a great pitcher

Baseball is ninety percent mental and the other half is physical.

—Yogi Berra

CONTENTS

A Fan's Notes xi

PART ONE

Screwballs and Blazers 3

Mighty Mo and the Rating System 7

Mariano Rivera's Childhood 13

The Yanks' Biggest Riddle 17

Pitch Count Phil 23

What Pitch Count? 29

Memory Lane: Bob Feller and the Motorcycle 33

Assembling the Bullpen in the Off-Season 35

Spring Training 45

The Yankees' Minor Leaguers 49

Between the Lines: Why Grades? 57

Behind the Scenes: Visiting the New Yankees' Bullpen 61

PART TWO

APRIL 2010 67

Memory Lane: The Home of Champions 101

MAY 2010 107

Memory Lane: A Truly Blown Save 153

JUNE 2010 157

Memory Lane: Yogi, Joe, and Knuckleballers 189

JULY 2010 193

JULY 12–15, ALL-STAR BREAK 203

JULY 2010 AND OLD-TIMERS' DAY 207
A Hot August Night, Triple-A Ball, and Yankee Hopefuls 235

AUGUST 2010 249
Memory Lane: Johnny Mize's Bat 283

SEPTEMBER–OCTOBER 2010 287

PART THREE
Memory Lane: An Imperfect Day, Don Larsen, and Me 319
Bullpen Grades for the Entire Regular Season 325
The Playoffs 331
The Yankees' Winning Formula: *Past* 349
The Yankees' Winning Formula: *Future* 353
My Stadium Misadventure 361
Memory Lane: All the Way Home 365

Acknowledgments 369

A Fan's Notes

Any baseball is beautiful. . . . It is a perfect object for a man's hand.
—ROGER ANGELL

Baseball is the only American sport where the defense has the ball.

Moreover, there's a case to be made that no action in sports puts into play more possible outcomes than a baseball thrown from a pitcher's hand, and, arguably, no team player in all of sports is more on the spot than a relief pitcher.

Indeed, with the game on the line, *all* eyes in the stadium and at home are fixated on that lonely soul on the mound. He's even elevated a foot or two above the other players to emphasize both his importance and solitude. Yes, the starting pitcher has a ton of pressure, but while he has time to work things out, the reliever has to come through ASAP. We also watch the hitter, of course, but there will be many of them in succession.

If relief pitchers are unable to take full advantage of favorable matchups at least 80–90 percent of the time, they are liable to get canned faster and more often than any other players.

IN WRITING this book, I have conducted hundreds of hours of in-person and phone interviews with people throughout the Major League Baseball community. Every quote or anecdote you read in these pages comes to me firsthand or from verifiable sources. All of the opposing-team scouts spoke to me on the condition of anonymity.

I charted *every* Yankee reliever's pitch of every game in the 2010 season, but for the sake of my sanity (and yours) I recount in detail only the most important or eventful games, especially those against the Yankees' most intriguing foes: the Red Sox, Rays, Rangers, Mets, and Dodgers, as well as the games that were turning points in the season—or in a reliever's career. I grade every reliever's performance, and also reveal baseball's own pitch-grading system.

Every 2010 game is touched on in some fashion; it's a long season but, as they say, every game counts. (Updates and commentary on 2011 can be found at BullpenDiaries.com.)

⚾ AT APPROPRIATE points throughout this book, I insert player and coach interviews, scouting reports, goings-on with other teams, and current perspectives on player evaluation and game strategy, as well as the Yankees' bigger plans, from the Bronx to the minor leagues. My primary focus is on the bullpen, but one cannot separate their role from that of the starters, defenders, and yes, the hitters.

Still, the bullpen is first and foremost. And as a former athlete myself, I am fascinated by the mechanics of pitching, especially the difficulty of repeating the throwing motion, particularly under in-game pressure. This is similar to the workaday efforts that a basketball player spends on his shooting stroke or a QB on his own throwing motion.

I will also provide several historical perspectives: the evolution of the relief pitcher in baseball, stories about eccentric relievers over the years, some myths about pitch count, a little Yankee trivia, and true stories about all-time Yankee pitching greats (including a wonderful conversation about knuckleballers between Yogi and Joltin' Joe).

Lastly, I have resurrected several personal memories, hopefully for your nostalgic enjoyment, concerning my boyhood proximity to Yankee Stadium.

The 2010 season ended up being a disappointment for the Yankees, and for Yankee fans, but much can be taken from last year as we look ahead to 2011, particularly the future of the bullpen. Additionally, *any* baseball fan has to admit that 2010 was a pretty amazing year—the Year of the Pitcher, a year of bizarre walk-offs and blown calls, with both broken records and broken legs—and many of these reminders and recapitulations will surprise you.

TODAY'S PROFESSIONAL athletes have it easier than ever, but they still put in a full day's work, often late into the night, in front of adoring or heckling crowds, then head off to a 2 A.M. flight to another city, another hotel. Long gone are the easier days of travel in a geographical box circumscribed by the original major league cities of Boston down to DC, over to St. Louis and up to Chicago, an area only one-twentieth the size of this country.

Ballplayers today make a ton of money, and we think we would trade places with them in a second, but it can all go away in a heart-beat: a torn elbow or knee ligament, a string of bad games, and then it's over, someone always ready to take their place on the field.

It is of utmost importance to me to be true to those who play their hearts out for a game that I love, a game that is also a business, but one that we still call our national pastime. I have a journalist's—and a fan's—impatience with a player who isn't successful, but I still root for them, always.

I've been lucky enough to make sports my vocation and avoca-tion. I set several basketball records at Hunter College in New York, coached in the Continental Basketball Association alongside Phil Jackson, and then went on to coach on my own. I coauthored a bestselling book with Phil, penned many more books and magazine articles, and now make my pro hoops column deadline several times a week for two national sports websites. And I still get a thrill out of the tension in a basketball locker room, hearing the noise of the crowd just outside the door. The joy of teamwork, the sweat, the winning. And yes, the badges of injury: a broken nose, a few loose teeth, an achy knee.

Even so, baseball was my first love. Since I grew up in the shadow of Yankee Stadium, my childhood was measured by the dozens of Yankees games I attended every spring, summer, and fall. If I wasn't good enough to play the game on a professional level (I had a pitching tryout at Yankee Stadium after college), I've always wanted to capture the humanity of big league baseball as well as the universe of numbers that governs the game—some real, some overstated in importance. Baseball is a game of fractions and emotion, stats and action, head and heart.

Here is the account of a year in the life of a bunch of guys—some famous, some not-yet, some already out of the game as you read this—who put on Yankee pinstripes, grabbed glove and ball, warmed up in the bullpen, and then walked out into the glare of the most intense spotlight in professional sports to try to throw a ball past the game's best hitters, and won or lost.

⚾ THE BOOK concludes with my predictions for 2011—as well as an overview of the Yankees' team-building strategy over the years—but first a brief comment about the firing, within a few days of the season's end, and while I was finishing this book, of pitching coach David Eiland.

Every player or scout I spoke to had nothing but praise for Eiland, and as you will see, it runs throughout this book. His firing, for unexplained personal reasons, does not diminish one iota what he accomplished for his players and team. It remains to be seen how his successor, Larry Rothschild, performs, but I was hoping Eiland would be succeeded by Mike Harkey, whom I spoke to this year and got a good feeling for.

Let's see how it all plays out in 2011, hopefully a season where the Yankees can put all the pieces together for another run to the World Series.

First, let's see how we got to this point in baseball bullpen history.

PART ONE

Great relievers of the past, Mariano Rivera's
impressive stature, spring-training preparations, the
farm system, and a quiet Stadium moment

Screwballs and Blazers

Baseball is a game where a curve is an optical illusion,
a screwball can be a pitch or a person, stealing is legal, and you can spit
anywhere you like except in the umpire's eye or on the ball.

—JIM MURRAY, SPORTSWRITER

The first reliever to achieve a measure of distinction was Firpo Marberry (Washington, Detroit, NY Giants/1923–36). A sometimes starter, he relieved in 365 of his 551 lifetime appearances. Six times he led the American League in games pitched, and he also was MLB's leader in "saves" in five seasons.

Note: Saves didn't become an official stat until 1969, and Marberry's accomplishments in this category were made retrospectively.

In the early 1930s, Johnny Murphy was the Yankees' designated reliever, earning the nickname of "the Fireman."

Murphy was succeeded in the 1940s by another Yankee, Joe Page, who took over the nickname. Though he was possessed of a blazing fastball, Page's career was abbreviated by his raging alcoholism. Yet primarily because of his successes, other ball clubs began looking for specialists who could douse fires ignited by shaky starters.

In the early 1950s the Cleveland Indians added a new twist—using Ray Narleski (R) and Don Mossi (L) to match up against opponents on a batter-for-batter basis.

More and more, relievers were employed to finish ball games.

❿ JUST ABOUT every successful relief pitcher had at least one super-duper weapon.

The following were the "junk men":

- With his spectacles, his serious mien, and his lack of notice-able musculature, Jim Konstanty looked more like an ac-countant than a baseball player. But his slow-motion palm ball helped propel the Phillies to the World Series in 1950. *RIP, June 1976.*
- Luis Arroyo saved innumerable games for Whitey Ford with his screwball.
- Hoyt Wilhelm dazzled hitters with his knuckleball until he was forty-nine.
- Bruce Sutter used his signature split-fingered fastball to amass 300 career saves.
- Mike Marshall was a screwball who also threw a screwball. It was Marshall who appeared in a record-setting 106 games for the LA Dodgers in 1974. Because he insisted on using his own personal training methods, Marshall also alienated every manager he ever had.
- Dan Quisenberry had a unique submarine motion. "I discovered a delivery in my flaw," he once said. He also claimed to have seen the future: "It's much like the present, only longer." *RIP, 1998.*
- Just retired, Trevor Hoffman had a wicked change-up of an out-pitch.

Then, the fastballers:

- Goose Gossage had a belligerent presence on the mound and a pea-sized fastball to back up his scowls. (The controversial Gossage has nothing but scorn for today's relievers and has said that it's too easy just having to pitch the 9th; he pitched the 8th *and* 9th.)

- From 1962 to 1965, Dick "the Monster" Radatz absolutely terrorized hitters with his electric fastball. But the strain began to overpower him, and he spent the last three years of his abbreviated career nursing a sore arm.
- Lee Smith used his slider and a rising fastball to set the all-time saves record at the time.
- Ryne Duren wore thick glasses and had a warp-speed fastball. He'd routinely throw his initial warm-up pitch ten feet over the catcher's head just to scare the hitters. Like many closers, Duren sought to alleviate the terrific pressure he pitched under by trying to find solace in alcohol. *RIP, 2011.*
- Rollie Fingers sported a handlebar mustache, a fierce independent nature, and a devastating slider.
- A unique approach: Phil Regan was famous for letting the opponents even the score, then getting credit for the win when the Cubs eventually surged back to win. That's why he was called the Vulture.
- Dave Righetti and Dennis Eckersley became relievers after their starting careers ran out of gas. Eckersley in particular benefited from his time with Tony LaRussa and the A's; LaRussa is often credited with coining the term "closer" just for the 9th-inning guy.
- Both Righetti and Eckersley were, and continue to be, controversial and outspoken about the ills of the game and how contemporary pitchers are handled.

Closers have become so important to the modern game that several have won Cy Young Awards: Eckersley, Fingers, Sutter, Marshall, Sparky Lyle, Eric Gagne, Mark Davis, Steve Bedrosian, and Willie Hernandez. Several won MVPs: Eckersley, Fingers, Hernandez, and Jim Konstanty with the 1950 Phils. (Konstanty actually started Game One of the '50 World Series against the Yanks, and came to the Yanks for a couple of years in the mid-'50s.) Closers in the Hall of Fame include Gossage, Sutter, Eckersley, Fingers, and Hoyt Wilhelm.

As for relievers who garnered World Series MVPs: Fingers, John Wetteland (with the Yanks)—and, of course, Mariano Rivera in '99.

Courtesy of Keith Allison

Mariano Rivera

Mighty Mo and the Rating System

Rivera can hit a gnat in the ass.

—AN OPPOSING TEAM'S SCOUT

Simply put, Mariano Rivera is a freak of nature.

Closers usually have one great pitch and another change-of-speed pitch. From time to time there have been one-pitch closers, but these guys have always been knuckleballers. That makes Rivera's almost exclusive use of his cut-fastball totally unique.

In his prime Mo could throw his cutter in the 95–96 mph range. These days it's clocked at 89–91. The movement is more lateral than vertical, and more than anything resembles a very fast, late-breaking slider. Not until the ball reaches the dirt cutout in front of home plate does Rivera's cutter suddenly dart in to lefties and away from righties. And despite losing velocity over the years, the late action and pinpoint command ensure that Mo's cutter remains virtually unhittable.

He can also shorten or lengthen the movement of his cutter by either slightly raising his release point or lowering it. He'll use the wider break only when the count is in his favor and he wants the hitter to chase a ball out of the K-zone.

The Rating System

Every team in MLB employs an evaluative scale for pitchers that ranges from 20 to 80 (although some use 2.0 to 8.0). Nobody seems to know how, why, or when this rather quirky numerical range was adopted.

In any case, it is universally agreed that a 50 rating is the major league average in the various categories that include the overall effectiveness of a given pitch (whether it be fastball, curve, sinker, slider, change-up, or cutter), how much (and when) the pitch being rated moves in its travel to the plate, and how accurately the pitch can be thrown.

The range for the average collegiate pitcher varies from 35 to 45, which means most have absolutely no chance to ever play in the major leagues. A rating of 80 in any category is the best possible—and rarely achieved—grade, and practically assures that any pitcher who features such an elite weapon is a bona fide All-Star.

Most clubs rate an 89-mph fastball as 45, 90 mph as 50, and 91 mph usually translates into 55. The slight variations inherent in this system depend on the standards set by a specific team's scouting director and/or general manager.

Furthermore, a fastball in the 92–94 mph range is routinely graded in the 60s; 94–96 in the 70s; and a fastball above 96 mph is awarded an 80. In their halcyon days, Randy Johnson, Roger Clemens, Nolan Ryan, and Kevin Brown were the only pitchers in recent memory whose fastballs rated 80s.

But that's just velocity.

The modern scoreboards and televised games all display the radar gun's reading of every pitch thrown in every game—a tendency that has overemphasized velocity. Speed is, after all, the only absolute, inarguable measure, besides the final score. But though most organizations favor power arms (including the Yankees) that are capable of striking out hitters with runners on third base and less than two outs, major league pitching gurus believe that other aspects of a pitcher's arsenal are more important.

The first priority is command of every pitch, then movement. Next is a pitcher's ability to throw all his pitches with the same motion—and velocity is actually last on the list.

The crucial category of command is concerned with accuracy within—and around—the strike zone. Command, however, is a different category than control, which is totally quantitative and judged by the number of bases on balls a pitcher issues. (While an average of three walks per nine innings is an acceptable number, power pitchers can usually exceed this limit with minimal damage because of their propensity to accumulate strikeouts. However, exceeding three walks per game is dangerous for control pitchers who lack blowout stuff. If nibblers can't paint the corners, they must necessarily come in with pitches that are eminently more hittable.) Command is strictly about whether a pitcher can routinely hit the target provided by the catcher's glove.

There are several criteria used in evaluating movement. For a fastball: does it rise, tilt, run, and/or sink? Rising fastballs produce strikeouts and pop-ups. Fastballs that move only laterally produce called strikes, but also line drives. The natural movement on any right-hander's fastball is to run away from a right-handed hitter (RH), and the principle is reversed for lefties pitching to lefties. It's usually the case that sinking fastballs have more depth on the pitcher's-arm side of the strike zone. Roy Halladay is the rare current practitioner who has equally devastating sinking action on both sides of home plate.

Sinkers obviously result in groundballs or swinging misses. However, the fact that catchers must turn their gloves to receive most sinkers has its downsides: the glove's late movement can often cause the umpire to call a ball (the opposite of when a catcher can nudge the glove into the K-zone to get the borderline strike call), and late-breaking sinkers can result in jammed thumbs or, worse, the pitch getting past the catcher.

In evaluating a slider, scouts value depth more than tilt—with the latter being acceptable only if a pitcher deliberately throws one out of the K-zone to tempt a hitter to chase it. In his prime, John Smoltz had the only 80-rated slider in recent times.

The optimum curveball is likewise one that drops more than it swerves. The late St. Louis Cardinal rookie Darryl Kile had an 80 curve. The same vertical action is used to judge change-ups, with Greg Maddux also topping out at 80.

And the universally acclaimed all-time master of the cut-fastball is Mariano Rivera.

⚾ MO'S MOVEMENT of cutter = 80. Movement of his two-seam fastball = 50, which is only average, but good enough to keep batters guessing. This latter pitch will run in on righties and also show some sink. For every twenty cutters, Rivera will throw one two-seamer.

Mo's command of his cutter and two-seam fastball = 80. Only Dennis Eckersley and Trevor Hoffman have reached this top-of-the-line rating. However, in his prime, Satchel Paige's command was off the charts. Instead of using home plate to tune up his command in his pregame warm-ups, Paige had the catcher place a baseball atop the plate and then proceeded to deliver pitches that would nip the tight column of space *over* the corners of the baseball!

While he's not quite in Paige's class, command is the key to Rivera's effectiveness. Indeed, since 2005, Rivera has been extended to a three-ball count by only 14 percent of the hitters he's faced.

Rivera is equally adept at painting the black on both sides of the plate. Generally, he'll keep the ball down but can go up the ladder when this tactic is appropriate. He also likes to jam lefties and throw backdoor cutters to righties. Everybody knows what's usually coming, but his late movement and incredible command still make Rivera so dominant.

Scouts are likewise impressed by Rivera's instincts, athleticism, competitiveness, psychological stability, and work ethic. Plus, another unsurpassed aspect of Rivera's is the ultrarepeatability of his delivery. All of his pitches are made with the exact same motion, release point, and follow-through. With his smooth, effortless delivery and total mastery of the K-zone, Rivera can single-handedly control the pace of an inning.

Rivera never dissembles with the media. Not even after the worst outing of his career, when he "blew" the game that clinched the 2001 World Series for Arizona. Never mind that there had been a freak rain shower during the game that caught the Arizona grounds crew by surprise so that the retractable roof was never closed. Never mind that the ball that was bunted right back to him was slick from rolling through the wet grass, and that Rivera's off-target throw to second base was therefore highly compromised. Never mind that he was eventually beaten by a broken-bat bloop single, aka a "duck fart." Rivera made no postgame excuses or off-the-record complaints even then.

"Mo's a straight-up guy," says one sportswriter. "Even though I'm supposed to be objective, there's no way I can avoid rooting for him. I hope he pitches forever."

⚾ HOWEVER, SOME scouts say that Rivera's forty-year-old pitching arm is, well, forty. But one of MLB's most senior Yankee watchers predicts that Rivera will continue being the game's prime-time closer for another three years. His 2010 season was pretty impressive, despite some surprising ups and downs for him. More on that later.

If he pitches too much or too often, Rivera's arm will sometimes drop and he'll lose his late bite and pinpoint command. But this is a rare occurrence, made even more infrequent because Rivera has the ability to make quick in-game self-corrections—he is one of the few pitchers anywhere who can do that.

In 2007, Boston's lefty sluggers backed off the plate a few inches to prevent Rivera from hammering them inside—and they hurt him on several occasions, until he drew them back toward the plate by routinely clipping the outside corner.

A hitter's game plan? Over the course of his career, righties have hit .218 and lefties .206 against Rivera, so there's no foolproof way to center one of his pitches. The only approach is to be patient and hope he makes a mistake.

YANKEE INSIDERS likewise affirm that Rivera is tops across the board for his honesty, compassion, and humility. He routinely takes the young Latino players under his wing, treating them to meals, advising them on how to deal with the media and the fans, constantly encouraging them, and teaching them the tricks of the trade. His character took shape in Panama.

Mariano Rivera's Childhood

Fishing is a hard job.
—MARIANO RIVERA

Baseball was the most popular sport in Panama. When Rivera and his young buddies first started playing the game, their baseballs were made of fish net and tape, while their bats were fashioned from tree branches and cardboard served as their gloves. Because he was the best athlete and had the best arm, Mariano always played shortstop.

His father, Mariano, Sr., was a fisherman by trade and famous among his fellow residents in the small town of Puerto Caimito for his generosity; he was always eager to lend money, extend credit, or provide whatever assistance he could in emergencies. Indeed, he lived the Christian credo that he so strongly professed. But his father was also committed to raising his four children—Mariano being the second oldest—with a firm hand. Rivera credits the many disciplinary spankings he received for keeping him humble. At the same time, his mother, Delia, was always there to provide comfort and forgiveness.

As a teenager, Mariano worked on his father's fishing boat and was expected to pursue the same livelihood. Mariano later told the New York *Daily News*: "Fishing at night in the rain. You have to be smart and quick. You can't fall asleep on the job because you might get in an accident."

Money was scarce. "But," Rivera continued, "my childhood there was wonderful. Oh man, I didn't have much. Basically I didn't have anything. But I was happy with whatever we had. I tell you what . . . if I can do it all over again, I wouldn't change it. I'd do it exactly the same way we did it back then."

Even though he grew into a gangling 6'4", 160-pounder, casting the nets and pulling on the lines strengthened his biceps and forearms. Yet despite his father's wishes, Mariano abandoned the fisherman's life after three years. His ambition at that time was to study to be an auto mechanic.

MARIANO WAS first noticed on the ball field in 1987 by a local scout named Herb Raybourn, who was then working for the Yankees. When he began his scouting career with the Pirates in the '60s, Raybourn had found and signed such notable Panamanian players as Manny Sanguillen and Rennie Stennett. But as he watched the eighteen-year-old Mariano play shortstop for a local amateur team, Raybourn categorized him as another classic case of good field, no hit.

When Raybourn next saw him a year later, Mariano had become a full-time pitcher. His lively four-seam fastball traveled to home plate at an average speed of only 85 mph, but Mariano also had a loose arm and excellent control. In 1990, and mostly on the basis of Mariano's long-shot potential, Raybourn signed him to a contract worth $3,500.

As he relentlessly progressed through the Yankees' farm system, Mariano was strictly a starter. Adding ten pounds also added 10 mph to his fastball, which was his primary weapon. His repertoire also included a strictly average slider and an extremely hittable change-up.

In 1992, his right elbow required minor surgery, but three years later he was finally called up to the big club. Mariano's major league debut came against the Angels in California, when he was racked for five runs and eight hits in 3⅓ innings. His fastball was certainly a high-quality pitch, and his slider was serviceable, but his change-up was useless and he also lacked any semblance of the fourth pitch that major league starters required. Still, he showed enough stuff to start another nine games in 1995 before being sent to the bullpen for the last two weeks of the season.

In 19 total games with the Yankees in '95, Rivera compiled a record of 5-3, a 5.51 ERA, and in 71 IP yielded 71 hits and was credited with 51 strikeouts. Interesting enough, in his nine late-season relief appearances he failed to record a save.

THEN SOMETHING magical occurred in June 1996. For some still unexplained reason, Rivera was suddenly unable to throw his four-seam fastball in a straight line. Even though he never flipped or twisted his wrist, the ball kept dipping and darting.

For a few weeks, Rivera and then Yankees pitching coach Mel Stottlemyre tried to tame the pitch, but without success.

Then Rivera finally told Stottlemyre, "I'm tired of working at this. Let's let it happen."

That summer and early autumn of 1996, Rivera's cutter became the most devastating pitch in the bigs. His job at that time was to pitch the 7th and 8th innings as the bridge to closer John Wetteland. The following season, after Wetteland signed a free-agent contract with Texas, Mo registered 43 saves as the Yankees' fail-safe closer.

In so doing, he gradually refined the delivery of his spontaneous money pitch. He now consciously holds his index and middle fingers close together with his thumb underneath the ball.

"To me," Rivera told Sports Illustrated's Tom Verducci, "it's really a four-seam fastball with pressure on the middle finger. I don't move my fingers, but at the end it comes off the middle finger. I try to keep that finger on the ball as long as I can."

These days, Rivera is a highly respected, and even a revered, senior citizen of the pen. After doing his preliminary loosening up in the Yankees clubhouse, he'll usually appear in the bullpen by the

6th inning. Then he'll sit beside one or two of his younger compatriots and talk about the theory and practice of relief pitching. In his willingness to share his knowledge, Rivera is even eager to teach the young 'uns how to throw his version of the cutter.

HIS GENEROSITY extends to the residents of Puerto Caimito, where he still maintains a home. Rivera tries getting back every Christmas to present gifts and money to the less fortunate families there.

Rivera is reluctant to discuss his beneficence. All he is willing to say is this: "What I have and what I have accomplished . . . thanks to God . . . it won't change me. No. Because I have a little bit more, that means I'm better than you? No. Unacceptable. That's just the way I am."

He'll continue being the only major leaguer to wear number 42 until he hangs up his spikes. Rivera also possesses five World Series rings, and 559 regular-season and 42 postseason saves.

In addition, Rivera rates 80s across the board for his generosity, humility, and intelligence. All the pitching numbers add up to Rivera's being the number-one closer in the history of the game.

The Yanks' Biggest Riddle

The secret of my success was clean living and a fast-moving outfield.
—LEFTY GOMEZ

Joba Chamberlain has dynamic stuff, and an inventory that could someday conceivably qualify him to be a number-one starter. One scout goes so far as to state: "Chamberlain has the potential to be another Roger Clemens."

Chamberlain's rising fastball usually has extremely good life, hence the movement rating of this pitch is 70. Even though his command of his fastball is only 50, when he pitches high in the K-zone hitters simply cannot catch up with it. That's why his ace gets an overall rating of 70.

His slider is often his out-pitch. Movement = 70; command = 50, which is only average. Still, because of its extraordinarily late and extra-sharp break, what one scout calls Joba's "slider from hell" is rated overall at 70.

On the other side of the ledger, Joba's delivery is anything but smooth. "A lot of grunting and farting and overthrowing," says a scout. "When he misses his intended spot, he misses by plenty."

Yankees pitching coach Dave Eiland is more specific: "When he wants to pitch down and away, he tends to pull his head off-line, which causes him to overstride and rush his delivery. At the same time, doing this will open up his front side prematurely, which will cause the ball to be up and over the plate. Also, his back leg sometimes breaks down, which lowers his arm slot and makes his release angle very inconsistent. It's just that he's still only twenty-four, and in the heat of battle he wants to try harder. He has to stay tall and concentrate on a good finish. He also has to learn that sometimes less is more."

Everybody agrees that Chamberlain is a power-oriented pitcher. "Trouble is," says a scout, "he's too power-minded. So much so that what he really wants to do out there is to embarrass hitters with his velocity."

Courtesy of Rachel Hood

Joba Chamberlain

When he did whiff a hitter to finish an inning, Joba often resorted to making a fist, pulling the chain, and shouting triumphantly. "That's bad shit," says a scout. "It's like a hitter pimping after blasting a homer. Sooner or later, Chamberlain's going to be the cause of a fight."

After having a sensational rookie season coming out of the bullpen in 2008, the following season Joba was shifted into the starting rotation with disappointing results. He began 31 games, pitched 156 innings, allowed 167 hits, walked 76, struck out 113, had a 4.75 ERA and a record of 9-6. Put in the bullpen for the playoffs, Chamberlain responded with 1 walk, 7 whiffs, and 9 hits in 6⅓ innings and substantially reduced his ERA to 2.84.

Out of the bullpen, Joba could hump up his fastball to 97 mph and above—as a starter he routinely threw 89–91 mph. The primary reason was his desire to pace himself and to save his superheat for emergency situations. Unfortunately, he frequently got himself in trouble in the very first inning and could seldom amp up the fires high enough to get the critical strikeouts he needed.

"As soon as a guy got on base against him," a scout observes, "Joba tried to throw 120-mph fastballs, started to rush his delivery, and then his mechanics fell apart. He reacted by rushing his delivery more and more. That's why as a starter he had so much trouble getting out of the first inning without giving up a bunch of runs. I mean, the guy's not a thinker out there. The game speeds up for him mentally. It'll take him a while to mature, and there's always the possibility that he'll never get there. But I wish we had him!"

Eiland also notes some drawbacks that Chamberlain exhibited as a starter: "Sometimes when he falls behind he wants to show the hitter all of his pitches. Yes, Joba does have four pitches, but he doesn't have to use them in every at-bat."

Eiland likewise insists that Joba is very coachable. "During a game, he'll look into the dugout when things start to get out of whack. His look tells me that he knows he's doing something wrong, but he can't quite figure out what it was. I'll make a little gesture to illustrate where he's off, and if I go out to the mound, I'll say to him, 'Stay back. Stay clean.' And more often than not he'll respond."

If Chamberlain's immaturity negatively impacts his performance, his youthful emotionalism makes him overly defensive about his pitching. September 20, 2009, was a Sunday afternoon in Seattle, wherein Joba started and got pounded for seven runs in three innings. Despite his abominable outing, he was jocular when speaking to the postgame media, talking as though he'd just thrown a complete-game three-hit shutout. His attitude was so inappropriate that Yanks skipper Joe Girardi had to lecture him about humility.

Still, everybody agrees that Joba is a nice guy with a good work ethic. Indeed, he always gets to the ballpark before most of his teammates to get his running in, and he's spent many hours in the weight room to harden what used to be a somewhat flabby physique.

Moreover, he chooses to live in New Jersey in order to avoid the party-time temptations of New York, and there are no rumors of his carousing until the wee hours. For sure, his arrest early in 2009 for DUI is a red flag. But, says a scout, "Political correctness aside, Indian youths from Nebraska tend to drink too much."

Hitter's game plan: upset his comfort zone by frequently stepping out of the box. Because he's not a very good athlete, Chamberlain doesn't field his position well, so he can be bunted on. If there's a runner on first, making him throw over will also help shake his concentration. Otherwise, make him throw strikes and be prepared to attack the mistakes he usually makes in the middle of the plate. When/if he gets ahead in the count, hitters will have to swing early to avoid getting his devastating slider.

IT WAS an erratic 2010 for Joba, with him ultimately losing his 8th-inning slot to Kerry Wood. How that all transpired, and what the future holds for him as a Yankee, will be covered in the subsequent game-by-game sections.

Above all, Joba Chamberlain is not likely to ever become a starter because he has a reliever's personality.

The Psychology of Starting vs. Relieving

From 1971 to 1978, Tom House was a savvy reliever for the Braves, Red Sox, and Mariners, and he later earned a Ph.D. in psychology. He is currently the pitching coach at the University of Southern California and has come up with a psychological profile of relief pitchers that MLB teams take for gospel.

"Starters are craftsmen," says House. "They have a plan and can concentrate for long stretches. Relievers shit, fire, and go, and are powered by adrenaline rushes. Relievers are here-and-now guys who would go crazy if they had to sit during the four days between their scheduled starts, especially after a bad outing. Chamberlain fits this profile to a T."

The focus of relievers is strictly of limited duration, and they need unusual stimulation to maintain their concentration.

"They're at their best," says House, "when the excitement in the ballpark is at a maximum level. They embrace bases loaded in the bottom of the ninth in a one-run game. Relief pitchers are gunslingers."

If Joba Chamberlain was too laid-back and lacked intensity as a starter—and if he was barely passable when he started in 2009—then why did the Yankees make such an issue of his competing for the number-five slot in spring training last year? Especially since Phil Hughes would be working to master his change-up?

Because they were interested in appeasing Chamberlain, in keeping his competitive chops up. And they were well aware that the main reason why Chamberlain wanted to be handed the ball at the beginning of a game was that he knew that top-of-the-line starters get paid much more than setup guys.

Still, if Hughes had won the bogus competition even before a pitch was thrown in 2010, there was one scenario that would compel the Yankees to shift Chamberlain's role. Considering the heavy workload that Sabathia, A. J. Burnett, and Andy Pettitte carried in 2009, it was entirely conceivable that at least one of them would suffer a serious injury during the season. Otherwise, Chamberlain already had a seat reserved for him in the bullpen before a pitch was thrown in spring training in 2010.

Let's see if and how he works his way back into a key role this year, but as we know, it's a long season, players get hurt, others are called up, and some, like Joba, could see a comeback.

Pitch Count Phil

It's all about putting the thought in a hitter's head that he's not going to see just two or three different pitches.

—JOE GIRARDI, TO GEORGE KING III OF THE *NEW YORK POST*

Generally speaking, with a few concerns and caveats, Phil Hughes came through as a starter in 2010. A Cy Young–like first half, a subpar second half, and media-obsessed pitch-count tracking, but still, he is a big reason why the Yankees got as far as they did in 2010.

Of all the horses in the race to claim the last starting position at the beginning of last year, virtually all of the Yankees' decision-makers hoped, and expected, that Phil Hughes would emerge as the winner. Hughes had been used exclusively as a starter in the minor leagues as well as in his rookie season in the bigs. In 2009, he became a setup man for the Yankees strictly by accident.

The team kept Hughes on the 2009 opening day roster as insurance against Chien-Ming Wang's being unable to make a complete recovery from the ankle injury that had caused him to miss most of the 2008 season. To give Hughes the pitches necessary to keep his arm strong and his stuff sharp, he was sent to the bullpen, where a vacancy already existed since Chamberlain had been moved into a starting slot.

Hughes' work as a reliever was a revelation. He proved to be so valuable that the Yankees went elsewhere to find a replacement for Wang.

Still, the Yankees remembered Hughes' 7-inning, 1-hit start against Cleveland in 2008 that was cut short only by his suffering a twisted ankle. It was also anticipated that the 2010 season would be Pettitte's last, so Hughes would eventually be moved back into the starting rotation anyway.

"Having both Hughes and Chamberlain in the bullpen in the upcoming season," said Yankees GM Brian Cashman, "would be our strongest team we could have."

And Cashman had the stats to back this up. As a starter in 2009, Hughes had a 3-2 record with a 5.45 ERA. He also notched 31 strikeouts in 34⅔ innings, while batters hit him to the tune of .276. Out of the bullpen, Hughes was 5-1, sported a 1.40 ERA to go along with 65 strikeouts in 51⅓ innings, and held hitters to .172.

"But," Cashman added, "we have to think of the future."

⚾ HUGHES CERTAINLY has enough stuff to be an effective starter. He regularly threw his fastball at 96 mph as a reliever, and ranged from 90 to 94 when he started. His two-seamer sinks and has better movement than his riding four-seamer. Hughes has deceptive arm speed when throwing his down-breaking curve and his strictly average slider. The only catch is that starters usually need four reliable pitches and his change-up is woeful. Fastball = 60. Curve = 65. Slider = 50. Change = 40.

Hughes worked hard on the change-up and increased his change-up rating to 45 before the end of the 2010 season.

"I'm learning to throw it," said Hughes in spring training, "instead of pushing it. But it's a long way from being a finished project."

"Developing a usable change is critical for Hughes," says Eiland. "Last year he didn't throw a single change-up as a reliever. But as a starter, he absolutely needs this fourth pitch as a weapon against lefty hitters."

Overall command = 60. The problem here is simply that Hughes did not throw sufficient innings in the minors to develop pinpoint command.

Hitter's game plan: make him work deep into the count, lay off of his curve when it's down in the K-zone, and wait for him to make a mistake up in the zone with his fastball.

As Hughes comes straight to home plate, his arm action is exemplary, except that his back leg sometimes breaks down and he often overthrows. In addition, he uses a fair amount of effort to throw 92, and when he muscles the ball, he loses his feel, makes mistakes up in the K-zone, and also issues an inordinate number of walks. Because of this flaw, Hughes lacks the command and control to ever be a closer (plus he doesn't have that one super pitch that closers need), which means that if he weren't moved into the rotation, he would've been relegated to being a setup man.

Dave Eiland points to another part of Hughes' delivery that needs to be rectified: "It's all about how he holds his hands before he releases the ball. A pitcher's last balance point before moving into his delivery is when his hands are braced over the rubber. When he's set and balanced, he must be mindful of separating his hands before leaving the rubber. Too many times, Hughes holds his hands together too long and his balance is compromised. For Hughes, this is more of a mental challenge than a physical one."

Hughes, like every young pitcher, has several other critical areas that need to be improved. One is to firm up his somewhat soft body. Another is to overcome the questions that several Yankee watchers have about his work ethic. "Don't get me wrong," says a team insider. "Although Hughes does his assigned tasks and is far from being lazy, he tends to avoid spending that extra time that can greatly accelerate his education. In fact, there are plenty of scouts who believe that Hughes is accomplishing whatever success he has thus far achieved on his stuff alone."

In addition, despite Hughes' being well-grounded, unfailingly respectful, and polite, there's a psychological aspect of his makeup that several scouts are wary of. "He just about shit in his pants during the '09 postseason," says one well-traveled member of this anonymous fraternity. "Just look at his numbers in the playoffs as a whole. Six earned runs in 6⅓ innings. In addition, his delivery was more laborious and he made too many mistakes in the strike zone."

Eiland begs to disagree, although his demurral is a bit soft around the edges. "It's easy to sit behind the screen and make such judgments," he says. "I do not buy in to the opinion that Hughes was intimidated in the World Series. Besides, I have to believe in and protect my guys."

❂ WITH ALL of the pros and cons percolating in the media and in the Yankee organization, the unspoken truth was that Hughes was destined to become the fifth starter even before spring training officially commenced last year. Only a disaster of immense proportions could've sent him back to the bullpen.

There were, however, still several drawbacks to returning Hughes to the starting rotation: the bullpen would be severely weakened, with Dave Robertson having to be promoted into a setup role along with Chamberlain, leaving a huge gap in the 7th inning. This was something that Cashman had to address during the off-season.

The other problem was Hughes' proposed pitch count. He split the 2008 season between the majors and the minors, but his ankle injury limited him to throwing a total of only 69⅔ innings. And because of the time spent in the bullpen in '09, he pitched only 105⅓ innings. Consequently, if Hughes did become the Yankees' fifth starter, he would simply have to be limited to about 160 innings for the upcoming season.

Working back from that number, given an optimal average of 15 pitches per inning, Hughes had 2,400 bullets available. Since fifth starters are the ones whose turn gets bumped because of rainouts and travel days, Hughes could make approximately 25 starts—which would come out to 96 pitches and 6.4 innings per start.

But, given his often-erratic command, figure that five or at most six innings would be his upper limit—which, in turn, put an added burden on the relief corps.

The Yanks would need to monitor Hughes' pitch count, especially early in the 2010 season, and possibly again this year.

What Pitch Count?

You spend a good piece of your life gripping a baseball and in the end,
it turns out that it was the other way around.

—JIM BOUTON

During the 1883 National League season, the Buffalo Bisons played a total of 98 games. Their star pitcher, Jim "Bud" Galvin, started 75 of those games, finished 72 of them, and wound up hurling 656 innings.

These days, a pitcher who starts 30 games, records 250 innings, and registers three or four complete games is considered to be a workhorse.

In Galvin's day, and for many years thereafter, pitching staffs were composed of two or three starters and three or four relievers. These extra hurlers were usually composed of some combination of rag arms, boozed-up vets who went barhopping with the manager, and youngsters who were still strangers in paradise.

Old-timers like Bud Galvin, Jack Chesbro, Joe "Iron Man" McGinnity, Christy Mathewson, Walter Johnson, and Cy Young could pitch so long and so often for several reasons:

- They threw no elbow-wrenching sliders.
- Spitballs were legal and were thrown with little stress.
- In the dead-ball era, there were fewer hits, fewer runs, and therefore fewer pitches.

- There were no night games, and traveling was relatively easy. Every team in the league fit between Boston and DC, New York and St. Louis.
- Indeed, starting pitchers were so untaxed that many of the best moundsmen were frequently required to pitch double-headers and also in relief of faltering starters.

Today the Yankees, like every other team in MLB, fervently believe in the necessity of tracking and limiting their pitchers' pitch counts—especially with their youngsters. They are convinced that being a successful pitcher is much more difficult nowadays than ever before, particularly in the American League, where a designated hitter bats instead of a usually weak-hitting pitcher. Because the modern-day hitter generally eats better, refrains from smoking, and works diligently in the weight room, today's batsmen are bigger and more powerful than hitters used to be. That means pitchers have to bear down more on every pitch, and therefore exercising caution is both appropriate and necessary.

All of the current professional pitching gurus vividly remember how ruthlessly Billy Martin, in the name of winning *now*, overworked his young pitching staff when he managed the 1980 Oakland A's. Martin's starting rotation featured Rick Langford, Mike Norris, Matt Keough, Steve McCatty, and Brian Kingman.

In that season, Langford led the league with 28 complete games (CG) and 290 innings pitched (IP). Three years later, he developed a sore arm and was out of baseball by 1986. Close behind Langford was Norris, who had 284 IP and 24 CG (Tommy John was a distant third with 16 CG). Norris' arm problems forced him into retirement in 1983, although he did return to Oakland to appear in 14 games in 1990. Keough recorded 20 CG and 250 IP before his arm went dead in 1983. McCatty had 11 CG and 221 IP but managed to persevere despite a perpetually aching arm until 1985. For Kingman, the numbers were 10 CG, 211 IP, and an exit stage right three seasons later.

Or, as one crusty old pitching coach put it, "By the time Martin got through squeezing all the juice out of these kids none of them could wipe their ass without howling in pain."

Another memorable red flag was raised on Dallas Green, when he managed the Mets in 1999. Green allowed Al Leiter to throw 166 pitches in an extra-inning game. The next time out, Leiter threw 136, and then broke down.

If these are the proofs cited by the pitch-counting managers and coaches, there are several experts who take a contrary position.

"It's baloney," says an old-time scout. "Young pitchers aren't given enough time and aren't trusted to pitch themselves out of trouble, which happens to be the best way to develop them. There's no magic number at which a pitcher can break down. Everything depends on the individuals involved. Hey, Mark Prior had a perfect delivery and his arm fell off in a hurry. In 2009, Baltimore shut down its young pitchers with two weeks left in the season. It's nonsense. The biggest result is that too many pitchers look to the dugout when the scoreboard registers their one hundredth pitch."

HALL OF Famer Bob Feller wholeheartedly agrees. Discounting the four years he spent in the service, Feller was easily baseball's best pitcher from 1938 to the late '40s. At age ninety-one, he remains alert and opinionated.

"I used to throw from 120 to 125 pitches in a normal game and pitched over 300 innings several times. I was only hurt once, when I slipped on a mound one opening day in Cleveland. Tallying pitch counts is a sure sign of overcoaching and overmanaging. Pitching coaches are afraid that if one of their guys gets hurt they'll be fired. Today's young pitchers are babied too much, and that's why so many of them know how to throw but never really learn how to *pitch*."

Feller also denies the value of the weight training that today's pitchers undergo. "They're muscle men," he says. "They don't do enough stamina building, like running all-out wind sprints or pitching batting practice in between appearances."

Born and raised on a farm in Van Meter, Iowa, Feller claims to know the secret to avoiding sore arms and elbows: "Kids get into physical trouble due to a lack of strength in their triceps, shoulders, and legs. Doing manual labor builds up strength in the entire body. Look at what the average kid is doing with his time these days . . . playing electronic games, eating junk food, getting obese, doing everything possible to stay away from manual labor. It's a cultural plague."

The rarity of CGs in today's game especially disgusts Feller: "Any man in any profession should finish what he starts."

⚾ FELLER ALSO has a spot in baseball history in helping to measure the speed of a fastball, long before radar guns.

Memory Lane

Bob Feller and the Motorcycle

In the late 1930s and early '40s, Bob Feller was baseball's strikeout king and undisputedly the game's best pitcher. Although he had a backbreaking curveball, Feller's signature pitch was his heater.

In fact, his fastball was so fast that old-timers compared its velocity to the likes of Walter Johnson and Smoky Joe Wood. But without the instruments of modern technology, it was impossible to determine just how many miles per hour Feller's blazer could travel.

One day early in the 1940 season, Feller's Cleveland Indians were in Chicago for a series against the White Sox when Lew Fonseca approached him before a game. At the time, Fonseca headed the Major League Film Division, but he'd once been a player, good enough to lead the American League in hitting (.369) in 1929. Fonseca's idea was to have Feller throw his fastball in direct competition with a speeding motorcycle to determine whether the baseball or the cycle would reach home plate first.

Not knowing the details of the test (which Fonseca would film), Feller showed up wearing civilian clothes, dress shoes, long pants, a white shirt, and a necktie. The experiment was conducted on a street blocked off by the police near Lincoln Park, where the requisite sixty feet and six inches between the rubber and the plate were carefully measured and marked. In lieu of a catcher, the target was a cantaloupe-sized bull's-eye suspended from a wooden frame.

Feller took off his tie, undid the top button of his shirt, and warmed up with Fonseca for a few minutes. When Feller was ready, the driver started his machine and began his run far enough in back of the pitcher so as to pass Rapid Robert motoring at 86 mph just as the ball was released. But the timing was a bit off, and the motorcycle was about two feet beyond Feller when the ball came out of the pitcher's hand.

The test had a pair of incredible outcomes: Feller's first and only pitch zipped through the middle of the target. And the ball beat the motorcycle to the plate by 13 feet.

Using some basic math, the following equations—$86 \div 60.5 = 1.42$; $13 + 60.5 = 73.5 \times 1.42$—determined that the speed of the pitch was 104 mph.

Several years later, Feller was wearing a baseball uniform and pitching from a mound when his ace delivery was measured by an electric-zone device at the Aberdeen Ordnance grounds in Washington, DC, and was clocked at 107.9 mph, the second-fastest pitch ever recorded. (Nolan Ryan is first at 108.1 mph.)

For years afterward, Feller often showed the film of the event whenever he made a public appearance (followed by footage of Abbott and Costello's famous "Who's on First?" skit).

Seventy years later, Feller's fastball remains the standard of excellence. Although he's ninety years old, he told me this: "I can still throw strikes, and I believe I can at least throw as hard as Stu Miller used to."

Assembling the Bullpen in the Off-Season

*People ask me what I do in winter when there's no baseball.
I'll tell you what I do: I stare out the window and wait for spring.*

—ROGERS HORNSBY

In the off-season, every GM looks to upgrade his starting pitching *and* bullpen, and the interplay comes in when one of the long relievers might be ready for the move up to a starting slot. Long before any players, coaches, or fans make the annual treks to Florida or Arizona with sunscreen and high hopes, MLB brass have evaluated and reevaluated all of their pitchers, arranged a few trades, and made some key guesses and projections.

Last season, GM Brian Cashman and Manager Joe Girardi were all set to promote Phil Hughes to a starter, but they made a show of making it seem that Joba Chamberlain had a shot. Their not-so-secret agenda was fulfilled when Hughes excelled in Tampa, and Joba missed a few days with flu and didn't do well. Still, going into 2010, the Yanks had the luxury of a few other potential fifth starters to consider:

Since righty Alfredo Aceves was 10-1 with a 3.54 ERA in 42 mostly multiple-inning appearances out of the bullpen in 2009, his name was bandied about as being another possibility to fit into the bottom of the rotation in '10. In fact, he had been a starter for many years in the Mexican leagues and had a decent outing in his solitary start for the Yanks in 2009.

Fastball = 50. There's a slight but late sinking action. Cutter = 55. This is employed mostly to jam lefties. Curve = 50. When he's on, the break is a quick one and approaches being a slurve. Change-up = 50. Another pitch used almost exclusively to lefties.

With his decidedly mediocre stuff, his command (60) is the key to his effectiveness. He changes speeds, adds and subtracts on his fastball, and can shave the corners of the K-zone with every pitch he throws. In addition, he's a competitor and is unafraid of contact. Scouts describe him as "a real pitcher."

"I'd take him in a heartbeat" is the universal sentiment.

Like most long men, Aceves has a rubber arm and can get loose in a hurry if he must. In fact, he's usually the guy who steps out of the bullpen to help the Yankee outfielders warm up before innings with long tosses. And once a game reaches the sixth inning, Aceves can get comfortable, since he knows he won't be used. Even though he can go four to five days without game work, it's difficult for pitching coaches and managers to find sufficient innings to keep Aceves and his fellow long men sharp.

Off the field, Aceves is very popular with his teammates. Although he's listed as being twenty-seven, most insiders concede that he's at least thirty, and there are constant clubhouse jokes comparing him to the ageless Satchel Paige. Teammates also kid him about his uniform number, 91, which he's adopted because his favorite athlete of all time is Dennis Rodman.

Aceves' main flaw is the length of his backstroke. "When he drags his arm," notes Eiland, "he loses his leverage and his command, and that's when he gets into trouble. My constant message to Alfredo is 'Get it out and get it up.'"

His long arm action enables lefties to pick up his pitches early. Aceves also tends to quicken his motion on his change, while losing arm speed when delivering his curve. This latter flaw prevents him from getting on top of the ball and pulling it down, so that his curve sometimes breaks too early (or "rolls"). Indeed, it's the mechanics involved in throwing his curve that gets Aceves into his deepest messes.

Many scouts doubt that Aceves can function as a starter over long periods of time. "That's because he's also a bit of a head jerker," a scout notes, "so hitters can get used to his motion and see him better the second time through the batting order. Aceves has a history of pitching well early in the season and also against teams that haven't seen much of him before. The more hitters see him the more they hit him."

⚾ IN 2009, Sergio Mitre (*Mi-tré*) had two strikes against him: He had been suspended for fifty games at the start of the season for testing positive for an illegal drug. Plus, he was barely a year out of Tommy John surgery, when the normal recuperative time is eighteen months. Perhaps this is why, although he was 3–3 in 12 games, his ERA was a sky-high 6.79.

Before he injured his arm, Mitre was good enough to be a fourth starter (for the Cubs and Marlins), but even then he was far from overpowering. When he gets on top of his fastball, it has good sinking action, but when he throws it high in the K–zone it's as straight as the line drives that usually result. His subpar curve is rated 40.

Eiland indicated that Sergio Mitre's biggest problem is his delivery, but other scouts are more specific: there's too much motion in his delivery, including his bouncing hands, which make it virtually impossible to repeat his release slot from pitch to pitch. This particular flaw is a costly one because his stuff is barely average, and Mitre needs near-perfect command to be effective. If his delivery gets stronger and more consistent, his command will improve and he'll be able to get through a lineup two or three times.

⚾ IF ACEVES and Mitre had the lock on middle relief and spot starting potential, this much of the bullpen for 2010 was also set by opening day: Joba in the 8th and Mo in the 9th.

One-batter relievers, 7th-inning guys, and someone to give Joba and Mo an occasional rest would also be essential. Who else could play a factor in the '10 season, and help the Yankees in future years if they proved themselves worthy and sturdy?

Righty Dave Robertson is used almost exclusively in the 7th inning as a setup man to Joba and Mo. Robertson is still remembered fondly by management and teammates due to his strong play-off work in '09. He got the nickname "Houdini" for coming in twice with runners in scoring position, once each in the ALDS and ALCS, and getting out of the inning.

Robertson's specifics: At 5'11", he uses a unique over-the-top delivery that's the key to his success, simply because there are so few pitchers with similar release points that hitters have trouble picking up the ball—which means they have less time to react. According to Eiland, "Robertson's fastball can get up to 92 or 93 and he has a late back-door cut that moves away from right-handed hitters. But although he has a loose arm, his backstroke can be too long, so occasionally his arm can't catch up with his body and his fastball tends to straighten out."

Several opposing scouts suggest that Robertson learn to throw a sinking two-seamer, something that can be mastered in a week's work of bullpen sessions. Robertson's curve breaks straight down and usually serves as his strikeout pitch. Yet since he quickens his delivery when he throws his change-up, Robertson seldom throws this pitch over the plate simply because hitters find it much easier to track.

Fastball = 50. Curve= 50. Change-up = 40. Overall command = 45.

Despite his average stuff, scouts admire Robertson's fearlessness and feel for the game. "He's an overachiever who routinely makes the unexpected pitch at precisely the right time," says one longtime scout. "If the catcher was solely responsible for calling these surprise pitches, then the whole staff would be following suit, which simply isn't the case. Robertson's still young, but he loves to work in clutch situations and he exudes a quiet cockiness.

However, since he's only five-eleven and 190, he's not big enough to throw on a down plane. It also remains to be seen if his body will hold up over the long haul."

Projected future: doesn't have the stuff to be a closer, but could eventually graduate into a setup role.

DAMASO MARTE (*Mar-té*) is the Yankees' lefty specialist. As a situational pitcher, it's imperative that Marte be able to warm up in a hurry, something that he can do in about five minutes.

Marte was with the Pirates when he first faced the Yankees in 2008, and after helplessly whiffing against him, lefty slugger Jason Giambi opined that he was unhittable. However, when he joined the Yankees as a free agent the following season, Marte was getting hit so hard and so often that Giambi said perhaps the Yankees had made a big mistake and had signed his brother.

During the 2009 World Baseball Classic, Marte suffered a sore elbow. As a result, his velocity was down and he had trouble throwing strikes even after he served a long stretch on the Yankees DL. However, some skeptics believed not only that had Marte injured his arm before signing his three-year deal with New York, but that he was still nursing the same injury even after he returned to active duty. "After all," said one insider, "if a guy has been throwing strikes for his entire career and he suddenly can't find the plate with a road map, there's no question that he's hurting."

Indeed, Marte was erratic for most of the '09 season until surprising the Yankees by excelling in the postseason. He struck out Chase Utley and Ryan Howard on three pitches each in Game Six of the World Series against the Phils.

Marte's biggest asset is his deceptive delivery, releasing the ball to lefties from a spot that's behind their heads. In so doing, he throws across his body, something that is much more characteristic of a lefty's deliveries than a righty's. Although this motion can cause arm problems, pitching coach Eiland says this: "He doesn't have a herky-jerky motion so his delivery is not so acute as to do him harm. What does happen, though, is that because of his delivery sometimes Marte's arm slot falls and his pitches flatten out."

In addition, Marte sometimes lands a couple of inches more toward the first-base line than he wants to, which causes him to get under the ball at the release point. The result is a flatter breaking pitch and a loss of command, and by carrying the ball farther to the plate before letting it go, righties see the ball earlier/better.

Fastball = 60. Marte sits on 92 mph but can muscle up to 93. He likes to elevate his fastball, which runs in on lefty hitters. Slider = 60. He actually throws a "slurve" that has a bigger break but less velocity than a slider, and more velocity but less break than a curve. This is his out-pitch against lefties. Against righties he tries to back-door his slurve. Command = 45. But since he mostly pitches to only a single lefty hitter who tends to bail out on his pitches, Damaso Marte can usually get away with making mistakes. Hitter's game plan: Be patient. Lay off the slurve when it's not in the strike zone.

Traditional Thinking

According to Eiland, Yankees manager Joe Girardi, like most managers, is fond of resorting to late-inning matchups, i.e., using lefty pitchers against lefty hitters, and righties vs. righties, but Rivera, Chamberlain, and Robertson are all righties.

"Having only Damaso Marte available," says Eiland, "would definitely inhibit Joe's options."

At the same time, very few teams can afford to carry two lefty specialists. But Eiland also notes that in '09 both Robertson (14-74 for a .189 average) and Alfredo Aceves (32-151 for .212), both righties, were extremely effective against southpaw swingers.

However, several veteran scouts believe that too many managers are slaves to the R vs. R and L vs. L routine.

"They do this," says one scout, "mainly because the media will always second-guess them if a righty gets a key late-inning hit off a lefty. The media's opinions are based only on statistics. Not only that, but the media in general proliferates statistics. And managers hate to be second-guessed. That's why you'll often see a manager using three relievers to get three outs in late-game situations."

This ADHERENCE to percentages ignores a pitcher's instincts and feel for the game, and whether the hitter is hot or not. As a result, several vital aspects of the game that cannot be quantified are vanishing.

"With the managers and pitching coaches making repeated visits to the mound," says the scout, "the game slows down and the fans get bored. I tell you, the whole thing is crazy. Making numbers and percentages the bottom lines comes straight out of the Bill James methodology. The error here is that all of this stuff works backwards from numbers to ability."

Hall of Famer Feller agrees. "All of this righty-righty and lefty-lefty stuff is nonsense," he insists. "Good hitters can hit anybody and good pitchers can get anybody out. Whichever side he bats from, a good hitter in a slump isn't nearly as dangerous as a hot .220 hitter. There's too much of a reliance on stats these days."

Pitchers on the Bubble

In any case, should Girardi decide to keep another situational lefty, the most viable candidate is Boone Logan, obtained from Atlanta in the Brian Bruney transaction.

At twenty-six, and measuring 6'5" and 215 pounds, Logan has appeared in 164 games with the White Sox and Braves, pitching to an astronomical 5.78 ERA and getting spanked by lefty hitters to the tune of a .266 average. If both totals are unacceptable, Logan also has a pair of serious flaws in his delivery: an inconsistent release point, and a propensity to straighten up after the ball leaves his hand, which prevents him from finishing his pitches. But his "ass-and-elbows" delivery sometimes keeps hitters from picking up the ball. Plus, his size enables him to pitch on a down plane and make the hitter feel that he lets go of the ball right in front of the hitter's face.

Even so, professional baseball mavens have long memories and can still recall when, in March 2006, Logan was summoned from a distant minor league field to pitch in one of the Chisox's intrasquad games—where he proceeded to strike out a pair of tough lefties, Rob Mackowiak and Jim Thome.

The Yankees are hoping that the rapture can indeed be recaptured.

Fastball = 60. Movement of fastball = 55. Command of fastball = 40–45.

Slider = 55. Command of slider = 45.

Obviously the Yankees believe that Eiland can smooth out Logan's delivery and therefore increase his command. "Every organization is convinced that they have the capability to cure every player's shortcomings," says another longtime advance scout. "But Logan isn't athletic enough to make the required adjustments. He's not a kid anymore, and he still hasn't gotten it."

At the start of '10, Logan was stashed in Scranton (their Triple-A farm team) as insurance in case Damaso Marte gets hurt or gets routinely bombed.

⚾ CHAD GAUDIN was used mostly as a spot starter in 2009 and only occasionally as a long man. On the plus side, he has long, loose arm action, and his best pitches are a deceptive fastball that shows late life and an above-average change-up. "He's only five-nine," Eiland notes, "and because he tends to leave the rubber before his hands separate he has a poor angle on most of his pitches."

Even worse, Gaudin's pitches are easy for hitters to pick up and he has very poor control of his slurve. "It's ugly when he gets hit hard," a scout claims, "with 450-foot homers launched to the outer reaches of the ballpark. His stuff isn't good enough for him to be anything other than a long man. He is a major league pitcher, but only as the tenth or eleventh man on a staff. He's definitely on the bubble because the Yankees simply don't trust him."

⚾ EVERY YANKEE fan knows the outcome of two key deals Cashman made early in 2010. Bringing back Javier Vazquez as a starter was a failure, and his spring-training acquisition of Chan Ho Park was also a big bust, especially dollar-wise, and Cashman has admitted as much. Both had their moments, just not enough of them. But while the midseason acquisition of Kerry Wood would prove to be huge, to staff an effective bullpen for 2011 guys will need to come off the DL and the Yankees will probably look to a fairly well-stocked farm system and glance at a few trades.

Spring Training

Spring training means flowers, people coming outdoors, sunshine, optimism, and baseball. Spring training is the time to be young again.

Getting Ready to Get Ready

While most organizations are happy to arrange for their young hitters to play winter ball, so they can experience as many at-bats as possible, young pitchers are generally forbidden to do more than limited and noncompetitive tossing. Pitchers, then, are on their own until mid-February, when pitchers and catchers (P&C) report for spring training.

By Christmas at the latest, pitchers will indulge in approximately ten-minute-long sessions of catch with a friend two or three times per week, graduate to long toss, then do some flatwork, i.e., duplicating their delivery and the 60'6" distance between the rubber and the plate on a level surface. After two to three weeks of these preliminaries, and depending on the pertinent geography and climate, the procedure is to locate a nearby port-a-mound (indoors or outdoors) and someone willing to squat and catch. By the commencement of P&C, pitchers are ready to throw anywhere from fifteen to thirty pitches at a time, using 90 percent of their in-game effort.

Throwing in the bullpen every other day once spring training commences, pitchers will quickly increase their load from a starting point of 15–20 pitches that consume 5–8 minutes, to approximately 40 pitches in 15 minutes. Strictly adhering to fastballs is the norm for most pitchers until the third and/or last such session. In between these bullpen workouts, pitchers will run wind sprints and half-speed jogs around the inside perimeter of one of the Yankees' four practice fields, which during P&C are used by both the big and the minor leaguers.

"The killer," says Joe Ausanio, an ex-Yankee (1999–2001), "are the various drills in the Pitchers Fielding Practice, aka the dreaded PFP. Especially when you're from a northern, winter-bound city like me, and the days are hot and steamy in Tampa."

PFP is conducted at several stations scattered among the four adjacent playing fields. Included in the drills:

- Covering first base on groundballs hit to the right side of the diamond, when the pitcher must sprint directly to the base and end up with his back foot placed against the 2B edge of the base as he stretches toward the expected throw.
- Covering first on routine groundball double plays when the first baseman is either fielding the ball or has moved too far from the base to return in time to secure the resulting throw for the second out. In this situation, the pitcher sprints on an angle toward the baseline and then pivots to race toward the base. Since there's an extra throw involved, the pitcher has time to straddle the base to increase his range in case the throw is off-target.
- Fielding situational bunts and throwing to the appropriate base.
- Fielding comebackers and throwing to the appropriate base.
- Fielding high-hoppers, which is especially tricky when the ball comes out of the sun.
- Backing up third base or home.
- Properly executing rundowns.

PFP will continue on a daily basis until the end of camp.

After just two or three bullpen sessions, pitchers must be prepared to throw live batting practice when the rest of the position players arrive in Tampa. After getting loose in the bullpen (20–30 warm-ups, depending on the individual), pitchers will throw from behind a three-quarters screen—with the top left section removed for a right-handed pitcher and the top right for a lefty.

In this procedure, the pitchers are throwing close to 100 percent while working on their mechanics and their stuff, but not necessarily their command. Hitters are alerted as to the identity of each forthcoming pitch, and the radar guns are operational. After throwing 30–40 earnest pitches, the pitcher can return to the bullpen if more work is needed on his mechanics.

Intrasquad games begin about a week before the start of the exhibition season. Given the large number of pitchers in camp, it's necessary to convene pregame bullpen sessions and live BPs until the first cuts and reassignments (to the minor league camp) are made around the Ides of March.

"EARLY IN the season," says one well-seasoned scout, "guys' mechanics are more easily upset than later on. Suddenly lots of pitchers come up with tired arms and instead of their fastball hopping, they're hopping to back up third base. What with the cold weather and the rainouts limiting live pitches, guys will get hurt. It's inevitable."

He continued: "As far as the Yankees' bullpen is concerned, the most important information to be learned in spring training is just how deep their minor league relief pitching is. Everything may be fine and dandy in Florida, but let's see where their bullpen is in April, May, and June."

The Yankees' Minor Leaguers

When and if one of these young men ever gets to the big club,
he can wear his socks any way he wants to.

—NARDI CONTRERAS, YANKEES' ROVING MINOR LEAGUE PITCHING COACH

Gray feathery clouds hang over the four contiguous diamonds that constitute the Tampa practice complex, but the morning is warm, so the young pitchers don't need much time to get loose as they move through their accustomed drills: running backward, then laterally, lifting their knees, walking while swinging their arms, undergoing various upright and prone stretches, climaxed by short and then long tosses.

All of the players are clean-shaven and wear midnight blue caps with the familiar intertwined *N* and *Y* emblazoned in white above the bill. Their matching short-sleeved jerseys feature the iconic NY logo positioned over their hearts, and there are large white-blocked numerals on the backs. Some of the pitchers have already been assigned to the teams in the various classifications where they will begin the season: Triple-A (Scranton/Wilkes-Barre), Double-A (Trenton), Single-A Advanced (Tampa), Single-A (Charleston), Single-A Short Season (Staten Island), or one of the two teams in the rookie league situated in the Dominican Republic. Since the groups are mixed at each of the PFP stations, many of the numerals are duplicated, which is surreal at times.

The uniform pants are adorned with the familiar Yankee pin-stripes and extend to just below the knees, leaving long spaces for the high dark blue stirrup hose. "In the past," says Nardi Contreras, the Yankees' roving minor league pitching coach, "the strike zone used to extend from the letters to just below the knees, and hitters wore their socks that high in hopes of preventing low pitches from being called strikes. But we have them dressed this way just to ensure uniformity. Guys with the big team can suit themselves, so C.C. Sabathia wears his pants down low around his ankles. We also insist that the kids be clean-shaven every day."

With his close-cropped white hair, his angular yet somewhat heart-shaped face, and his soft gray eyes, Contreras has a decidedly avuncular appearance. "I was born and raised here in Tampa," he says, "and Juan Marichal was my hero, so I grew up trying to mimic his delivery. The turned head, the high leg kick, and everything. It was a bad delivery for everybody except Marichal, and I battled a sore arm for most of my career."

Contreras signed out of high school with Cincinnati in 1969 and eventually reached the bigs eleven long years later with the White Sox. In thirteen innings spread over eight games, he pitched to an ERA of 5.93, while yielding a hit to every third batter he faced. He became a minor league pitching coach for Chicago in 1981.

"These days," he says in a voice that is surprisingly soft and lilting, "I see myself as a father figure to these young men." His sweeping gesture includes all of the ball fields, plus the shaded lunch pavilion where we sit. "Whether a kid has signed for millions of dollars or not a single penny, as long as he's in pinstripes I'll treat him like a son. Our aim is to develop them into big league pitchers, hopefully with the Yankees. But this doesn't happen too often."

Contreras takes his time in answering the most simplistic questions, never glancing at his watch, and always maintaining direct eye contact. He used to throw batting practice as he made his rounds of the Yankees' minor league clubs, until he hurt his left foot three years ago and was forced to wear a small brace. "I really miss being out there and communicating with the kids on a totally active level. But I gladly accept God's will in all things."

During the season Contreras will occasionally join the big team's coaching staff for a few days. "I'll do this when a kid that I've been working with in the minors has been called up. Phil Hughes, Joba Chamberlain, Jeff Karstens, Tyler Clippard. I can familiarize the Yankees pitching coach about what to expect from the kid, but my main job at times like those is to make the kid feel as comfortable as possible."

In general, the Yankees look to draft tall pitchers who have power arms. (A guy like Stu Miller, who was a standout reliever from 1952 to 1968 for Baltimore, St. Louis, San Francisco, Philadelphia, and the Mets, would never be drafted these days. That's because his repertoire consisted of only four pitches: slow, slower, slowest, and dead-stop.) But the Yankees generally take their time in differentiating between starters and relievers.

"Just about every pitcher drafted was a starter in Little League and high school," Contreras says. "When he gets to college, though, there might be four holdover starters on scholarship ahead of him, so it's easy to put the new guy in the bullpen. The really high draftees in every organization get the most money, so they need to be starters. If a guy from a small college is drafted, teams can afford to plug him into the bullpen."

A pitcher's repertoire is also a major factor since starters need four "out" pitches while relievers require only two. "In the low minors," Contreras continues, "we'll give most of the kids a first look as a starter and we'll make sure they pitch a lot of innings. But you can't have nine starters on one team. Once it's decided that a youngster's future is in the bullpen, we'll give him extended work. Two or three innings and at least fifty pitches an outing, even if he's predicted as being a closer. The extra work helps him develop his command. The entire organization is committed to doing everything correctly at every level."

No wonder there's a constant focus on protecting young pitchers' arms by attending to their deliveries. "The mechanics are the same for starters and relievers," says Contreras, "but since relievers have to go all out on every pitch, they have more potential for fatigue, which leads to injuries. So we concentrate on maintaining balance. The most critical checkpoints are keeping the chin over the belly and not arching the back before initiating the delivery motion. We want our kids to always separate their hands before moving forward and to keep their heads still. Avoiding unnecessary head movement allows pitchers to read hitters swings. Tom Glavine and Jimmy Key were the best at doing this."

Yet there are some mechanics that the Yankees don't mess with.

"We never change a kid's back-arm swing. The longer the backswing the more power he can generate. And if a kid has a short-arm delivery, we let him be."

(It should be noted that a former major league pitcher and pitching coach vehemently disagrees with this laissez-faire attitude toward short-armers: "A guy needs to use his muscles to get into his release position, and this causes early fatigue. In addition to a loss of power, short-arm deliveries are also conducive to injuries.")

While faulty deliveries can certainly produce injuries, Contreras believes that the main cause is genetics. "A kid can have big, strong muscles," he says, "but weak ligaments."

Much is made in the media of savvy catchers being able to pick up flaws in a pitcher's delivery, but Contreras minimizes this possibility. "Catchers can only see if a guy opens up too early simply because he has to pick up the ball in order to catch it. Anyway, a major league pitcher should be able to make some of his own in-game adjustments. But Rivera is the best at doing this."

Meanwhile, Bob Feller pooh-poohs the modern-day focus on mechanics. "The whole thing is overrated," he says. "The truth is that you can't get out of a pitcher's arm what the Good Lord didn't put in. At best, tweaking a kid's mechanics may add another one or two miles per hour on his fastball. And that's it."

◑ IN ANY case, the Yankees' modus operandi for their neophyte pitchers includes much more than attending to their mechanics. Their game plan ranges from designing individualized off-season exercises aimed at building arm strength, core strength, and cardio endurance to monitoring the caloric and protein content of the breakfasts and lunches provided at the minor league pavilion. The organization has a consulting staff of psychologists available to help kids who may be at risk, and even a director of mental conditioning (Chad Bohling), who teaches relaxation techniques.

"We also have personalized programs for some in-season exercises," Contreras says, "depending on a pitcher's body type and injury history."

In addition, the Yankees are the only MLB team that videotapes their minor leaguers' bullpen sessions, and also times their young pitchers when they run around the inner perimeter of the field to conclude their daily workouts.

"It's all about paying attention to details," says Contreras.

◑ AFTER TOPPING my heartfelt thanks for his time and courtesy by thanking me for my attentions, Contreras resumes his roving: talking to players who wait their turn at the practice stations, conferring with one of the younger coaches to make sure the subsequent drill will be conducted exactly according to procedure, and mussing one guy's hair as they laugh at something Contreras said to him in Spanish.

The other coaches only have what one of them calls "functional Spanish." When a young Latino turns too quickly and makes an off-target throw to second base, the coach says, "Bueno, but too much rapido."

Meanwhile, the groups of pitching hopefuls eagerly trot from station to station for the next stop in PFP routines. Just as quickly, an attendant ground crew rakes, waters, and undertakes whatever minor repairs are necessary to minimize bad bounces and caught spikes. And the coaches at each station make sure to thank the ground crew for their quick and efficient work.

Rating the Future Yankee Relievers

The jewel of the organization's prospective relievers is Romulo Sanchez. Measuring 6'5" and 260 pounds, the right-handed Sanchez has the makeup of the quintessential power pitcher. No surprise, then, that his high-rising, late-moving, 94-plus-mph fastball is rated at 65. Nor that his hard-biting curve is a 55. Throwing these awesome pitches where he wants to is Sanchez's continuing problem. His control rating: 20! And his command: 30! His abysmal lack of accuracy is due to several flaws in his delivery: when he rocks back at the start of his windup, his body has too much lateral movement. His land leg is so stiff that it acts like a wall and causes Sanchez's delivery to be over-the-top and effortful.

"The only possible way to help him," says a scout, "is to have him pitch as many innings as possible." Some observers believe that such poor control and command can never be brought up to major league requirements. Others cite Sandy Koufax and claim that these faults can be fixed, but only if Sanchez has sufficient body awareness and athleticism. Too bad his athleticism rating is 30.

Still, Sanchez will remain on the Yankees' forty-man roster simply because his incredible arm must be protected. Since Sanchez is already twenty-six, it may already be too late for him to realize his full potential, but indeed, if he ever clicks, then he'll be a truly special pitcher. Another consideration is that his trade value could be very high.

- Jason Hirsh once was a starter with a promising future with Houston and Colorado, until he suffered several arm injuries. Both his fastball and his curve are back to 50s, but neither is overpowering. Early in the exhibition season, the Yankees pitched Hirsh a single inning every other day, giving him the opportunity to build back to where he was while trying to develop him as a reliever. He'll be stashed in Scranton and will return to the bigs only in a dire emergency.
- Twenty-three-year-old Ivan Nova stands 6'4" and tips the scales at 210. He's a big youngster with a big arm. His motion is smooth and effortless, which makes him sneaky-fast. His fastball and curve are both rated at 55 to 60. His change-up is below average. Although he's not quite ready for the majors, in the long run he has enough stuff to be a middle man capable of doing an average or even slightly above-average job in the 6th and 7th innings.
- Wilkin De La Rosa is a lefty with a history of starting in the minors but is being groomed as a situational reliever. However, his overall rating = 40, so it's doubtful that he'll ever make the bigs.
- Christian Garcia is a 6'5" right-hander who's been stuck in the mid-minors for several years. Since he's already twenty-five, scouts project Garcia as possibly developing into being a decent pitcher on the Triple-A level.
- Mark Melancon also relies on a 50-rated sinking fastball, but he's very slow getting to his release point, which makes his command much too erratic. Also, this flaw gives base-stealing runners an extra half-step.
- Both Jonathan Albaladejo's fastball and slider are 50-rated. His fastball has a sinking action that's good enough to routinely induce groundballs, but his command of this is a 40. His command of his slider isn't much better: 45. Albaladejo's primary problem is his delivery. When his front side can stay

closed, his fastball has better depth, but the tendency to have his left shoulder fly open flattens his money pitch and makes it hittable. Yet his flaws are ultimately fixable.

- By far the most intriguing pitcher in the organization is 6'11" Andrew Brackman. His 95–97 mph sinking fastie as well as his big-breaking curve both are rated 70—and this is less than two years after undergoing ligament-replacement Tommy John surgery.

Since the Yankees originally signed him for $4.45 million out of North Carolina State, they have always visualized him as eventually being a starter—a number-one starter at that. Too bad his overall control and command are rated between 35 and 40.

Because he's so unusually tall, Brackman's moving parts are bigger than normal, and it's extremely difficult to get his upper- and lower-body mechanics in sync—which means that his development will be agonizingly slow. Brackman worked hard during last off-season to shed twenty pounds, and both Eiland and Contreras devoted many hours in spring training to rebuilding his delivery.

Even so, many scouts affirm that Brackman is essentially a two-pitch guy whose future, if he can ever get his control/command together, is in the Yankees bullpen. The Yanks have exercised his option for 2011.

Between the Lines

They both (statistics & bikinis) show a lot, but not everything.
—TOBY HARRAH

As you read on, it will certainly be reasonable to ask why I employ grades to evaluate each reliever's performance instead of using saves or ERA, the universal measurements.

Here's why:

First of all, many sports have developed a wealth of statistics—maybe too many—but baseball relievers are stuck in a time warp. They have all the same measurements as a starter (except for starts, saves, and inherited runners who score), but there are so many things, good or bad, that can happen to relief pitchers that are unique and that usually go uncounted.

On one side of the ledger:

- Every baseball fan knows about the reliever who comes in with a three-run lead, gives up two runs, and still gets the save—in nail-biting fashion.
- Take the case of a lefty specialist who's inserted into the game to end an inning by getting a lefty hitter out. But the batter walks, is clocked by a pitch, or gets a base hit—and

the manager is forced to burn another reliever. It's a negative appearance that goes uncounted.

- What about the reliever who gets the save, but in doing so gives up a pair of line-drive base hits before the next three batters all crush the ball but the various fielders make circus catches so that no runs score? In this instance, his ERA is lowered, but he certainly didn't pitch well.
- Or the reliever who enters a game with the winning run on second and two outs, coughs up a single to lose the game, but the previous pitcher gets the L—and his own ERA is not impacted at all. Stat-wise it's as if he never played, but in reality he deserves a grade of D or worse (if he's a lefty specialist and the hitter is a lefty).
- Most infuriating is when the reliever blows the save but gets the win when his team comes back.

On the other side of the ledger:

- The middle-inning guy who comes in, keeps the score down, and emerges with nothing except the lowering of his ERA.
- What about the pitcher who's victimized by a broken-bat bloop hit, a checked-swing hit, a swinging bunt, or a hundred-hopper seeing-eye single that brings in the tying run, but otherwise got the other guys out in dramatic fashion. In this instance, the guy's ERA makes a big-time jump.

Too often ERAs, holds, and saves can be bogus numbers. Batting average against a pitcher tells only part of the story, failing to differentiate between clutch hits and meaningless ones. But subjective grades (mine) that (hopefully) border on objectivity are the most inclusive measures of whether a pitcher accomplishes the task his team has asked of him.

How a reliever pitches—not just the outcome—is certainly how managers and coaches judge a reliever and determines whether they can trust him in the next game.

Pitching coaches each have their own evaluative systems, either on paper or in their heads, plus a gut feeling. Dave Eiland seemed to have a good handle on his staff and kept Girardi honestly apprised of who is ready to go on any given day, in any given inning.

Scouts on Pitching Coaches

Several scouts spoke to me about the qualifications of a pitching coach:

> Generally speaking, minor league pitching coaches are better than their counterparts in the majors. That's because they're better teachers, and have less pressure to produce instant results. Major league guys, however, have mastered the proper terminology. Open shoulders, late hand action, and all that. For sure, these things are important, but they can also become catchphrases that gloss over more serious problems. When it comes to hiring a pitching coach, the buddy system too often remains in force.
>
> There's no right way to be a successful pitching coach in the bigs. Dave Duncan, for example, only tweaked mechanics and mostly concentrated on teaching pitchers to read the hitters' swings. Bob Peterson focused on the fine-tuning of mechanics as a way of keeping his guys functional and healthy. Bill Connors, the Yankees guru stationed in Tampa, wants to keep everything simple. He only wants his pitchers to throw strikes. Trouble is, a guy can't throw strikes without good mechanics, and Connors never wants to mess with a pitcher's mechanics.
>
> Catchers rarely become pitching coaches. You'd think that this would be a natural progression, but Duncan is the only one that I can think of offhand. The only other one I can recall is Rube Walker with the Dodgers and the Mets.

Mel Stottlemyre was a wonderful pitching coach for the Yankees, but eventually got fed up with the late George Steinbrenner's interference and quit. I mean, if a young kid had one bad outing, the Boss wanted him sent to Siberia.

Ron Guidry succeeded Stott and was absolutely the worst ever. Guidry never studied videos, never consulted advance scouting reports, didn't like to work, had no communication skills, and didn't have a clue about fixing mechanical flaws. But he had been "Louisiana Lightning," a Yankee icon. Joe Torre wanted Guidry after Mel left, and Joe was too popular, so the brass didn't object. These days, Guidry still shows up in spring training, puts on a Yankee uniform, and helps work out the pitchers in PFP.

The Yankees gambled on Eiland even though he had never coached in the bigs. He got the job primarily on the basis of his work with guys like Chamberlain and Ian Kennedy in Triple-A. But he never flinches, is incredibly honest, and can give positive pep talks and still chew ass in private. He's a tireless worker who's always in the hunt for information. C.C. really likes him, Burnett swears by him, and he's highly respected all around the majors and minors.

"The Yankees got lucky with Eiland" is what one scout said.
Alas, he was pink-slipped immediately after the 2010 season, but was quickly signed by Tampa Bay as a consultant.

Behind the Scenes

Bullpen conversations cover the gambit of male bull sessions.
Sex, religion, politics, sex. Full circle. Occasionally, the game—
or the business—of baseball intrudes.

—JIM BROSNAN, FROM *THE LONG SEASON*

The home team's bullpen at the old gone-but-not-forgotten Yankee Stadium was a long open-air alley situated between the towering right-field grandstand and the much lower edge of the right-center-field bleachers. The players, whether warming up or sitting on the bench parallel to the front gate, were vulnerable to being verbally abused by nearby fans. In the new Stadium, however, the bullpen corps has much more privacy.

It is situated directly below the Mohegan Sun Sports Bar, adjacent to Monument Park, and bordering fair territory in right-centerfield almost exactly between the 385- and 409-foot markers, and I visited one cool spring morning when the Yankees were on the road. I was escorted to, and through, the backstage doorway and left to my own devices as I entered a fully enclosed, air-conditioned room with a bench across the back wall.

To my immediate left was the private bathroom, curiously marked with symbols indicating it could be used by men and women; it was also wheelchair accessible. Probably in accordance with some state law.

Next in my sight line was a small cabinet that was topped by a pile of fluffy white towels alongside a coffee urn. Feeling like a detective, I opened the cabinet and saw several packets of sunflower seeds, some bubble gum, cans of Red Bull and Gatorade, a container of powdered cream, three kinds of instant coffee (vanilla, decaf, and regular), and a half-empty pouch of chewing tobacco.

The players' bench was long and well padded, and there were bright fluorescent lights overhead and a rubberized floor below. From the bench I had to look through a Plexiglas window, past the two outdoor warm-up mounds, and through another Plexiglas window to get a distant view of the infield. From back here it would be impossible to discriminate between balls and strikes.

At the other end of the bench was a water fountain, and a red telephone was mounted on the wall above. Of course, I lifted the receiver and listened to the ringtones, but there was nobody in the Yankees dugout to answer my call.

A stationary bike sat beside the fountain, and a short wall at the end of the room housed a large glass-doored cooler that contained more cans of Red Bull as well as several plastic bottles of water.

I did it all: sat on the bench, sipped from the fountain, then mounted the bike and pumped away for ten seconds. Then I walked through the door next to the cooler and entered the outside area. My reveries were suddenly interrupted by the rumble of the elevated trains behind and above the bleacher wall.

Another red phone was mounted to the wall just outside this door, and a crunchy carpet of fine gray gravel bordered a pair of warm-up mounds on all sides. A long swath of incredibly green manicured grass separated the mounds from the gravel-enclosed home plates.

Three hard-backed wooden benches were set before a low wall holding the Plexiglas window that offered an unobstructed view of the playing field. Since the window was in fair territory, it was topped by a length of thick blue cushioning. Players who had lounged on these benches were apparently in the habit of leaning back and resting their spiked shoes against the window, as the thoroughly scratched Plexi was no longer transparent along the bottom edge.

A rolled-up tarp and a few garden rakes leaned against either sidewall, and three spike-scarred steps led to the gate that opened onto the field.

I've been on this planet for three score years and a few, but my inner child of Yankee worship emerged. Here I stood in what was at least the outer sanctum sanctorum. A blessed pilgrim. An eager supplicant.

What could I do to show my devotion?

Only one act seemed to be appropriate: climb one of the mounds, toe the pitching rubber, and throw a phantom 100-mph fastball that would noiselessly whack into the ghostly glove of the catcher who received my painfully tossed pitches during my tryout at Yankee Stadium so long ago.

I glanced around. Nobody was on the field. Nobody in the stands. I was alone in paradise. I could do the deed and then rake away any signs of my transgression.

Yes! I'd do it! It would be perfect justice! My symbolic atonement for nearly killing scout Johnny Johnston with a ball I threw over the catcher's head and into the stands! A different stadium, but Yankee Stadium nonetheless.

I stepped toward the blessed mound—the same one trod by Mariano Rivera. Yes! Some personal-cum-cosmic circle would be closed! Yes!

But, no. I just couldn't convince myself to tread on sacred soil.

Ah, but just being there was enough to lift my spirits and warm my soul. It is a blessed state to be a Yankee fan in the springtime. We all always feel the season ahead will be a good one, and we can even hope for greatness.

PART TWO

The roller-coaster 2010 season, player interviews, a
Bronx childhood, Yogi and knuckleballs, tales of other
Yankee greats, and an eye-opening Triple-A trip

April 2010

- Interviews with Joba Chamberlain and bullpen catcher Roman Rodriguez.
- Walk-off madness around the league, and A-Rod breaks the code.
- The bullpen's early ups and downs against the Red Sox, Jays, Rangers, Angels, A's, and O's.
- The Yankees' regional marketing strategy, and the first Scranton call-up of the season.

The pitcher has only got a ball. I've got a bat. So the percentage in weapons is in my favor and I'll let the fellow with the ball do the fretting.
—HANK AARON

The Yankees and the Red Sox are the only American League teams that do not have players' names displayed on the backs of their home uniforms. As a corollary, the sales of scorecards at Yankee Stadium and Fenway Park are especially brisk.

The Giants also do not sport names across their shoulders at home, nor do the Yanks on the road, the only team to never say who's who. (Ichiro is the only player who has received approval to use his first name on his uniform.)

Every team in MLB, however, is required to have numbers on players' jerseys. This practice dates back to the mid-1920s and was begun by the Yankees (although the Indians lay claim to this distinction, too). At the time, the placement of a hitter in the batting order determined his number. So the leadoff batter was 1, the second-place batter was 2, and so on.

That's why Ruth wore 3 and 4 was Gehrig's.

April 4, 6–7 @ Fenway Park

The collapse of the bullpen on 2010's opening day in Fenway was a major surprise and cast doubt on several off-season decisions.

C.C. Sabathia threw 6⅓ shaky innings, made 104 pitches, and was lifted with a slim 5–4 lead, one out, and Kevin Youkilis on third base. Girardi's first call to the bullpen summoned righty Dave Robertson to face Adrian Beltre.

Robertson's very first pitch was a belt-high, straight-as-a-string fastball that had too much of the plate—and Beltre promptly lined it into right field for a single that tied the game at 5-5. Robertson did settle down after that, inducing successive groundouts on curveballs. Robertson's grade for this outing: C-.

The Yanks responded by scoring two runs to reassume the lead at 7-5, but the next culprit-on-the-mound was Chan Ho Park. The first batter he faced, Marco Scutaro, lined a poorly located breaking pitch up the middle for a single. After whiffing Jacoby Ellsbury with a lively fastball, Park grooved another fastball into Dustin Pedroia's high-inside wheelhouse; one quick swing and the ball was launched over the Green Monster to knot the score at 7-all. Victor Martinez grounded a 91-mph fastball to Robinson Cano for the second out before Youkilis pounded another off-target fastball down the left-field line for two bases. Park never got out of the inning. Exit Park; grade F.

Enter Damaso Marte to pitch to David Ortiz. Indeed, Big Papi was specifically the one lefty hitter that Marte was supposed to eat up.

Too bad Marte's first pitch was a slider that broke away from Jorge Posada's desperate lunge, a wild pitch that sent Youkilis scurrying to third base. Two pitches later, Posada asked for a fastball down and away—and Marte delivered it high and inside. Posada was crossed up, but it was still scored as a passed ball, enabling Youkilis to score what turned out to be the winning run. Girardi had seen enough of Marte; grade F.

The ball was then handed to Joba Chamberlain.

Joba's fastball was clocked at 91–93 today, but lacked sufficient movement. To compound his miseries, his slider was likewise a bit flat, and he lacked command of both of his pitches. The outcome was a disaster. A single, a walk, and another single provided an insurance run. Joba's grade: F.

Boston 9, New York 7

Losing Pitcher: Park (0-1)

Bullpen diary: Whatever spring training tweaks Eiland applied to Robertson's fastball, it still lacked acceptable movement. Park's command of his fastball was inadequate. (Last season with the Phillies, Park didn't cough up a single homer during his 50 IP in relief. Welcome to the American League.) Damaso Marte's control was awful, raising the distinct possibility that his arm was hurting—again. Joba's fastball was up and he failed to push the radar gun past 93, a noticeable comedown from past seasons.

⚾ CHAN HO Park's previous teammates, coaches, and managers never succeeded in predicting whether the "good" Park or the "bad" Park would show up. "He has some very quirky characteristics," a scout adds.

"He can only sign contracts on a Monday. He insists on a certain uniform number. Some days he's full of energy. Some days he's in a fog. Nobody knows if he's just superstitious or if there's something about the South Korean culture that's the difference. But whatever it takes for Park to feel just right on a game-to-game basis is a mystery."

"He can be as good as anybody," adds the scout, "or as bad as anybody, and there's usually nothing in between. It's easy to tell which way he'll go by how he does against the first hitter he faces. If he gives up a walk or a hit, things will get away from him very quickly. If he overpowers or badly fools the hitter, then he'll cruise. Either way, though, Park also tends to get in trouble when he pitches away from contact. It's as though he doesn't really trust his stuff."

Game Two @ Boston, April 6

A complete about-face for the men of the 'pen.

Alfredo Aceves came to Burnett's rescue in the 6th. Throwing his change-up to good effect, pumping up his fastball to 93 mph, and sneaking in an occasional sinker or cutter, Aceves kept the Sox off-balance for two innings, preserving the 4-4 tie. How good was his control? Of his twenty-three pitches, only seven were out of the K-zone. Aceves' grade: A.

Dave Robertson started the 8th inning after the Yanks squeezed out a run to take a 5-4 lead. After three fastballs to Youkilis for a 2-1 count, his fourth fastball had as much motion as a still-life painting—and was lined into center for a solid single. Another quick hook for the righty Robertson. His grade: F.

Damaso Marte was then called upon to pitch to—who else?— Ortiz. Damaso quickly induced Ortiz to loft a weak flyball to medium centerfield. Mission accomplished. Grade: A.

After the day off and his miserable thirty-three-pitch opening day outing, Joba took the mound to complete the 8th inning with fire in his eyes. Beltre went down swinging on a 96-mph fastball, and J.D. Drew fanned on a crooked slider. Chamberlain celebrated his two Ks with two fist pumps and one loud scream. His grade: A.

The Yanks added two runs—so it was Mo-time for the first time in the young season.

A rare two-seamer that broke into righty Mike Cameron's fists produced a pop-up to Derek Jeter. But then Scutaro laced a 93-mph cutter for two bases—bringing the potential tying run to the plate. Not to worry. Rivera painted the outside corner with a cutter that fooled Ellsbury into taking a called third strike. Then another cutter ended the game when Pedroia lifted it to center. Ho-hum. Rivera's grade: A-.

New York 6, Boston 4
Winning Pitcher: Aceves (1-0)
Save: Rivera (1)
Bullpen diary: Four scoreless innings from the relief corps turned frowns into smiles throughout Yankee Land. Credit Aceves for setting the tone; also, kudos to Marte for so easily disposing of Ortiz. Most important, Joba reverted to the overpowering form he demonstrated in '08. However, Robertson was still out of sorts. Even though his confidence had always been a big factor in his success, could he now be doubting himself?

Game Three @ Boston, April 7

After the hitters dominated in the previous games, this one belonged to the pitchers. Pettitte was masterful in his six-inning stint, limiting the Bosox to a single run on a two-out RBI single by Ortiz.

Park made his entrance in the bottom of the 7th with the score 1-1. This was a crucial outing for Park. Was he still shell-shocked from his disastrous performance in game one? How would he fare against that all-important leadoff hitter—which, in this case, was the pesky Scutaro?

No problem. A slurve got Scutaro on a medium flyball to right, and the "good" Park was in attendance. His fastball topped out at 93, his slurve shaved the edges of the plate, and his change consistently fooled Boston's sluggers. After two more cans of corn, Park had a hugely successful inning under his belt.

But Girardi had a critical decision to make in the bottom of the 8th after Park got Martinez and Youkilis, and Ortiz loomed in the batter's box. To bring in Damaso Marte (who was up and throwing in the bullpen), or to stick with Park?

Girardi chose the latter option, and Park responded by striking out Ortiz with three consecutive change-ups that broke away and out of the big man's reach.

In Park's third and final inning, he got away with several mistakes. A 93-mph fastball to Beltre was up in the zone and resulted in a hard-hit liner that Nick Swisher corralled at the warning track in deep RF. Then Cameron made solid contact with another middle-up fastball, but just got under the ball and hit a sky-high drive that Brett Gardner gloved in front of the Green Monster. The last out of the inning resulted from another liner, this one off a rolling curve that Scutaro hit within easy reach of Gardner. Park's grade: A.

In the Yankees' half of the 10th, Curtis Granderson took a fastball from Jonathan Papelbon and deposited it halfway up the right-centerfield stands. Three subsequent walks and an RBI groundout by Mark Teixeira gave the visitors a 3-1 lead that Rivera sealed with three quick outs. The game, and the season-opening series, was history. Rivera's grade: A.

New York 3, Boston 1 (10 innings)

Winning Pitcher: Park (1-1)

Save: Rivera (2)

Bullpen diary: A courageous effort by Park to squeeze out a third inning. Even though he had some trouble locating his fastball, he changed speeds magnificently. Rivera survived a pair of highly uncharacteristic mistakes, including a high-inside two-seamer that widened Pedroia's eyes, but Pedroia was so overeager to tattoo the pitch that he only managed to foul it off.

STARTING THE season by taking two of three from the archrival Bosox was a wonderful way to begin the 2010 season—especially after the bullpen failed so dismally on opening day. By any measure, eight consecutive shutout innings delivered by their relievers in the hitter-friendly confines of Fenway Park was absolutely encouraging.

With the three games averaging over 3½ hours each—typical Yanks/Sox midnight madness—both teams needed to get on to their next series, if only to play shorter games. (The AL record for longest nine-inning regular season game, according to *Baseball Almanac*? Yanks vs. Sox at Fenway, August 18, 2006. 4 hours, 45 minutes. But they all seem to run that long; plenty of value for the ticket payer's dollar.)

Three games down, 159 to go, including the season-ending series against the Sox—the first time since 1950 the Yankees and Red Sox will start *and* end the season against each other.

Around the league: Three pitchers have already had balls called on them for licking their fingers while on the mound. In a confusing rule change, MLB allowed pitchers to moisten up in cold weather— if they then wipe off their fingers right away, which would seem to contradict the whole idea.

April 9–11 @ Tropicana Field

The Yankees flew to Tampa for a three-game set against what was arguably the best young team in the American League. After the Boston marathons, the Yanks would need Javier Vazquez to pitch deep into the opener of their next series in order to avoid stretching out their relievers too soon. But David Price's 97-mph fastball and wicked slider shackled the Yanks, while Vazquez-redux was simply pounded.

With the Yanks down 7-2, Sergio Mitre was sent to the mound with two out and one on in the bottom of the 6th. After crossing himself with the baseball in his right hand and then planting a kiss on the horsehide, Mitre faced Carl Crawford—who proceeded to smack a flat sinker for a five-hop RBI single through the middle. Ben Zobrist followed with a line-drive two-bagger that drove Crawford home and increased the debit to 9-2.

For the next 2 ²/₃ innings, however, Mitre kept the bases empty. His fastball topped out at 92 mph, his sinker sank, and his change-up was well located at the bottom of the strike zone. Mitre's grade: B.

Tampa 9, New York 3

Bullpen diary: Most of Mitre's previous appearances in the bigs have been as a starter or as a long man, so taking the ball from Girardi in the middle of an inning with a runner on base compelled him to immediately pitch out of a stretch—not to mention being forced to make his season's debut inside the claustrophobic domed space of Tropicana Field. No wonder it took Mitre two batters and eight pitches to find his comfort zone.

He took the signs from Posada with his hands held still and at the level of his chin, then he dropped his hands to armpit level as he began his delivery. As a result, his hands didn't bounce and his motion was much more economical than it had been in '09. Girardi used Mitre in a perfect mop-up situation where even if he had gotten creamed, the outcome of the game would not have been altered.

Mitre's contribution should not be overlooked, since it enabled Girardi to keep the rest of his bullpen idle and well rested.

Game Two @ Tampa, April 10

This was a laugher.

The second time through the lineup, the Rays' young starter, Wade Davis, was thoroughly battered from pillar to post. Conversely, C.C. was literally unhittable. By the 6th inning, the Yankees led 8-0, and the only suspense was supplied by the possibility of a no-hitter—but that was rudely ended with two out in the bottom of the 8th when he delivered his 111th pitch, a 93-mph fastball that Kelly Shoppach slapped into LF for the Rays' first hit.

Before the ball landed in front of the charging Brett Gardner, Girardi was out of the dugout and on his way to the mound, waggling his right hand to summon Robertson into the action.

With an overwhelming lead so late in the game, Robertson could simply throw fastballs without worrying about trying to fool or finesse the first batter he faced, Gabe Kapler. Indeed, Kapler lofted Robertson's seventh consecutive fastball to Gardner in LF, and the 8th inning was in the books. In the 9th, Robertson was great. Fastballs and curves got two quick outs, and even a double by Zobrist didn't matter. A groundout followed to end the game. Dave's grade: A.

New York 10, Tampa 0

Bullpen diary: With Robertson back in the groove, every member of the relief gang now seemed to be in top form. Not for long, turns out.

Game Three @ Tampa, April 11

Burnett was roughed up for a brace of runs in the bottom of the 1st, but then underwent a Mr. Hyde–to–Dr. Jekyll transformation and shut the Rays down over the next six innings.

With the Yankees comfortably ahead by a 7-2 margin, Joba's task was to snuff out the Rays quickly and efficiently. But he encountered a world of trouble in dealing with the leadoff hitter in the home 8th, Jason Bartlett. A steady diet of 93- and 95-mph fastballs, two mini-breaking sliders, and four foul balls ended with Bartlett clocking a lifeless 93-mph fastball into CF for a single.

Obviously flustered after Bartlett's eight-pitch at-bat, Joba rushed his first pitch to Crawford and came in with a fat 91-mph fastball in the middle of the plate that was blasted into left-center for a stand-up RBI triple. Uh-oh. The feisty Rays were down by only 7-3, but Joba battled his way through the rest of the inning to keep the Rays at bay. Still, not an overwhelming appearance; Chamberlain's grade: D+.

To close out the game, Girardi called upon the Sandman, even though the four-run lead didn't qualify as a possible save situation. But Rivera wasn't very sharp. He gave up a leadoff single but induced a double-play groundball. The inevitable conclusion of the game and the series was delayed by a surprising development, that is, Rivera walking the light-hitting Sean Rodriguez. However, Mo finally lowered the boom in whiffing Bartlett on a trio of cutters. Rivera's grade: B-.

New York 7, Tampa 3

Bullpen diary: Joba had major difficulty locating his fastball, throwing two in the dirt and centering several others. Also, except for four 95-mph fastballs—two fouled off, two for balls—Chamberlain's velocity was relatively ordinary. With this inferior outing, Joba has regressed to where he was in his opening day appearance in Boston. Can he be trusted?

A scout in attendance at the game offers this assessment: "Chamberlain had trouble repeating his delivery, so his arm slot was moving from pitch to pitch. This led to his poor command and reduced velocity of his fastball, as well as a diminishment of its usual movement. At times he looked very tentative, as though he wasn't fully committed to his pitches."

JOBA

Joba Chamberlain sprawls rather than sits in the chair that faces his dressing cubicle.

"I'm from Nebraska," he says, "so it was a given that I'd play peewee football. For the same reason the color of the first car I ever owned was Nebraska red."

Joba has reasons for everything: "I started playing baseball when I was four years old, and then I moved on to tee-ball. When I was still a little kid I loved to play dress-up, and since catchers got to wear the most stuff, that's the position I wanted to play."

Eventually he became a heavy-hitting catcher and part-time pitcher in high school. "Nine homers as a senior," he recalls, "and thirty innings pitched."

He was still wearing the tools of ignorance when he matriculated at Nebraska-Kearney (a Division II school) and also when he initially transferred to the University of Nebraska in 2005. But before his sophomore year was over, Chamberlain had become a full-time pitcher and star of the Cornhuskers staff—going 10-2 with a 2.81 ERA, while also ringing up 130 strikeouts in 118 1/3 IP. After another stellar season in Lincoln, the Yankees drafted him in 2006, and he's been with the big club since the end of the 2007 season.

Still, pitching doesn't always come easy for Joba.

"I've always been susceptible to rushing my pitches," he says. "I tend to leave the rubber too early, but I can mostly get away with it because my arm action is really quick and it can catch up with the rest of my body. This is something that I have to be constantly thinking about, even when I'm throwing on flat ground or in batting practice. Just going straight down and straight out. But I'm never quite there on a consistent basis."

Chamberlain must also pay strict attention to delivering his slider. "I sometimes hold the ball too long," he says. "Then I wind up yanking the pitch and burying it in the dirt. Thankfully, Dave Eiland is right on top of everything."

The problem is that while starters have plenty of time as a game unfolds to get their mechanics straight, Joba understands that relievers have to "do it right then."

He discounts critics who maintain that his erratic efforts are primarily due to his stiff front leg. "A lot of power pitchers don't bend their front legs," he says. "The key is to land softly and with a straight front, which is what I do."

As he speaks, Joba leans forward and picks up a baseball.

"I'm only twenty-three," he says, "and I have lots and lots of energy. That's why I have to at least play catch with someone every day, and also why I'll run laps around the field and then run steps before every game. I'll actually run more after I've pitched two days in a row to get rid of the lactic acid that's accumulated in my muscles."

He continually twists, twirls, and squeezes a ball in his big hands.

"That's my job," he says. "To bring energy to a game."

AROUND THE LEAGUE

By April 11, 2010, MLB had already seen eleven walk-off game-winning hits, plus one by a wild pitch. The rule of thumb is that it takes time for hitters to get their timing down early in the season. Not so much this year, it seems.

April 13–15, Los Angeles Angels @ Yankee Stadium

After the World Championship ring ceremony—which turned into a very emotional moment at the Stadium when Hideki Matsui, now with the Angels, received his—the Yankees' first home stand of 2010 got under way.

In hurling six shutout innings, Andy Pettitte got himself out of several jams by coming up with terrific pitches in clutch situations. Park assumed the pitching duties in the top of the 7th with the Yankees enjoying a 5-0 lead. Park's very first pitch—a called strike to Jeff Mathis—was a darting fastball, his liveliest one of the season so far. Then a nifty slider induced a groundout, but another slider was hit like a bullet by Brandon Wood, necessitating an excellent over-the-shoulder catch by Swisher in deep RF.

The hard-hit ball seemed to unsettle Park, as he rolled a slider that Erick Aybar promptly smacked into LF for a solid single. Park then was cautious in a seven-pitch battle against the dangerous former Yankee Bobby Abreu, nibbling with fastballs and sliders until a perfectly situated 93-mph dart on the outside corner resulted in a comebacker to end the inning.

Even so, as the 7th inning was under way, Park had trouble locating his fastball, and those that clipped the K-zone were mostly lifeless. Accordingly, he threw three sliders, one exceptional curve, and one change-up before whiffing Torii Hunter on still another slider.

(By the way, Hunter was not named after *torii*, the gates to a Japanese shrine. Hunter jokingly told a reporter back in 2006: "I think, when my mom filled out the paperwork after I was born, she accidentally put two *i*'s.")

Another seven-pitch at-bat terminated when Matsui grounded out on a slider. But then Kendry Morales jumped on an 88-mph meatball that cut the plate at belt level and sent it deep into the RF stands. Park ended the inning by getting Juan Rivera to pop to first on a 92-mph fastball. Actually, behind on the count 1-and-2, Rivera got himself out by trying to hit a 500-foot homer on a pitch that was on the outer third of the plate. Park's somewhat shaky effort reduced the Yanks' lead to 5-1. Park's grade: C-.

Before Robertson took the mound to begin the top of the 9th, the Yankees tacked on another two runs and now led 7-1. Here was an opportunity to demonstrate that his sterling outing in Tampa was no fluke—and that the battering he'd absorbed a week ago in Boston was merely a blip. Unfortunately, Robertson got into trouble with his third pitch to Howie Kendrick, who led off the inning. Kendrick was way late on a pair of 93-mph fastballs, but Robertson's third pitch was a curve that Kendrick smashed up the middle for a single.

Robertson's faux pas was not reading Kendrick's swing. Since Kendrick had no chance against the fastballs, why would Robertson give him the opportunity to slow down his swing by launching an 85-mph curve? For sure, Posada bears some of the blame for allowing Robertson to make the mistake—but the pitcher is always responsible for agreeing to the catcher's call.

Suffice it to say that things went downhill from there—two singles loaded the bases. Then Abreu made solid contact with a belt-high fastball down the middle—and the resulting grand slam narrowed the Yankees' advantage to 7-5. Robertson's grade: F.

It was Mo-time once again.

After Rivera fell behind 3-1 to Hunter, the SRO crowd at the Stadium started to fidget. A walk would bring up the potential tying run in the person of Matsui, World Series MVP and always a fan favorite. But a sixth consecutive cutter eventually caught Hunter looking, for the second out.

Matsui popped up the first cutter he ever saw from former teammate Rivera, and the game was *fini*. An A for Rivera.

New York 7, Los Angeles 5
Save: Rivera (3)
Bullpen diary: Once again, Park failed to muster up his optimum blazer. He registered a single fastball at 93 (and got an out); otherwise

he maxed out at a mere 91. So far, only one of Park's three outings has been mistake-free.

Rivera's cutters lacked the movement that we've all been accustomed to seeing for lo these many years. But Mo righted himself in a hurry by slightly elevating his release point to improve his location, and both Hunter and Matsui were rendered helpless. Still, given the decrease in his velocity, the flattening of Rivera's cutter is something to keep particular track of.

Robertson's control was fine—only one ball in 15 pitches—but his command, his movement, and his awareness were all faulty. Another miserable outing and Robertson might find himself on the next bus to Scranton.

TRIPLE-A

While Yankee fans have taken it for granted that a wealthy club like theirs could easily and happily foot the bill for many, many flights in years past to and from Columbus, Ohio, and the Triple-A team there, it proved prudent financially for the Yanks to acquire the Phils' franchise in Scranton, Pennsylvania, in order to allow players, scouts, and management to make the four-hour drive as often as need be—and that would be a lot this season.

Additionally, the move gives the Yankees a regional footprint from which to keep building a loyal and local extended fan base, with their top minor league teams now circumscribing a wide arc from Scranton down to Trenton, and over to Staten Island. And all just a car ride away.

Game Two vs. the Angels in the Bronx, April 14

Vazquez had trouble locating his fastball and was yanked in favor of Alfredo Aceves with one out, a runner on second, and LA leading 3-1 in the top of the 6th. After he got a look at four different pitches—slider, cutter, curve, and change-up—Juan Rivera slashed the first fastball he saw on a line to the right side. But Teixeira make a sparkling diving catch and the inherited runner was forced to stay put on second. However, Maicer Izturis spanked a letter-high 88-mph fastball for an RBI single, before a groundout ended the inning with the Angels now up 4-1.

Aceves struggled mightily throughout the top of the 7th. A single by Aybar on another too-high, too-slow 88-mph fastball was followed by a comebacker that moved him to second, and then came an RBI single by Hunter on a two-seamer that never sank. Next up was an eight-pitch walk to Matsui (as Yankee fans fondly remember, Hideki excels at working the pitcher, especially late in the game) and a first-pitch fastball that hit Morales to load the bases. But Aceves escaped further damage when Juan Rivera took a mighty home-run swing, again, at a 2-0 fastball and popped up for the last out of the inning. Aceves: D.

Now down 5-1, Joba mounted the hill. Izturis lined a flat 92-mph fastball to CF for the first out and Mathis crushed an even flatter 95-mph fastball for a single. But a strikeout and a flyball maintained the Yankees' four-run deficit. Joba today: A-.

The Yankees lineup generated two runs in the bottom of the 8th, so Damaso Marte was down by only 5-3 when his number was called. Relying mostly on his slider, Marte got two flyouts and a strikeout. Marte: A.

Los Angeles 5, New York 3

Bullpen diary: Aceves hadn't pitched in eight days, so it's understandable that the pinpoint command he absolutely requires to be successful was AWOL. Even so, for him to issue a walk and then to hit a batter in the same inning has to prompt Eiland to find more innings for Aceves. Joba's fastball had minimum movement and wasn't well placed. It was obvious that Chamberlain was still having trouble repeating his delivery.

Like Aceves, Marte hadn't pitched since April 6 in Boston; unlike Aceves, he was razor-sharp. The four fastballs Marte unleashed were 92–93 and with late movement, and he got two key outs from his sharp, slicing slider. After his dismal debut in the opener in Fenway, Marte looks to be at least as effective as he was in last year's postseason.

OFF THE FIELD

The U.S. Congress held hearings this week about banning smokeless tobacco from MLB when the players' contracts come up in December 2011. All tobacco has been banned in the minor leagues since the '90s. Yogi Berra's childhood friend from St. Louis, Joe Garagiola, a longtime antismoking advocate, testified today, asking all players to stop carrying a can of dip in their pockets, for their own health—and as an example for kids.

Game Three vs. the Angels in the Bronx, April 15

On Jackie Robinson Day, marking the sixty-third anniversary of breaking the color line in a big league ball game, all of the players in MLB wore number 42. Mariano Rivera is the only active player who wears 42 every day.

Philip Hughes also conducted his own personal celebration, pitching five outstanding innings in his 2010 debut as a starter. Indeed, Hughes' lone mistake in the ninety-nine pitches he launched was grooving a mediocre fastball that Matsui clouted into the RF stands. However, the miscue seemed to be a minor one, since the Yankees had busted out to a 5-1 lead. For some unfathomable reason, though, Girardi sent Hughes out to start the 6th—whence he proceeded to issue a walk, yield a single, and add ten meaningless pitches to his count. Exit Hughes. Enter Robertson.

Robertson temporarily redeemed himself by retiring five of the six batters he faced. The only blemish was an eight-pitch walk. Robertson: A.

Damaso Marte was sent forth with two outs in the 7th to pitch to left-handed hitter Abreu, and got him looking. But in the 8th he gave up two quick singles and was lifted for Joba. Marte: C-.

Joba took over and threw only three snapping sliders to Kendrick.

The result was a dribbler back to the mound that led to a nifty 1-6-3 double play to end the threat and the inning.

When Joba walked Mike Napoli on a wild slider to start the 9th, Rivera was up and throwing in the bullpen. But Wood was caught looking at a late-breaking slider that nipped the low-inside corner, and Reggie Willits hit a 92-mph fastball to Granderson for the second out.

Since the theoretical tying run had been on deck when he entered the game in the 8th, Joba would be credited with a save if he finished the game. To do so, he had to retire Erick Aybar—but a 92-mph fastball was hit on the ground to Jeter's left and skidded off his glove into CF for a single. That was all for Chamberlain. B+.

With two runners on base and the potential tying run on deck, Mariano also came into a save situation. A cutter produced a meek groundout—and the Yankees had won their third consecutive series by identical 2-games-to-1 margins. Rivera: A.

New York 6, Los Angeles 2
Save: Rivera (4)

Bullpen diary: An encouraging performance by Robertson. This time he noted that Kendrick was late on a 2-2 fastball and eventually came back with another fastball for a called third strike.

Marte's ability to return to the mound the next day and breeze through a nine-pitch, 1-2-3 inning proves that there's nothing wrong with his arm.

Joba's velocity is still up and down: 90–92, with an occasional 93. The two successive sliders he threw to Wood in the 9th inning were significant. The first one fell off the table, rendering Wood helpless. The second one was overthrown, flat, and lined foul. Blame Chamberlain's variable release point.

⚾ THE BULLPEN was at the top of the news because Park was placed on the fifteen-day disabled list for what was described as a "low-level strain of his right hamstring."

To take Park's place, Boone Logan was summoned from Scranton, where the tall lefty had pitched to a sparkling 1.35 ERA in four appearances. Logan's success in the minors was due, the Yankees said, to Eiland's adjusting his delivery during spring training, that is, keeping his body lower after the ball leaves his hand, thereby regularizing his release point, which in turn would allow him to properly finish off his pitches.

If Logan does put a second lefty specialist at Girardi's disposal, the absence of Park created another problem: Since Park and Aceves (or as the Yankees call him, "Ace") had essentially the same role—to pitch two to three innings—Sergio Mitre would most likely inherit Park's innings. However, if Ace and Mitre were forced to go in successive games, then the Yankees would be without a long man for a couple of days.

April 16–18, Texas Rangers @ Yankee Stadium

In game one, C.C. (short for Carsten Charles) Sabathia pitched all six innings in a rain-shortened win. He made spectators of the relievers.

New York 5, Texas 1

Game Two vs. the Rangers in the Bronx, April 17

Both the lineup and Burnett were in top form. That's why the scoreboard favored the home team 7-1 when Aceves entered the game to commence the 8th inning. But Ace was a deuce from the get-go. Aceves had nothing, inducing nary a swing-and-miss. A single, force-out grounder, walk, and two-run homer later and Girardi had seen enough of Ace, summoning Marte to face LH Chris Davis. Ace: F.

Damaso got Davis looking and retired RH Joaquin Arias on a stinger to Cano. Marte: A. Since the Yanks still had a four-run lead, Mariano kept his seat in the bullpen while Joba was called upon to finish off Texas in a nonsave situation. A seven-pitch groundout and two strikeouts. Joba: A.

New York 7, Texas 3

Bullpen diary: Joba's slider accounted for all of the three outs he produced. In '08, Chamberlain's average fastball was clocked at 97 mph.
Except for three 94s, his fastballs today ranged from 89 to 91—and
all of them lacked movement. Also, his slider continued to be erratic,
ranging from flat to sharp in a single at-bat. Despite his latest success,
the Yankees have to be concerned about Joba's stiff front leg, the lack of
juice and movement on his fastball, and the inconsistency of his slider.

Game Three vs. the Rangers in the Bronx, April 18

Pettitte turned the Rangers' bats to straw, using 106 pitches to complete eight innings. With the Yankees sporting a 5-2 lead, Rivera
began his warm-up routine in the bullpen in the bottom of the 8th.

Having previously stretched his legs and torso, Mo now loosened
his right shoulder by swinging his arm in large circles while holding
a regulation-size weighted baseball. Then, after making three light
tosses to Roman Rodriguez, Rivera began throwing hard. With
each pitch, he checked himself to make sure that his mechanics were
A-OK. After 12–15 practice pitches, Mo is always ready to take the
mound, where another seven warm-up throws gets him locked in.

And he was certainly properly tuned when he fooled Vladimir
Guerrero with an 88-mph cutter that was skied to shallow RF and got
Nelson Cruz and Davis with cutters on the corners. Another A for Mo.

New York 5, Texas 2

Save: Rivera (5)

Bullpen diary: Rivera has already saved 55 percent of the Yankees'
wins. However, Mo was still not in midseason form. Of the fourteen
cutters he threw in this game, only two had the maximum vertical
and horizontal movement that Yankee watchers have grown accustomed to seeing. Still, his ability to paint the black on both sides of
the plate demonstrated that he was in command of his command.

This day in baseball history: On April 18, the Mets and Cardinals played
a twenty-inning game, the longest in the majors so far this year.

Twenty-nine years ago to the day, on April 18, 1981, the longest game in major and minor league history was played. Wade Boggs' Pawtucket Red Sox played Cal Ripken, Jr.'s Rochester Red Wings for thirty-two innings until four in the morning before being suspended; the game was finished on June 23 in eighteen minutes. Cal went 2-13 and Wade 4-12.

Twenty-three other future major leaguers played in the game, notably Bobby Ojeda, Bruce Hurst, Marty Barrett, Rich Gedman, and Chico Walker.

ROMAN RODRIGUEZ

As the Yankees' bullpen catcher, Roman "Don't Call Me Ramon" Rodriguez is officially listed as "Field Staff" rather than a "Coach." But Roman (as in the city) has a number on the back of his uniform—88—and as soon as he leaves the clubhouse he dons his shin guards and always has his mask and his chest protector within reach.

He's a native of Venezuela who was signed by the Pirates as a nondrafted free agent back in 1988. "I was a shortstop," he says. "Good field, no hit."

After spending eight years in the minors, Rodriguez was hired by the Kansas City Royals as their bullpen catcher (1997–2000). From there he moved to Boston's bullpen. "Rick Down was the Red Sox's hitting coach," says Rodriguez, "so when he came to the Yankees in 2002 he took me with him, and I've been here ever since."

Rodriguez pays absolutely no attention to how a pitcher warms up prior to entering a game: "You can pitch a no-hitter in the bullpen, but it's different when there's a batter up there and forty thousand people are screaming and yelling. Last year, just about everything that Phil Coke threw in the pen kicked up dirt, but he still did a good job when it counted. I mean, there's no way to predict how a guy's going to do by what he does in the privacy of the pen."

While receiving the relievers' warm-up tosses, Rodriguez wears the full catcher's regalia, including the mask. "Even though about seventy-five percent of the warm-up pitches are strikes," he says,

Courtesy of Rachel Hood

Roman Rodriguez

"sometimes a breaking ball can hit the dust and bounce up into my face."

He also reports that the number of get-ready pitches required by each of the relievers varies:

Robertson needs 15; Marte 10–11; Chamberlain 10; and Park 20. "Chan can actually get loose with fewer pitches," says Rodriguez, "but he takes longer to get the right feel."

As for Mo? "Eight to ten, but in an emergency he can get ready in five."

RODRIGUEZ'S WORKDAY begins before each game as the starters get their between-starts bullpen work in.

"These sessions take place on the third day after their start," he notes. "They'll each throw about fifty pitches using about seventy-five percent of their game-time effort. With Dave right there, they're mostly working on any mechanical problems they might be having, and they'll pitch to spots. It's like a working vacation for them."

But Rodriguez never takes a vacation. "I'll run and work out every day," he says, as he pounds his fist into his mitt. "And I'm ready to go out to the 'pen if anybody feels like doing some extra throwing. That's why I'm sitting here in the dugout so they don't have to go looking to find me."

Then he points out to the gleaming green field and the thousands of empty seats.

"Hey, man," he says. "I like being here. You know?"

April 20–22 @ Oakland–Alameda County Coliseum

The Yanks flew cross-country for the first time this year, and Alex Rodriguez would be in the news again—but not for any off-the-field misadventure.

In game one, after Vazquez gave up a two-run homer to Kurt Suzuki with one out in the bottom of the 6th, the Yanks still led 6-3, but he was pulled in favor of new arrival Boone Logan.

The first major league hitter lefty Logan faced this season was lefty Eric Chavez. At first glance, Logan's arm angle had been raised and his delivery was much smoother than at the start of spring training. Two quick outs, and kudos to Dave Eiland. So far.

Logan had no problem early in the bottom of the 7th—a flyout and a groundout. But Logan's difficulties began when Rajai Davis grounded a first-pitch fastball to Jeter's left; when Derek had trouble pulling the ball out of his glove, the speedy Davis beat out an infield single. Yes, Logan should/could have been out of the inning, but the lost opportunity seemed to fracture his focus. He gave up a sharp single to LH Daric Barton, and then a walk. Logan's grade: C-.

Here's what then confronted Joba: two outs, bases loaded, the

Yankees up by 7–3, and the power-hitting Kevin Kouzmanoff repre-senting the potential tying run. Joba ended the threat and the inning with a sharply breaking slider that Kouzmanoff missed by a foot.

A 1-2-3 8th for Joba featured 94- and 96-mph fastballs. His grade today? A.

With the Yankees still leading 7–3, Girardi didn't want to use Mo in a nonsave situation, so he decided to start the bottom of the 9th with Marte against a right-handed pinch hitter, Jake Fox. But both Marte's fastball and slider were uncontrollable, and Fox walked on five pitches. Marte: F. Girardi was forced to use his hammer to secure the win after all. Rivera moved his cutters in and out and the game was soon over. A for Mo.

New York 7, Oakland 3

Bullpen diary: Pitching from a full windup, Logan's long legs and medium-high kick give hitters a lot to see before they can locate the ball. But with a runner on, his delivery from the stretch wasn't quite as easy and his lead knee wasn't elevated nearly as much.

Joba's velocity was up, and both his command and the movement of his fastball were top-notch. But his slider was erratic: four of them were killers, and four were potential victims. Still, the season is barely three weeks old, and Chamberlain usually requires at least twice that time period to reach his peak.

Marte looked to be lost on the mound.

Rivera's velocity is still down, with his cutter sitting at 88 mph. But his location and late action are right on.

MIRACLE MAN?

Edwar Ramirez worked the 7th and 8th innings for the A's, issuing three walks, striking out two, and giving up one run when the infield botched what should have been an inning-ending double-play ball.

Ramirez had several cups of coffee for New York in the past two seasons, and was lopped off the forty-man roster when Park was signed. Just as quickly, Ramirez was given a contract by Oakland.

Then as now, Ramirez is a change-up pitcher in the mode of Trevor Hoffman and Stu Miller. Ramirez's arm action looks like he's about to throw a fastball, but his off-speed deliveries have terrific late movement in that they sink and move laterally away from right-handed hitters. And it's primarily the depth that fools both LH and RH hitters as the ball changes planes so quickly and in such a short distance. Ramirez can throw his change anytime—even when he's behind 2-0 or 3-1. One scout goes so far as to rate his change-up a 75.

"He's a one-inning guy you can use when you're looking for a groundball," says the scout. "And he does have the fortitude to get an out in the last three innings of a tight game."

However, Ramirez's slider spins, hangs, and is rated at 40. His fastball is rated 55—although it's fairly straight, it does have a slight cut at the end that jams lefty hitters.

All told, his command of his fastball is sometimes iffy, enabling hitters to sit on his change, thereby removing the surprise factor.

Even so, what endears Ramirez to so many baseball people is the fact that he came from nowhere. Indeed, he was a mediocre prospect in the low minors constantly on the verge of getting cut. But over the course of several off-seasons, he worked on his change-up strictly on his own. Making up a grip that felt comfortable, then throwing literally hundreds of balls against a wall, willing himself to find his way into the bigs.

If Ramirez is a one-pitch pitcher with limited potential, his love for the game is nothing short of inspirational.

Game Two @ Oakland, April 21

In his second start, Phil Hughes was simply incredible. He had a no-hitter through seven innings, with 10 Ks on 101 pitches, but then he yielded a single and a walk with one out in the top of the 8th. Joba came to Hughes' relief with the Yankees leading 2-0. A dead-red fastball was laced for an RBI single, but Chamberlain got out of the inning with no further damage. Joba: B-.

The Yanks tacked on an insurance run and now led 3-1, so

Mariano was summoned to do what he does. Still, Mo needed nine cutters to finally get Daric Barton to lift a harmless pop-up that A-Rod easily corralled in foul ground. Then Rivera barely escaped a mistake pitch to Ryan Sweeney—a high, flat, middle-of-the-plate slider that was knocked into CF for a single. Next up was Suzuki, whose home-run power threatened to tie the score. Rivera fed him a steady diet of 91-mph cutters that darted over the outside corner, but when he tried to close out the RH Suzuki with a jammer, the ball was too far inside—and Suzuki was awarded first base after being hit on the arm. Now Chavez represented the winning run.

Chavez moved off the plate to prevent Mo from crowding him with cutters (just like the Red Sox did in the 2004 ALCS). Yet, after fouling three inside cutters, Chavez barely got his bat on an outside cutter and tapped it back to Rivera, who threw to second for the force-out.

Two out, two on, two runs behind. The A's last chance was Kouzmanoff, their primary long-ball specialist. The game ended when he broke his bat on an inside cutter and looped the ball to CF. Rivera's first so-so game in a while; a B.

New York 3, Oakland 1
Save: Rivera (6)
Bullpen diary: Joba was pitching for the second consecutive day, and his slider wasn't consistently sharp and his fastball lacked sufficient hop. Fox's RBI single produced the only inherited runner who scored off Chamberlain so far this season.

Rivera didn't have his A-stuff. Even though he served up twenty-six pitches and only six of them were balls, Mo only induced a single swing and miss. And how often does Rivera hit a batter? Only 2.5 times per season.

Game Three @ Oakland, April 22
C.C. didn't get away with his solitary egregious mistake—a life-less fastball right down the pike that Suzuki clouted for a three-run

homer in the first inning. Even so, he hung on—battling his control all the while—to pitch an eight-inning complete game in absorbing the loss.

Oakland 4, New York 2

Bullpen diary: Too many innings for the relief corps is a problem, but so is too *few* innings. Robertson hasn't thrown a ball in anger in more than a week; Mitre hasn't made an appearance since April 9; Aceves has been collecting splinters since April 17 and hasn't had a good outing since April 6, the second game in Boston; and Park's injury is perhaps not as "mild" as initially announced. It's already been three days longer than the original "three or four" day prognosis, and he's still limited to long toss and is nowhere near ready to throw off a mound.

The Yankees, like most teams, habitually minimize the severity of injuries, especially to pitchers. Their reasoning is as follows: if they do need a quick fix to replace the injured player, potential trading partners won't take advantage of the Yankees' desperation by demanding the moon and the sun in return.

Footnote: In the 6th inning, A-Rod had his infamous breach of baseball etiquette, crossing over the mound on his way back to first base after Teixeira's long flyball curved foul. A's pitcher Dallas Braden yapped at Alex, who returned the favor. A-Rod laughed it off the next day, but the media was all over him for breaking one of baseball's codes.

April 23–25 @ Angel Stadium of Anaheim

In game one, Burnett's fastball against the Angels was consistently up and his curve was mostly nonfunctional. The Yankees were fortunate that the game was tied at 4, with one out and a runner on first, when Robertson relieved in the bottom of the 7th. The Yankees got an easy out when a strong throw by Posada caught Abreu trying to steal second. Then Robertson blew away Hunter with a 92-mph fastball to earn an A.

Joba took over in the bottom of the 8th and was roughed up. First Matsui lined a poorly placed fastball for a single. Then Joba hung a spinning slider to Morales that wound up in the RF stands. The Angels now led 6-4. Another line-drive single was followed by a soft fly, but then came two well-hit line-drive outs. Joba: F.

Los Angeles 6, New York 4
Losing Pitcher: Chamberlain (0-1)
Bullpen diary: Joba's worst outing of the season was characterized by poor location, an abundance of mistakes, and no movement on his fastball. In eighteen pitches, he achieved nary a swing and miss. Even a toss to Teixeira to hold Juan Rivera close at first was wild and high.

Of his gopher pitch to Morales, Chamberlain later said this: "It started where I wanted, but it just didn't get there."

Game Two @ Anaheim, April 24

Pettitte had another exceptional performance, whiffing eight, walking none, and baffling the Angels for eight innings. The Yankees had an insurmountable 7-1 lead, but after Andy had thrown 114 pitches, Damaso Marte was called upon to close out the game, which he did, giving up only a harmless single. Marte: A.

New York 7, Los Angeles 1
Bullpen diary: Francisco Cervelli was behind the plate for the Yankees, resting Posada on a day game following a night game. After Morales took strike one, Marte shook off Cervelli four times before uncorking a change-up that Morales lunged at and missed by several inches. This was the first pure change-up that Marte has thrown so far this season.

With the Yankees up by six runs in the bottom of the 9th, why didn't Girardi use Sergio Mitre? After all, Mitre hadn't pitched in seventeen days and could've used the work, whereas Damaso Marte had seen action only four days previous. The fact that Sergio Mitre's number wasn't called raises the question of exactly why he's still on the roster.

Were the Yankees still dubious about Hughes' effectiveness as a starter?

And was Mitre still deemed to be their insurance policy in case Hughes did ultimately fail?

Game Three @ Anaheim, April 25

An important day; the last day of the west coast swing. Good to get on the plane on a win. Not today.

Once again, Vazquez showed nothing. His poor command and low-velocity fastballs contributed to his blowing an early 3-0 lead, and he was replaced by Logan in the bottom of the 4th with a runner on third, two outs, and the Angels ahead 5-3.

Pitching from a windup, lefty Logan got lefty Abreu to line his first pitch—a 93-mph fastball—to Jeter to end the inning. The Yanks got a run back in their half of the 6th, but in the bottom of the 5th, Logan, pitching from the stretch, got a strikeout and a flyout, and his fastball was faster than it had been (mid vs. low 90s), but then he gave up a sharp single. Logan's grade: B+.

Girardi called on Aceves to keep the game within reach and to pitch to RH Juan Rivera—even though he hadn't pitched in over a week. But Ace had his A-game working. He finished the inning by inducing a groundout on a late-breaking cutter.

In the bottom of the 6th, Aceves threw nothing but cutters, coaxing a pair of groundball outs and a pop-up. In the 7th, the first batter lined out to Cano, but with the LH Abreu due up, Girardi signaled for Marte. Aceves' grade: A.

But Marte wasn't up to the task. His fastball was beyond his control—either outside or below the K-zone—and he delivered a five-pitch walk to Abreu. His wild streak got even worse when he hit Hunter in the knee with another errant fastball. Marte was lucky to record the first out when Matsui checked his swing and bounced into a force.

Kendry Morales' subsequent at-bat led to confusion—and the end of the Yankees' chance to win their sixth consecutive series.

Even though there were runners on first and second, Rivera was on deck and Robertson was already loose in the bullpen. Girardi's initial impulse was to deliberately walk Morales and call in Robertson to face Rivera, so he signaled for an intentional walk. Cervelli stood, stepped out, and caught the looped ball one. Girardi then changed his mind and motioned for Cervelli to get back behind the plate and directed Marte to pitch to Morales. When Damaso's next two fastballs missed, he looked into the dugout for further instructions. Since the count was 3-0, should he throw another wide one or still attempt to get Morales out?

Girardi clearly indicated that Morales should be pitched to. "Don't give in!" the Yankees manager shouted.

Ah, to pitch or not to pitch; that was the question.

Morales provided the answer by blasting a fat fastball into the RF stands to give LA an 8-4 lead. Marte: F.

Guess who pitched the bottom of the 8th? The all-but-forgotten Sergio Mitre. And he was erratic, with two flyouts mixed with two walks, ending in a strikeout. Mitre: C+.

Angels 8, New York 4

Bullpen diary: Aceves had total command of his stuff, nipping the corners, moving his pitches up-down-in-out. Considering his long layoff, his stint was remarkable. Logan's velocity was up but two of the four batters he faced belted line drives. Marte had nothing, and also needed a map to find the K-zone, but Girardi must share the blame for the botched intentional walk–cum–home run.

Sergio Mitre did manage to get through the 8th, which was a considerable accomplishment after his extended inactivity. However, back on April 6 when he faced the Bosox in Boston, Mitre's delivery was smooth and quiet with no unnecessary movement in his hands or legs; this time, however, Mitre reverted to his old habits. His hands never stopped moving, while he sometimes tapped his lead foot and shivered his back foot.

Back to the drawing board.

After the Series

Here's the on-site report from another team's advance scout:

Chamberlain's mechanics were a mess. His velocity was down, and both his fastball and his slider were flat. The only consistent aspect of his appearance was that he opened up too soon and consequently his arm slot dropped. Chamberlain is still a work in progress.

Robertson had more deception in his delivery and a bit more cutting action on his fastball because his delivery was more over-the-top than it was since I last saw him in spring training.

Logan's increased velocity was due to his shorter arm action, but his breaking pitches were too inconsistent. Also, he threw his change-up with too much force so there wasn't the kind of difference in speeds between his curve and his change that he needed. In the past, Logan always pitched out of the stretch, even when the bases were empty. But he came at Hunter from a wind-up with a runner on third in the seventh inning of the first game. Pitching this way reduces Logan's velocity, but improves his command.

Aceves has become strictly a two-pitch guy. He throws his cutter about ninety percent of the time. It's often fatally straight, but this time he had some good movement away from the lefties. And he uses his change-up that moves away from righties. He had the on-target command that he absolutely requires, but in the long run, Aceves has to work both sides of the plate. Not just keeping his cutter away from lefties and his change away from righties.

Marte's velocity was there, but he tried to be too fine and consequently walked one guy and hit another. He usually throws two kinds of sliders—a looping slurve-type pitch to righties, and a flatter pitch to lefties that lacks depth but has more horizontal action. The fastball that Morales nailed was meant to be near the outside corner but was right down Broadway.

Sergio Mitre's rust was showing. And his relapse into his nervous delivery prevented him from getting on top of his pitches. So his curve was straight and his fastball had no discernible sink.

In other words, the Yankees bullpen really isn't in very good shape.

⚾ THE OFF day, April 26, 2010, saw the Yankees at the White House to meet President Obama in celebration of their 27th World Championship. Obama congratulated them, but still got in his plug for his hometown White Sox, doffing the cap with the calligraphic S.

From there the Yankees went to Walter Reed Army Medical Center to connect with patients for a few hours.

Alas, after the cross-country flight from LA and their day off spent in the hoopla of the Pennsylvania Avenue ceremony, the team was not rested.

⚾ MANY DIEHARD Yankee fans don't know that the franchise actually began in Baltimore in 1901 and then moved to New York in 1903. Ancient history, especially considering the state of the Orioles now.

A quick recap of the three games in Baltimore.

April 27–29 @ Camden Yards

In the first game, Hughes struggled, but still left with the Yanks up 2-1. Logan and Robertson both got F's for blowing the lead. Robertson's ERA is now an astronomical 10.80. An even more startling stat is that he has allowed hitters to reach base on 60 percent of balls put in play against him, compared to the MLB average of 29.2 percent. Aceves came in late and earned a B for good, not great, stuff.

Baltimore 5, New York 4
Losing Pitcher: Robertson (0-1)

Game Two @ Baltimore, April 28

In game two, C.C. was nicked for eleven hits in 7 2/3 innings, but he induced a pair of double plays that got him out of jams. Meanwhile, the lineup was blasting the ball all around the yard and jumped to an 8-3 lead. Joba took over with two on and two out, and got a bounce-out on a nasty slider. Grade: A. Mop-up duty fell to Mitre. Three exquisitely sinking fastballs led to three groundball outs and the game was in the books. Grade: A.

There was bad news after the game on Park's sore right hamstring. While another MRI uncovered no new damage, the soreness was unrelieved and the doctors were mystified. As a result, Park's stay on the DL was downgraded to "indefinite."

New York 8, Baltimore 3

Game Three @ Baltimore, April 29

In the third game, Burnett had his mojo working. His fastball topped out at 97 mph and his curve was crackling. After eight innings, he retired with a 4-0 lead. Even though this wasn't a save situation, Mo hadn't pitched in a week and simply needed the work. A handful of lively sliders eased Mo to a grade of A.

New York 4, Baltimore 0

At Month's End

The Yankees concluded the road trip at 5-4, bringing their overall record to 14-7 and placing them just 2½ games behind the first-place Rays at the end of April. The Yankees' W-L record is even more impressive since they've played fifteen games on the road and only six in their home grounds just off the Major Deegan Expressway. So far the Yanks have been mostly carried by timely hitting and sterling starting pitching.

The inconsistency of their bullpen must be resolved ASAP.

Bullpen Scorecard for April

Here are the average grades for the relievers thus far:

Mariano Rivera (9 appearances): 3.72 = A–
Joba Chamberlain (11): 2.72 = B–
Sergio Mitre (3): 2.91 = B–
Alfredo Aceves (6): 2.40 = C+
Boone Logan (3): 2.30 = C+
Damaso Marte (9): 2.21 = C+
Chan Ho Park (3): 2.17 = C+
Dave Robertson (7): 2.00 = C

The composite grade over 48 total relief appearances is C+ (2.54). Without Rivera, the average works out to C– (2.27).

Memory Lane

The Home of Champions

A mystique of history and heritage surrounds the New York Yankees.
—PAUL BLAIR

As the old Yankee Stadium was being sadly torn down last winter and spring and fans could see the "progress" on websites, in the papers, and as they walked into the new stadium, I was prone to some serious nostalgia.

THIS WAS a deal neither my parents nor I could resist. If I could scrape up the meager sum of $1.35, I would be permitted to be out in the world on my own recognizance for about nine hours—which meant that I'd also be out from underfoot for the same period. For twelve-year-old me, the agreement was even better: an opportunity to spend a thrilling afternoon eyeballing the Bronx Bombers at Yankee Stadium.

My parents could afford to fork over the necessary funds only once or twice a week. But in addition to my fifty-cents-per-week allowance, I was paid a dime every time I swept the floors in my family's two-bedroom railroad flat, plus an extra nickel for the tedious job of dusting my mom's collection of miniature and oddly shaped perfume bottles. And on Saturday when the Yankees were on the road, I worked for fifteen cents an hours plus tips delivering orders from a local grocery store.

This is how my game finances broke down:

Ten cents for the bus rides each way, including one free transfer with every fare.

Eighty cents for general admission to the sunbaked bleachers.

Ten cents for a scorecard. *"Scorecard here! Yankee scorecard here! Can't tell the players without a scorecard!"* Not that I was particularly interested in keeping score, or that I hadn't already memorized each player's and coach's uniform number. It was just a souvenir, something to flash in the jealous faces of my buddies when I returned back to Fulton Avenue later that day.

Ten cents for a good-sized bag of salted peanuts. A good deal for a snack that lasted for several innings once I got the knack of soaking each peanut, shell and all, in my cheek for at least one at-bat.

Coupled with the solitary, barely gurgling water fountain that was available to the three thousand denizens of the bleachers, the salty nuts made purchasing cups of "orange drink" mandatory. This minimally flavored, lukewarm beverage was carried about in large metal canisters strapped to the backs of the ever-present vendors, and was dispensed by plastic taps set at the end of long metallic tubes.

These wandering vendors carted two sizes of paper cups—"large" and "medium"—for ten- and five-cent portions. The large cups encouraged gulping and never lasted long enough. Two medium cups contained slightly more of the pale orange stuff than one large cup. So pacing my usual consumption of three cups was a major undertaking that was frequently complicated by extra innings and doubleheaders.

Beer was also for sale from mobile vendors, but only Ballantine, the Yankees' TV and radio sponsors. *"It's a Ballantine blast,"* Mel Allen would intone whenever a good guy reached the seats. (Giants fans always drank Knickerbocker beer, while Dodgers fans routinely inhaled Schaefer beer.)

Besides my jingling coins, I also carried a tuna salad sandwich in a small greasy paper bag and my autograph book. To quickly lighten my burden, I usually ate my sandwich as soon as I transferred at 161st Street for the crosstown bus. I also carried several dozen self-addressed penny postcards for the pregame business at hand.

This had to do with my being an autograph hound. That meant I'd arrive at the House That Ruth Built at about nine bells, just when the visiting players and the hometown heroes would arrive. Then I'd join the desperate, bustling dozens of similar fanatics trying to get close enough to the Mick, the Scooter, Yogi, Battling Billy, Steady Eddie, the Chief, or whomever we could intercept during their thirty-yard walk between the players' parking lot and the cops who kept us away from the players' entrance.

The same relentless elbow-flailing, pushing-often-coming-to-punching melee would be repeated when the visitors' bus arrived.

"Who'd ya get?"

"The Mick!"

"Wow!!"

"Andy Carey."

"Aw, he's no big deal. I got a million of him. He always stops and signs for everybody."

"Who'd ya get?"

"Casey?"

"Where? How? When?"

"Just now. He took the train and got off the el."

"And he was signing?"

"For everybody."

Some of us would then make a mad dash for the train station at River Avenue and 161st Street in hopes of intercepting Stengel before he ducked into one of the Stadium's private entrances. I never did catch up with the wily Ol' Perfessor. In fact, the only celebrity subway rider whose autograph I ever did capture was on Old Timers' Day when I came across a squat, burly, middle-aged man and asked, "Who are you?"

Turned out to be Jimmy Foxx.

When players wouldn't pause to sign, we'd try to thrust a post-card into their hands, pockets, belts, whatever. As a last resort, we tossed postcards through open windows on the team bus. About 50 percent of the postcards were returned with bona fide signatures. The rest vanished.

Once inside the Home of Champions, I made a beeline to my accustomed position in the middle of a certain long, frayed wooden bench situated precisely ten rows up from the home-run fence and directly behind where the leftfielder would be stationed when a power-hitting righty was at bat. That's because my absolutely favorite player, Gene Woodling, was a dependable .300 hitter, as well as the undisputed master of playing all the angles necessary to survive in the Stadium's infamous sun field. Of course, this also meant that I'd be sitting in the sun for the entire game.

At the same time, Hank Bauer's fans sat in the partially shaded right-field section, Mantle's in the middle, and the gamblers claimed the always-shady spot just under the NO BETTING sign.

Once a month, when the neighborhood gang of street urchins made a collective trip to the Stadium, we always sat in the centerfield section because our cigar-smoking thirteen-year-old leader, Bobby Jeff, was a diehard fan of the Mick's. When I flew solo, though, broiling in the summer sun was well worth the sweating just to be able to shout encouragement to Woodling.

Being naturally shy, though, all I ever yelled to him was "Atta boy, Gene!" And even though I tried to duplicate a right-handed version of his corkscrew batting stance whenever my buddies and I played stickball in Crotona Park, he never turned around to acknowledge my undying loyalty.

Another surefire way for me to ensure that I was always in the seat of my choice had something to do with the fact that, during every game I ever attended, I used my trusty Boy Scout knife to crudely engrave the appropriate date in the soft wooden bench. After the forty to fifty games I attended each summer until I became a high school senior at age fifteen, my dated tallies would extend the entire length of the bench.

Of course the engraved section was always removed during the off-season, but I still managed to make a temporary keepsake of my own particular mania last until the Yankees inevitably won the World Series.

After each and every game, cops cordoned off the infield, the dugouts, and the bullpens. Otherwise, children of all ages could run amok in the outfield, making fantastic diving catches and sliding into imaginary bases. I couldn't begin to count how many times I'd robbed Ted Williams of line-drive doubles hit into the right-centerfield gap.

When the cops started clearing the field, I sometimes pulled a crushed orange drink cup out of my pocket—in planning this procedure, I'd make sure to buy a large—then fill the cup with as big a divot as I could dig from right field. Never left field, lest Woodling catch his spikes in pursuit of a flyball and wrench an ankle.

By dint of diligent watering, I could keep my Yankee Grass alive for about a week.

May 2010

- The Phils get caught with binocs in the bullpen, the Yanks visit old friend Johnny Damon, and Papelbon gets advice from Rivera.
- A wild pitch walk-off, broken leg walk-off, and a balk-off.
- Interviews with Damaso Marte and Boone Logan.
- Joba earns 7 A's but 2 F's, and Triple-A call-ups Nova and Sanchez impress.
- Lastly, a robbery, followed by the story of a truly blown save.

Baseball is almost the only orderly thing in a very unorderly world.
If you get three strikes, even the best lawyer in the world can't get you off.
—BILL VEECK

April 30–May 2, Chicago White Sox @ Yankee Stadium

Pettitte got in trouble in the first when he was touched for two bloops and a bang. But the Yankees pecked away, and by the time Aceves relieved in the top of the 7th, the score was knotted at 4–all.

Ace got away unscathed when he unloosed an 0-2 change-up to Alexei Ramirez that was high and in primo hitting zone. Fortunately, Ramirez is a Punch-and-Judy hitter who punched a timid groundball to Teixeira. After missing with a pair of fastballs, Aceves snapped off the best slider he's thrown so far this season—and

Gordon Beckham took a mighty swing and did nothing except create a minor breeze. Beckham then popped up a fastball to Cano. Alex Rios, however, lined a 3-1 cutter to LF for a solid single, and on the first pitch to Paul Konerko, Rios stole second base; blame Aceves' big leg kick and long-armed backswing.

Still, the strategy was a questionable one for Ozzie Guillen. With two out and Rios now in scoring position, Aceves had no rationale for pitching to Konerko, who happened to be leading the American League in RBIs. Sure enough, Aceves (and Guillen) took the bat out of Konerko's hands when he was deliberately walked.

The Yankees' strategy eventually worked, as Aceves snuffed Carlos Quentin on a soft liner to A-Rod. Ace's grade: B.

After Jeter lashed a two-run triple in the bottom of the 7th, the Yanks led 6-4, and Damaso Marte was brought in to initiate the 8th inning with the expectation that he'd ring up LH Mark Teahen. Marte got the job done when Teahen grounded the sixth consecutive fastball he saw to Cano. Marte: A. It was now Joba Chamberlain's job to hold the fort and turn the 9th inning over to Mo.

And Joba came out with a light in his eyes and fire in his right arm.

Mark Kotsay dribbled a 95-mph blazer to Jeter, and A.J. Pierzynski bounced a devilish slider back to the mound to complete Joba's A-rated outing.

Mo time one mo' time.

But this time Rivera's cutter was moving too much for him to hit his spots. Even so, Juan Pierre bumped a soft liner to A-Rod. Ramirez whiffed on a 92-mph two-seamer that broke down and in. Mo then ended the game with a flourish, striking out Beckham with a cutter that moved as though it were alive. Rivera: A.

New York 6, Chicago 4

Winning Pitcher: Aceves (2-0)

Save: Rivera (7)

Bullpen diary: Aceves had command problems, and of the four batters who made contact, two hit whistling line drives, but he still got the win, thanks to Jeter. Marte also battled his command. His velocity varied from 89 to 92 and he threw all fastballs. His last pitch to Teahen, however, was picture perfect as it painted the outside corner. Joba's heater was smoking, and his command was fantastic—all five of his pitches were Ks.

Mo's velocity was also up, reaching 93 mph six times. It also seems that he's trying to compensate for the overall diminishment of his velocity by throwing more two-seamers than usual.

Game Two vs. the White Sox in the Bronx, May 1

Still another sad-sack outing by Vazquez created a nightmare for the bullpen. As in his previous starts, Vazquez threw lots of dead pitches that jumped to life only when they hit the visitors' bats.

With the Yankees down 5-1, Sergio Mitre was called upon to stop the bleeding. Against Beckham, Mitre was still a captive of his bad habits—tapping his front leg so noticeably before coming to a set that his body had barely stopped trembling before he began his delivery. Moreover, from the stretch position, his glove came to the required stop for only a fraction of a second, tempting a balk call.

Nevertheless, Mitre's sinker was dropping as though the ball turned to lead when it approached the plate. Beckham subsequently struck out swinging on said sinker. Mitre pitched very carefully to Andruw Jones, a wise tactic since Jones had already smacked a pair of homers against Vazquez. But the Yanks caught a break when Omar Vizquel danced too far off first and Posada picked him off. Mitre carefully completed a ten-pitch walk to Jones. The ever-dangerous Konerko was up next, but Mitre put him away with a change-up that was bounced to A-Rod.

After walking Teahen to start the 5th, Mitre resumed his lights-out performance, getting a pair of harmless groundouts and a routine flyball. Mitre then easily retired the next six batters he faced, most of them on sinkers that bottomed out. Mitre for the day: A.

The Bombers' lineup roused itself in the bottom of the stretch inning; a three-run HR by Swisher gave the Yankees a 6-5 edge.

Robertson was called upon to hold the lead, but he failed miserably. After Swisher made a great running catch on a Jones shot, Konerko sat on Robertson's fastball and lined a double. Teahen then creamed a 93-mph fastball down the 3B line, but A-Rod made a nifty catch and throw for the out. Robertson then threw a curve in the dirt and another one high and outside before Girardi ordered him to finish his stint by deliberately walking Quentin. Men on first and second; Robertson: D.

Damaso Marte was called upon to safeguard the one-run lead by erasing LH Pierzynski, except that Pierzynski cracked a two-run double to left-center that put the Chisox up by 7-6. It was decidedly anticlimactic when Marte retired LH Kotsay on a flyball. Marte: F.

Aceves worked a 1-2-3 8th. In the top of the 9th, Aceves faced the two most dangerous hitters the Chisox had to offer. But he mixed his cutters and his change-ups and got Jones to bang an off-speed pitch to Jeter. Then Konerko popped out on a cutter. Aceves: A.

Lefty Boone Logan became the sixth pitcher of the game when he was summoned to deal with LH Teahen—and he simply blew him away. Logan: A. The Yanks didn't rally in the 9th, but there were several positive developments to take from this game.

Chicago 7, New York 6

Losing Pitcher: Robertson (0-2)

Bullpen diary: Even though there was occasional movement in his lower body, Mitre certainly got on top of his sinker. One has to wonder: since Mitre has been a starter for most of his career, and since Vazquez was stinking up the mound, should Girardi be considering switching their roles?

At a minimum, since next Thursday is an off day before the Yankees make a return visit to Fenway and Vazquez is due to open the series, his next turn should be unceremoniously skipped.

While Robertson's velocity was up—sitting at 93–94 mph—his location was off and his fastball continued to be straight. How long before he's wearing a Scranton uniform?

Marte's fastballs were flat and he's increasingly unreliable.

Even though it lasted for only four pitches, Logan's stint was an eye-opener: 95 for a called strike; 95 just missing the outside corner; 95 for a swinging strike; then the 97-mph heater that Teahen was a mile behind.

It seems obvious that Logan is ready to usurp the erratic Marte as the primary lefty specialist.

BOONE LOGAN

Q: You're six-five and 215, so you must have played some hoops when you were a kid back in San Antonio.

A: I never did get into basketball. Not at all. I started out playing baseball when I was about six and I never was interested in any other sport.

Q: Being so tall must be a big advantage to a pitcher.

A: It can be if I can stay on top of the ball. That would let me throw on a down plane and make it harder for hitters to pick up my pitches because the ball wouldn't stay at the same

Boone Logan

Courtesy of Amanda Rykoff

eye level. Also, a longer stride gets a taller pitcher closer to the plate when he releases the ball.

Q: You said "if" you can stay on top of the ball.

A: Before Dave Eiland worked with me in spring training to get my arm up quicker, my arm was dragging. That meant my release point was too far behind the opening of my front shoulder.

Q: And since then?

A: I used to only be effective when I threw to my arm side.

Q: Being a lefty, that means throwing inside to lefty hitters and outside to righties?

A: Correct. But now that my arm action is quicker I'm comfortable throwing to both sides of the plate. Also, my four-seamer doesn't run back over the plate like it used to.

Q: In basketball, it's axiomatic that young players will usually revert to their bad habits in pressure situations. Are you locked into your new arm action yet?

A: Not really. It's something I constantly have to be thinking about, even during games. Actually, I've kind of hit a plateau with this. Sometimes I stay back too long before I move forward, and that leads to my bringing my arm up slower than I'm supposed to be doing. Then I'm back to my shoulder opening, my arm dragging, and then I'm behind 2-and-0 too much. This makes pitching at this level very hard. But I'm getting to the point where I can usually make corrections while I'm out on the mound.

Q: Several weeks ago, you had a game against the White Sox where your fastball was up to 97 and 98. Now you're usually around 92 or 93. What's the difference?

A: My velocity just seems to fluctuate. I usually sit at 93 and top out at about 97. I happened to be well rested that day and the weather was perfect, warm but not humid. Also, I was probably a bit psyched because I was drafted and signed out of high school by the White Sox in 2002, and then they traded me to Atlanta six years later. I guess guys always get a little psyched when they play against teams that gave up on them.

Q: Where are you now in terms of your career?

A: I think I'm in a good place. I have a lot of respect for the Yankees and the way they pay attention to every detail. Dave is a terrific pitching coach. I think I'm making significant strides being here.

Q: Aside from totally getting used to your new arm action, what other aspects of your game are you working on?

A: Sometimes I have trouble totally concentrating when I'm put into games where we're down by a lot of runs.

Q: With the Yankees' potent lineup?

A: Yeah, you're right.

Q: What else?

A: I need to be more aggressive. I have to trust my stuff and attack hitters. I can only hope that the Yankees trust me to continue developing.

DAMASO MARTE

The protocol in the Yankees clubhouse is that players are available to the media only when they are sitting or standing at their dressing cubicles. They're off-limits when sitting on the plush leather couches watching something on the huge wall-mounted TV screen—some ball game or other (maybe theirs from the day before), or a fishing show that, today, particularly entranced Sabathia, Robertson, and Chamberlain.

Players' privacy must also be respected when they are gathered around the long, centrally placed table where, on this day, they try on sunglasses freely provided by an earnest sales rep.

Meanwhile, Marte sits by himself by his cubicle and vaguely expresses his willingness to be interviewed. Born and bred in the Dominican Republic, Marte speaks fluent English, but doesn't have much to say.

"Throwing across my body comes naturally to me," he avows. "No problem."

Damaso Marte receiving his 2009 World Series ring

Courtesy of Amanda Rykoff

However, after signing his first pro contract with a team in the Dominican Republic at age sixteen and subsequently spending parts of eight seasons in the minors, and eleven (including this one) in the majors (with the Yankees, Pirates, White Sox, and Mariners), Marte has been on the DL a total of eight times. His disabilities included tendinitis and strains in his left elbow, left forearm, left biceps, left trapezius, and left shoulder.

"No problem," he repeats.

According to Marte, the only serious problem he faces is on the mound when he drops his elbow and his slider "doesn't work." Sometimes he can correct this problem during the game, and sometimes not.

"When it's three-and-two and the slider doesn't move," he says, "then it's too late."

⚾ SINCE THE bullpen was burned out after throwing six innings in relief of Vazquez, the Yankees recalled Mark Melancon from Scranton—where he had pitched to a sparkling 1.76 ERA in ten games.

It should be noted that Melancon relies almost exclusively on a

50-rated sinking fastball, but he's very slow getting to his release point, which makes his command much too erratic. Also, this flaw gives base-stealing runners an extra half-step.

However, this is an incredible opportunity for Melancon. Should he do a merely adequate job, look for Robertson to take his place in Scranton's bullpen.

⚾ CURTIS GRANDERSON strained a right groin muscle on the bases and had to be put on the DL. Note that the Yanks traded away phenom CF Austin Jackson to the Tigers for Curtis, and that Jackson is burning up the league.

Game Three vs. the White Sox in the Bronx, May 2

Hughes had everything working. He even used his newfangled change-up to induce a few outs. Meanwhile, the lineup enjoyed a run-fest. Melancon entered the game in the 8th inning with the Yanks up 12-0.

The young man celebrated his return to the big club with a perfect inning, using his change-up to get a strikeout and his fastball to produce a pair of flyball outs. His delivery was smooth but, except for a curve that was fouled by Jayson Nix, his pitches were somewhat lifeless.

But when Beckham led off the 9th with a hot shot that went through the legs of Ramiro Peña (who played third to give A-Rod a day off), Melancon's poise was clearly compromised. The error was followed by a hard single by Andruw Jones, and then a solid HR by Konerko that landed deep in the second deck in LF. Melancon escaped further damage by using his sinker to get two groundouts and another flyball. His grade: a disappointing D+.

New York 12, Chicago 3

Bullpen diary: In all, Melancon threw 24 fastballs and nudged the radar gun up to 94 mph. However, most of these pitches sat at 92 and very few of them showed significant depth—as witnessed by the three outfield outs and two line-drive hits, against only three groundballs. At first glance, then, Robertson's spot on the roster is not in danger. In fact, Melancon will most likely be demoted as soon as the bullpen corps has a chance to catch its breath.

May 3–5, Baltimore Orioles @ Yankee Stadium

A quick recap of the sweep against the woeful O's, though it almost wasn't so, and Andy and Mariano are going to miss a few days.

In the series opener, Sabathia made one bad pitch in his eight innings on the mound—a HR to Matt Wieters—and otherwise clipped the Orioles' wings. Joba had little control of his sliders but pitched an uneventful 9th to earn a grade of A- and record his first save of the year.

New York 4, Baltimore 1
Save: Joba (1)

Game Two @ Baltimore, May 4

In game two, Burnett's curveball was the best he's had so far this season. The only run he allowed was unearned and caused by his own throwing error. He was relieved by Marte with one on and one out in the top of the 8th. The only batter Damaso faced was Wieters, a switch-hitter whom Girardi wanted to bat righty because of the homer-friendly proximity of the right-field porch. Mixing his sliders and his fastball, Marte whiffed him with a powerful 93-mph blazer, thereby earning an A. Alfredo Aceves came on to pitch to the dangerous Miguel Tejada and barely escaped disaster when a cutter was blasted to deep CF, where Gardner made a nifty catch on the warning track. Although he did get the final out of the inning, the long drive reduced Aceves' grade to B. Joba worked the 9th using his curve in lieu of his still useless slider, and easily retired the O's after yielding a groundball single up the middle. In so doing, Joba earned an A.

New York 4, Baltimore 1
Save: Joba (2)

Game Three @ Baltimore, May 5

Girardi had to use all five available relievers in game three, but the worst news was Pettitte's having to be lifted after five innings with a stiff elbow.

Was this just normal early-season soreness for Pettitte? Or a recurrence of a chronic problem that was the real reason why the Yankees made only a minimal attempt to re-sign Pettitte when he became a free agent in 2005? The Yankees announced that Pettitte "would probably" miss one turn.

A 6-1 lead seemed safe, especially when Mitre cruised through two innings with a drop-dead sinker. But with one out in the 8th, he gave up an infield single and his mojo seemed to desert him. He resumed his little toe-tapping dance with his back foot just before starting his motion, and he delivered a flatline sinker up in the zone that Ty Wigginton deposited deep in the LF stands. Exit Marte with a C-, and the Yankees' lead reduced to 6-3. The Yanks tacked on another run in the bottom of the 8th, and then Robertson was next. After he struck out Nick Markakis, the next four batters hit bullets. One landed in Swisher's glove in deep RF; another dropped in front of Gardner in CF.

But both the third and the fourth were caught by paying customers in the LF grandstand.

Robertson made another ignominious departure with another F, and only two outs away from the sweep, Logan came on and walked his first batter. But then he started firing darts; his fastball varied from 94 to 96 mph, and he even let loose one that raised the radar reading to 97. But instead of relying on his overpowering velocity and more than adequate movement, Logan kept trying to hit the corners of the K-zone. When he walked the light-hitting Julio Lugo, who had managed to foul off a 99-mph blazer, Boone was yanked. For putting guys on and letting the potential winning run come to the plate, Logan is awarded a D-.

With Mo out, Melancon back in Scranton, and Joba having pitched two days in a row, Aceves was the final available reliever. Fortunately, Wigginton lofted a flyball to RF to end the game. Ace gets an A.

New York 7, Baltimore 5
Save: Aceves (1)

Bullpen diary: Worse news than Pettitte's elbow was that Joba was used in save situations the first two games instead of Rivera because Mo had a slight stiffness in his left side. Indeed, it turned out that Rivera had suffered a pulled forty-year-old muscle in his rib cage and would be incapacitated for several days.

After the Series
The Yanks were fortunate to finish their mini home stand at 5-1, but next on the itinerary was a three-game series in Boston.

It was definitely decided that Vazquez would skip a turn and

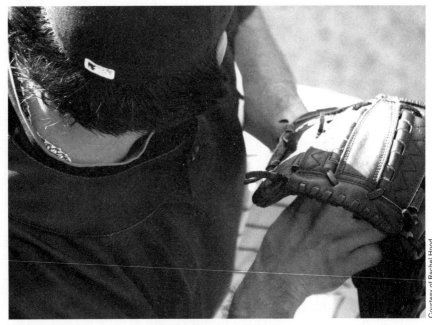

Courtesy of Rachel Hood

Sergio Mitre in the bullpen

work on his mechanics in the bullpen with Dave Eiland. This would presumably save Vazquez the humiliation of being pounded by the Bosox in the bandbox confines of Fenway Park. It was also reported that Mariano would "almost certainly" be ready for action in Boston. But who would substitute for Pettitte in the subsequent series in Detroit? Unless he was put on the injured list to allow a minor leaguer to be called up, the most likely candidate appeared to be Sergio Mitre.

Hmmm. What did that scout say in spring training about the apparently awesome Yankees bullpen eventually coming to grief in April and/or May because of injuries?

May 7–9 @ Fenway Park

Hughes continues to pitch like a top-three starter, completing seven effective innings and leaving with a 10-2 lead.

David Robertson replaced Hughes in the bottom of the 8th and began his stint by whiffing the tough Dustin Pedroia on a sharp-breaking 12-to-6 curve. Unfortunately, Robertson followed this by bouncing his next curve, throwing a subsequent bender high and wide and walking the next two hitters on eleven pitches.

Robertson seemed afraid to challenge the hitters with his fastball, and looked to be overthrowing. When he tried to get ahead of Big Papi with a super-duper fastball, he stumbled as he released the ball and wasn't near the K-zone. Even so, Robertson came back to get Ortiz looking at a bottom-heavy curve. But then Beltre lined an RBI single to right-center, before Jeremy Hermida fouled out to A-Rod to close the book on the 8th inning. Robertson gets an F because three of the five batters he faced reached base.

Logan was the next candidate, and his fastballs continued to push the radar gun into the mid-90s. Conscious that he was on the long end of a 10-3 lead, nine of Logan's eleven pitches were fastballs. After getting behind 2-0 against Victor Martinez, Logan assumed that the take was on, so he tossed a straight-as-an-arrow 94-mph fastball right down the middle—whereupon Martinez laced it into CF for a single.

But the Bosox had their scrubs in the game, so Logan ended the game with three stress-free outs. Logan: B+.

New York 10, Boston 3

Bullpen diary: OF Greg Golson was returned to Scranton, and since Sergio Mitre would be taking Vazquez's turn in three days, Romulo Sanchez was called up to add another arm in the bullpen. In spring training, a scout evaluated Sanchez as possessing a superior 65-rated fastball and a 55-rated curve. But his control was rated 20, his command 30, and his mechanics were awful.

Meanwhile, Robertson continued to regress.

Game Two @ Boston, May 8

In the bottom of the 5th, Sabathia was nursing a 6-3 lead with two outs and a 3-2 count on Victor Martinez when the sky filled with rain and the game was delayed. Only one strike away from a probable win, C.C. was already showered and dressed when the game resumed after a seventy-four-minute delay.

The bullpen now had full responsibility to preserve the lead and claim the win.

Aceves was the first candidate, getting Martinez on a harmless groundout that made the game official. However, after giving up two hits and gaining two outs in the bottom of the 6th, Aceves threw a cutter for a strike to Hermida and then asked out of the game.

At first, the message was simply that his back had stiffened up. Later it was announced that he had felt a tweak while running to cover first on Martinez's groundout. Next, the Yankees claimed that Aceves had been bothered by a sore back all through spring training. The last word was Aceves' belief that he had a bulging disk.

The results of a subsequent MRI were never publicly disclosed, but Ace was placed on the fifteen-day DL. Aceves for this game: B-, but he ended up lucking into his third win.

Boone Logan finished off LH Hermida by whiffing him on a fastball. Grade: A.

With the Yanks having extended their lead to 8-3, Girardi took the opportunity to see if Robertson could get back on track under minimal pressure. But Robertson's fastball remained flat and poorly located. Two more solid hits in two-thirds of an inning derailed him again. F.

Joba cruised through the next five outs, issuing only a meaningless walk. His velocity ranged from 94 to 96 mph, and with such a significant lead, Joba kept his slider in his pocket. An A for him. Damaso Marte mopped up without creating more of a mess. He only needed twelve pitches to record the final five outs. Also an A.

New York 14, Boston 3

Winning Pitcher: Aceves (3-0)

Bullpen diary: Ouch! With Mitre scheduled to start to open the upcoming series in Detroit in lieu of Pettitte, the bullpen lacked a long man. That's precisely why the call went to Scranton for Romulo Sanchez. In order to get Sanchez as many pitches as possible, he had been starting in Scranton, and the Yanks had been pleased with his progress.

DL news: The second of the two hitters the Yanks brought to the team to compensate for the loss of Damon and Matsui—Nick Johnson—went on the fifteen-day DL today with a wrist injury. He and Granderson are both on the shelf.

Game Three @ Boston, May 9

The team wasn't scheduled for an off day until May 24, so it was imperative that A.J. Burnett save the already shorthanded bullpen by pitching at least seven creditable innings. Unfortunately, A.J. was wild in the K-zone and coughed up nine runs before he was yanked with two outs in the bottom of the 4th. Burnett's replacement was Romulo Sanchez, and although the Yanks never got back in the game, the rookie did a fantastic job.

Sanchez started off by getting Darnell McDonald to whiff on a 96-mph fastball. After a walk, a liner to deep CF by Pedroia ended the inning.

Sanchez's 6th inning featured another hard-hit out (by Martinez), a bullet base hit (by Drew), a topped groundball out (by Youkilis), and a futile third-K swing by Ortiz trying to catch up with a 97-mph fastball.

In the 7th, Beltre got under a 96-mph fastball and lofted a flyball to LF. Hermida whiffed on another 96-mph heater. Then McDonald just missed blasting a fastball into the stands, sending Swisher to the wall in RF for the catch.

Two more hard-hit outs and a routine 6-3 grounder, and Sanchez finished with admirable numbers: one hit, one walk, no runs, and three strikeouts in 4$\frac{1}{3}$ innings. But because six of the thirteen batters he faced smashed line drives, Sanchez's grade is "only" A-.

Boston 9, New York 3

Bullpen diary: Obviously, the extra pitches Sanchez threw as a starter in Scranton have done wonders for his control and his command. His fastball routinely reached an impressive 97 mph, but without much movement. He threw three sliders, one in the dirt, three out of the K-zone, and two that were swung at and missed. The rest of his total of 51 pitches were fastballs.

Triple-A: Since Sergio Mitre would be starting tomorrow in Detroit—and wouldn't be expected to throw more than 70 or so pitches—another fresh arm was needed. Sanchez was sent back to Scranton. But he'll certainly be back with the big club sooner rather than later.

The latest arm to get called up was attached to the right shoulder of Ivan Nova, a starter in Scranton's rotation who sported a 2-0 record to go with a 2.43 ERA. Nova's arsenal included a low-90s fastball with sinking action, a change-up, slider, and excellent command. The plan is to use Nova as an emergency long man in case Mitre gets shelled early.

Spoiler alert: The Yanks would lose three of four to the Tigers, but the series in Detroit wasn't a total waste simply because Sanchez and Nova would make such good impressions.

May 10–13 @ Comerica Park

Sergio Mitre had flown to the Motor City the day before, but the rest of the Yankees traveling party got to the hotel at 4 A.M. And the well-rested Mitre performed slightly better than his teammates did. In 4⅓ innings Mitre yielded four runs (one unearned) and left behind a 4-2 deficit. Robertson took over with still another chance to redeem himself. He breezed through the 5th and, having established the threat of his curve, went almost exclusively with his fastball to cruise through the bottom of the 6th for his best outing in two weeks. A for Dave.

Logan was ineffective against the two lefties he faced in the bottom of the 7th—a walk to Johnny Damon and an RBI triple to Brennan Boesch. Logan: D. But Joba blew through the 8th, striking out the side on a devastating assortment of invisible fastballs and disappearing sliders. Grade: A.

Detroit 5, New York 4

Losing Pitcher: Mitre (0-1)

Bullpen diary: Robertson used his fastball to get five first-pitch fastball strikes against the eight batters he faced. Logan's velocity was down from the 97–99 level from his last few appearances; 93–95 this time out. Joba showed the best consistent velocity since the 2007 season—96 to a blistering 98. In addition, Joba's slider was nasty.

If Chamberlain has gotten his stuff together, then, in tandem with Mo, the Yankees can force opponents to try to beat them in only seven innings.

Around the league: The Phillies got caught using binoculars in the bullpen to allegedly steal signs on the Rockies. Nothing was proved, but it's the latest chapter in a very, very long tradition of fielders and batters trying to steal the catcher's signs since, oh, the first game in Cooperstown (or Newark, depending on whom you believe).

Doing any sort of looking or listening in has become such a preoccupation of the team on the field that an entire generation of Little Leaguers will certainly emulate their favorite pitchers and cover their mouths when talking to the catcher.

Game Two @ Detroit, May 12

Because of yesterday's rainout, this was the first of a day-night twin bill. It also marked the return of Vazquez to the starting rotation. His fastball was still clocked from 89 to 91, a few yards short of last season's readings, but his breaking stuff was moving and he had almost total command of all his pitches. Trailing 2-0, Vazquez left after seven innings, having allowed five hits and recording seven strikeouts.

Logan made easy work of the bottom of the 8th. Once again his fastball sat at 93 and touched 94 mph only once, but his control was much improved. Logan: A.

Joba came in for the bottom of the 8th, and once again had his optimum stuff. Except, that is, for overthrowing a pair of wild fastballs, and then escaping trouble when Scott Sizemore ripped a hanging slider down the 3B foul line that A-Rod snatched after a full-body dive. Teixeira then made a nifty scoop of A-Rod's off-target throw. Joba: A.

Detroit 2, New York 0

Bullpen diary: This constituted the first shutout suffered by the Yankees as well as their initial three-game losing streak. But the loss was more easily swallowed because of Vazquez's effectiveness, Logan's control (seven strikes in his ten pitches), and Joba's 95–97 mph fastballs and wicked sliders.

And after striking out Magglio Ordonez on an unhittable slider, Joba put the finishing touches on his outing with one loud scream and two fist pumps.

It should be noted, however, that in the previous game as well as in this one, Detroit's closer, Jose Velarde, broke into a mini celebration after every out he managed to get.

A MYSTERY reliever—probably Jonathon Albaladejo—was stashed in a local hotel to be quickly activated in case the bullpen was overly taxed during this series. But with Vazquez surviving for seven innings, this move proved to be unnecessary.

Game Three @ Detroit, May 12

Once again Hughes was brilliant, hanging up zeroes through eight innings. The Yankees then padded a slim 2-0 lead with a six-run top of the 9th. Even though this wasn't a save situation, Rivera returned to action with a 1-2-3 inning. Mo gets an A.

New York 8, Detroit 0

Bullpen diary: Except for a couple of straighter-than-usual cutters, Rivera didn't skip a beat. His velocity ranged from 89 to 91 and his command was superb. Only three of his twelve pitches were out of the K-zone.

DL update: With Aceves on the DL and Mitre unavailable for a few days, the Yankees may have to bring up another reliever. Park is scheduled to pitch in an extended "spring training" game today, then throw an inning in Scranton on Thursday, and if there are no problems, they will activate him over the weekend.

Game Four @ Detroit, May 13

C.C. didn't have much going for him, and the Yankees bats were full of holes vs. Justin Verlander. So the visitors trailed 6-0 in the bottom of the 7th when Ivan Nova made his major league debut.

Nova showed a well-rounded, bottom-heavy curve that fooled the first major league hitter he ever faced, producing a called third strike against Adam Everett. Subsequently, Nova induced two harmless

flyballs and three groundouts. The veteran Damon was the only op-
ponent who got good wood on one of Nova's pitches—an 85-mph
sinker that flatlined and was smashed into CF for a single. Ordoñez
followed by bouncing another single through the middle. But Nova
got the dangerous Cabrera on a high-hopper to short—also on an
active, well-placed curve. The natural movement of Nova's fastball
was to sink and move into a right-handed hitter. So he wasn't afraid
to jam Gerald Laird with a 93-mph heater that was nudged to Cano to
complete Nova's highly successful two-inning stint. Nova's grade: A.

Detroit 6, New York 0

Bullpen diary: Except for a few fastballs that Nova understandably
overthrew, Nova's number one averaged 92 and topped out at 95 mph.

Here's a scout's eyewitness report on Nova: "He's more of a
thrower than a pitcher and his arm action is much too long. The

Ivan Nova with the Scranton Yankees

second time around the league, he'll have a tough time getting hitters out. Although he's not quite ready for the majors, in the long run he has enough stuff to be a middle-man capable of doing an average or even slightly above average job in the 6th and 7th innings.

"I wish we had him."

Around the league: There have been 48 walk-off game winners through May 13, but none against the Yanks . . . and none *by* the Yanks.

May 14–16, Minnesota Twins @ Yankee Stadium

In game one, Burnett had trouble locating his fastball and was fortunate to be on top of a 3-2 score when he was lifted with a runner on second and two outs in the top of the 7th.

Damaso Marte's task was to handle one of the toughest lefty hitters in the league—Joe Mauer, last year's AL MVP—in what appeared to be a game-deciding at-bat. But Marte failed to get under a 1-1 slider that spun lazily over the middle of the plate—and that Mauer lashed into CF for an RBI single that tied the game.

Next up was Justin Morneau, another dangerous lefty swinger. (Morneau is one of only a handful of Canadian players in MLB; others include Jason Bay and Russell Martin.) Morneau jumped on another limp slider and smashed it into left-center for a two-base hit that put the Twins ahead by 4-3. After intentionally walking Michael Cuddyer, Marte finally got his slider under control and retired LH Jason Kubel on a flyball.

For sure, Minnesota's M&M boys are prodigious batsmen, but there's no excuse for Marte's sloppy performance. Grade: F.

However, a dramatic grand slam by A-Rod in the bottom of the 7th propelled the Yanks into a 7-4 lead—and Joba was called upon to keep the Twins quiescent until Mo could put them to sleep in the 9th.

And Joba was magnificent. While he lacked the ultravelocity of his past few outings, his 95-mph blazers were extremely well placed. Also, after throwing his first two sliders in the dirt, Joba and Posada kept the faith, and with Delmon Young understandably sitting on a fastball, he unleashed another in-the-dirt slider that Young missed by about a foot.

Alexi Casilla whiffed on a 94-mph fastball, then Nick Punto hit nothing but air on a 2-2 slider. Three hitters, thirteen pitches, and Joba had struck out the side. Joba: A.

The Yankees tacked on another run that increased their lead to 8-4 and ruined a save situation for Rivera. Even though Mo hadn't seen action in two weeks (April 30 against the Chisox), he breezed through the last three outs.

His cutter was alive, and after nipping the low-outside corner, he concentrated on throwing high-inside to change the hitters' eye levels. Mo: A.

New York 8, Minnesota 4

Winning Pitcher: Joba (1-0)

Bullpen diary: Even though Marte was technically the pitcher of record when A-Rod launched his bases-clearing dinger, the official scorer was within his rights to discount Marte's claim to the win because of his dismal performance.

This was the 8th consecutive A performance that Joba has achieved.

All told, Mo threw eleven pitches, nine of them strikes.

Now if only Robertson could take care of the 7th inning.

Yankee history: Bronx fans of a certain age remember our own M&M Boys, Mantle and Maris—and the strange baseball season that is 2010 would continue. A *USA Today* article reported that an official scoring error on July 5, 1961, gave Maris an RBI too many (the run scored on an error) and a mistake on September 10 that same season gave Mantle an incorrect run scored (Bill Skowron scored it).

As a result, Maris drops into a tie for the '61 RBI title with Jim Gentile, but he picks up the run-scoring title that year; he had been tied with . . . Mantle.

Around the league: The Mets' Fernando Nieve uncorked a wild pitch that let the winning run score in the bottom of the 9th. This season would see more of these variations on the walk-off theme.

Game Two vs. the Twins in the Bronx, May 15

Pettitte celebrated his return to the rotation with 6⅓ sterling innings. The Bronx Bombers' lead was 3-0 with one out and the bases empty in the top of the 7th, but Girardi decided not to push Pettitte past the ninety-five pitches he had already thrown.

Another chance for Robertson, and another near disaster.

His fastballs were snappy and well situated at the bottom end of the K-zone. Cuddyer bounced an easy hopper to A-Rod. But Delmon Young worked a nine-pitch walk. After Brendan Harris drilled a first-pitch fastball on a line into CF, pinch hitter Jim Thome now represented the potential tying run. Even in the twilight of a career that has produced 579 home runs, Thome was still a long-ball threat—especially with the short porch.

Good-bye, Robertson (with still another F on his report card). Hello, Marte.

So far this season, Marte has allowed four of the six runners he has inherited to safely cross the plate. And after the previous day's debacle against Mauer and Morneau, Girardi was extremely desperate, didn't believe in Logan, or else had great faith in Marte.

This was the key at-bat in the game.

A 91-mph fastball missed outside. Then the catcher, young Francisco Cervelli, called for another fastball and gave Marte a target that was low and outside. But Marte threw it high-inside, right in Thome's wheelhouse.

Two years ago, Thome would have launched the pitch into the stands—but his mighty swing only ticked the ball foul. Two more 91-mph fastballs were fouled off, and a sharply breaking slider missed the outside corner, before Thome took another potent slider for a called third strike to end the threat, the inning, and, as it turned out, the ball game. Marte: A.

Driven by long home runs by Teixeira and Posada, the Yanks muscled to a 7-0 lead in the bottom half of the inning.

With precious few options available, Girardi entrusted Logan to finish the game—and he did with minimum damage. Drew Butera plopped a duck-fart single into RF, advanced to third on a couple of routine groundouts, then scored on a solid single by Mauer. Morneau also added a single, but Logan recovered by blowing away Cuddyer on a 92-mph fastball. There were no dramatics in the Twins' last licks. Just three harmless flyouts and a meaningless single. Logan: C.

New York 7, Minnesota 1

Bullpen diary: If Robertson's location was a mite better and his movement was slightly improved, his velocity was notably decreased— mostly 89–91 with only a pair of off-the-plate 93-mph hummers.

Marte's revived slider was a very good sign. In fact, his release point was slightly higher than it had been in the opening game of the series, thereby allowing him to get more on top of the ball.

Marte must share the credit with Dave Eiland. Even though his velocity and his movement were diminished, Logan's strike-to-ball count (28 to 10) kept him ahead of the hitters.

With the loss, the Twins' lifetime record at Yankee Stadium is now a dismal 3-25.

Triple-A: Last night Park pitched a scoreless inning in Scranton, and he'll be activated for tomorrow's game. Who will get demoted? Robertson or young Nova?

Game Three vs. the Twins in the Bronx, May 16

Today would end up being one of the worst days for the Yankees so far this season.

Sergio Mitre started, had his sinker working, and through five innings limited the Twins to a solo homer by Morneau. After giving up a ringing base hit to Orlando Hudson leading off the 6th, Mitre was replaced by Robertson with the Yankees up 3-1.

This was a critical outing for Robertson, especially since the first two batters he'd face were lefties Mauer and Morneau. Since Logan had logged thirty-eight pitches in yesterday's game and Girardi wanted to save Marte for later in the game, Robertson was in the pressure cooker. He walked Mauer with six straight (literally) fastballs that ranged from 90 to 92 mph. Morneau worked the count to 3-2, then Robertson launched a 92-mph fastball that seemed to be several inches off the outside corner, but which the umpire saw as a called third strike.

A huge out for Robertson. Huge enough to turn his season around?

After Cuddyer smacked a liner into Jeter's glove, Hudson was doubled off second and Robertson was out of the jam.

Thome grounded to short to start the 7th. After LH Kubel was late on a 93-mph heater, Robertson correctly read Kubel's swing and whiffed him on a duplicate pitch. A walk and a pop-up ended the inning.

Robertson was getting on top of his pitches and finishing his release. Although the only two curves he threw were useless, Robertson finally gained the honor roll with a solid A.

Joba took over in the top of the 8th with the Yankees still nursing their 3-1 lead. Denard Span started the trouble by looping a slider into LF for a single. Then Hudson bounced into a force play, before Mauer drew a five-pitch walk. Then, after being set up with a blazer off the outside corner, Morneau struck out on a down-and-in slider. A great job of pitching by Joba—so far.

Unfortunately, Cuddyer followed with a blooped infield single that Teixeira couldn't field cleanly. Out came Joba, having earned a solid B-, because he only gave up a pair of bloops and a semi-intentional walk, and in came Mighty Mo to close the door. Right?

But there were omens of disaster right away when Rivera's first two pitches to Thome missed inside and didn't have much movement. A strike clipped the outside corner, a couple of fouls, then a 3-2 delivery that was six inches below the K-zone. Say what?

Rivera, he of the 80-rated control and command, walked a lefty hitter with two outs and the bases loaded?

While baseball fans of every persuasion were still dealing with the shock, Jason Kubel whacked a cutter deep into the LF grandstand! The grand slam put the Twins ahead 6-3. Casilla struck out to end one of the most unlikely innings in the season. Mo this time: F.

Ivan Nova was touched for a couple of base hits in the top of the 9th but escaped further damage when Mauer bounced into an inning-ending double play. Nova gets a C+ because all four batters he faced made solid contact.

Minnesota 6, New York 3
Losing Pitcher: Joba (1-2)
Bullpen diary: Robertson's two-inning effort was the longest stint of the season—and will make him unavailable when the Bosox come to town tomorrow. Even though Joba's fastball topped out at "only" 95 mph, he looked more like a pitcher than a thrower, but was fatally wounded by cheapie hits. Rivera's front shoulder was opening a bit too early, resulting in his yanking his cutters and losing his pinpoint command.

Rivera hadn't given up a grand slam in eight years.

Because Sergio Mitre started the game and was expected to throw only five innings or so, Park was kept inactive so that Nova could serve as the long man if necessary.

After the Series

Posada fouled a ball off his foot and would be day-to-day. Backup Francisco Cervelli is an adequate hitter who has been catching C.C. regularly, and they have a great rapport. (They are both Venezuelan, but Francisco's Italian grandfather gave him entrée to play for Italia on the World Classic team in 2009, along with Mike Piazza, Nick Punto, and—who knew?—Mike "Human Rain Delay" Hargrove.)

If Cervelli has to step in every day, how would the other starters—and the relievers—respond to someone besides fifteen-year veteran Posada crouched behind the plate?

In any case, at this point in the season the Yankees bullpen is overworked, inconsistent, and a minor disaster.

May 17–18, Red Sox @ Yankee Stadium

As is the case in sports, as in life, every day's a new one, and today would see a 180-degree change for the Yankees.

Hughes is the first Yanks pitcher with five wins and an ERA under 1.50 through his first six starts since "Bullet" Bob Turley in '58, when Turley went on to win the Cy Young.

But Phil had his worst outing of the year, primarily because he couldn't command his fastball. Even though he was presented with an early five-run lead, he was given the hook after five innings with the Yankees clinging to a precarious 7-5 advantage.

Since Robertson had pitched yesterday and Joba had thrown 14 pitches three days ago, as well as 23 pitches yesterday, Girardi called for Logan to begin the top of the 6th. Logan's velocity was down to 91–93, but as usual he had trouble getting ahead of the hitters. Victor Martinez led off by blasting a grooved fastball over the RF fence. David Ortiz then clubbed a slider that lingered in the center of the plate for a single. Logan avoided further damage when Beltre bounced a two-seamer to Jeter, who initiated a swift double play. In conclusion, Hermida tapped back to Logan.

As the inning unfolded, Logan's heater heated up to 94 mph, but he had more command of his breaking pitches than his fastball. Because Hermida's was the only ball that wasn't creamed, Logan: D-.

Park was activated prior to the game, with Ivan Nova returned to Scranton. And Park made his reappearance in the top of the 7th.

The first-batter blues struck when Darnell McDonald laced a fastball for a single. Park got Scutaro on an easy flyball to left, and Pedroia nailed a change-up but hit the ball right at Cano for a quick double-dip.

Somewhat of a close call, but whichever baseball deities have connected Park's immediate fortunes to his lack of success with leadoff hitters took notice when J.D. Drew initiated the top of the 7th by rocketing a single to RF.

It was obvious that Park didn't trust his fastball when he threw nothing but curves and sliders to Youkilis—the last being a hanger up in the hitting zone. Youkilis took a home-run swing—and made it so. The Bosox took an 8-7 lead.

A six-pitch sequence to Victor Martinez culminated in a 92-mph fastball being blasted into the RF bleachers. As me and my fellow bleacherites would have said of Park, "He shudda stood in bed." Too bad there's no lower grade than an F.

Damaso Marte finished out the inning by getting a pair of grounders sandwiched around a soft fly, and the top of the 8th commenced with another flyout, but then Scutaro drilled a 91-mph fastball up the middle for a base hit, and Pedroia sat back and enjoyed the gift of a four-pitch walk. Marte remained in place to pitch to Drew and erased him on a grounder to second. Because Marte easily retired all three of the lefties he faced and protected home plate from being invaded by foreigners, he rates a rousing B+.

Javier Vazquez had spent the entire game in the bullpen. Since Sergio Mitre had started and hurled five innings on May 16, Vazquez was ticketed to be the long man. Whenever the TV camera focused on him, Vazquez looked extremely unhappy. "What was I doing in the bullpen?" he moaned after the game.

But with the Yankees facing a 9-7 deficit in the bottom of the 9th, using Rivera would have been superfluous. So it was Vazquez to the mound for the duration, however long that might be. Getting excellent movement on both his curve and slider, Vazquez whiffed Youkilis on a well-placed deuce to earn his first A out of the pen.

Every Yank-o-maniac certainly remembers what transpired in the bottom of the 9th.

With Papelbon on the mound, A-Rod hit a dramatic two-run homer to tie the score, and shortly thereafter, Marcus Thames clouted an even more dynamic two-run homer to provide an extremely happy ending, the Yanks' first walk-off of the year.

New York 11, Boston 9

Winning Pitcher: Vazquez (2-4)

Bullpen diary: The K-zone seemed to be moving just as Logan released the ball, and he had trouble hitting his spots. While it's true that Park's two rehab appearances had been against minor leaguers who usually lack patience and are apt to swing at bad pitches, his fastball lacked juice and his command was strictly minor league caliber.

Marte's release point was up, which meant that his arm was dragging and his pitches were up—definite signs of fatigue. Vazquez looked sharp.

However, the Yankees' ultradramatic come-from-behind win overshadowed still another miserable performance from their relievers. Something—anything—has to turn this widespread malfeasance around or the Yankees' season will be a prolonged exercise in frustration.

Still, this was the first walk-off home run of Papelbon's career, plus the first-ever time he's allowed two HRs in one game, and his first blown save since the middle of last season.

Jonathan Papelbon is the only closer in the American League who is routinely compared with Rivera. But, throughout his career, Papelbon has had more trouble with the Yankees than with any other team: 11 saves, but a lifetime record of 0-5.

Here's a scout's take on Papelbon:

> He's very aggressive and likes to elevate his pitches. Both his fastball and his splitter are 60 and his command is 55. He has a straight-arrow delivery that's very repeatable and minimizes the strain on his arm. You have to zero in and hit his fastball before he gets ahead in the count and throws his splitter.
>
> What really makes him great is that he has the kind of electric stuff that normally allows him to get away with making mistakes in the strike zone. But so far this season, he's repeating some of the flaws he had last year. That is, getting too deep in counts and making more mistakes than even he can get away with.

Here's what Papelbon said to Dan Shaughnessy of the *Boston Globe* after a blown save: "It's all about being able to turn the page. I learned that from Mariano Rivera at my first All-Star Game in Pittsburgh [2006]. He told me that if I was going to be great, I had to learn to do that. And that's the first thing I took into consideration.

That's why starters are starters, and setup men are setup men, and closers are closers. You can't breed a closer. Closers are born. And I'm a born closer. This is what I was born to do."

Triple-A: Before the game, the Yankees optioned outfielder Greg Golson back to Scranton and recalled Mark Melancon. With Swisher day-to-day while nursing a sore biceps, the Yankees were temporarily short an outfielder.

Game Two vs. the Red Sox in the Bronx, May 18

Sabathia didn't have his A stuff, primarily because the game was played in a constant drizzle blown by high winds. Still, he battled through seven innings and left with a 5-1 lead.

According to the master plan, Joba would hold the Bosox at bay in the 8th and then Mo would close the deal in the 9th. But A-Rod made a poor throw on a groundball struck by Scutaro, and when Teixeira couldn't make the scoop, the error put the leading lady on first.

Then Boston's bats started to thunder. A solid single by Pedroia. An opposite-field two-bagger off the bat of Drew. Although Youkilis didn't mash the ball, he managed to bloop a single to RF. Ortiz then clouted a long drive to left-centerfield and broke into his home-run trot, but was easily thrown out at 2B. Still, when the inning was over, the Red Sox had tied the score at 5-5.

Joba's menu of fat, juiceless 91-mph fastballs and lazy sliders, along with his poor location, earned this performance an F.

Okay, surely Mo had shaken off that grand slam he'd yielded to Kubel two days ago, and would hold the fort until the Yankees found a way to get to Papelbon once more.

It looked like business as usual when Mike Lowell topped a two-seam fastball and grounded out. Then, even though Darnell McDonald *obviously* failed to check his swing on a 1-2 cutter that *obviously* sliced a considerable piece of the outside corner anyway, the umpire ruled the pitch a ball. Three pitches later, McDonald lined a 90-mph cutter for a single.

The key play of the game: Scutaro lifted an 89-mph cutter into short LF, where both Thames and Cano circled around the spot where the ball was expected to come back down to earth. Thames has never been accused of being a superior fielder, but with the departure of Golson, Girardi had no defensive specialist to replace him with. Of course, the wind caught the ball, and it bounced off Thames' glove for an error.

But when Pedroia dribbled a grounder that Teixeira easily handled for the second out, and with Hermida due up, it looked as though Rivera would pitch himself out of the jam. Alas, Hermida socked a 90-mph cutter for a solid double—and the Red Sox assumed a 7-5 lead.

The two runs were unearned, but Rivera got tagged with his second F of the year.

The Yankees did respond with a run in the 9th but failed to plate the tying run from third with one out when Papelbon made a neat pickup of a grass-cutter by Thames, and then struck out Randy Winn.

Boston 7, New York 6

Losing Pitcher: Rivera (0-1)

Bullpen diary: It's common knowledge around the league that Joba tends to get too comfortable when he's on a hot streak. That's when he loses focus and his already precarious mechanics completely break down. "I made some terrible pitches," Joba told the media postgame, which was certainly an understatement.

The news was even worse for Rivera, whose cutter frequently registered as low as 88 mph.

Both guys were victimized by errors, and Mo was hurt by a botched call by the ump. But errors and ump's mistakes are among the routine hazards that every pitcher must face—just as sensational diving catches that save multiple runs are routine bonuses. The most alarming aspect of this game is Rivera's gross inadequacies in consecutive games. He is, after all, forty years old.

And in baseball as in the real world, the older you get, the faster you get older.

DL update: As if the injury report could get any worse, Jorge Posada went on the fifteen-day DL with a hairline fracture in his foot, and Nick Johnson went to the sixty-day DL.

Triple-A: The Yanks called up catcher Chad Moeller again (Jesus Montero, the heir apparent to Posada, needs more seasoning in the minors) and recalled an infielder from Scranton who could also play outfield a kid named Kevin Russo.

May 19–20, Tampa Bay Rays @ Yankee Stadium

For the Rays' first visit to the Bronx this season, Burnett's fastball was disobedient and it seemed as though the Rays pounced on his every mistake. Still, Burnett took a beating for as long as he could in order to save the bullpen. He pitched 6 ⅔ innings and left on the short end of a 6-2 score.

Logan got the third out in the 7th with a sizzling 93-mph fastball that Gabe Kapler lofted to RF—but Kapler was the last out that Logan could manage. A seven-pitch walk to LH John Jaso was disheartening, but giving up a line-drive RBI double to weak-hitting Sean Rodriguez was even worse.

Girardi took no pains to hide his look of disgust as he strode to the mound and sent Logan to an early shower. Logan's tenure with the Yankees seems tenuous, as he registered his second F of the season.

Mark Melancon was called up from Scranton prior to the game and was immediately thrown into the fire. In quick succession, he gave up an RBI single to Jason Bartlett; a monstrous flyball out to Carl Crawford; an RBI single to Ben Zobrist; and still another RBI base hit, this one off the bat of Evan Longoria.

Melancon was missing spots and his ostensible out-pitch exhibited no discernible sinking action. B.J. Upton continued the onslaught by drilling a 93-mph fastball for a double. Kapler then took a 95-mph fastball over the outside corner to temporarily end Melancon's misery.

The Yanks now trailed 10-2, and rather than waste another re-liever, Girardi sent Melancon back into the fray and hoped for the best—and the best was what he got.

After Jaso singled, Melancon whiffed Rodriguez and induced Bartlett to bounce into a double play. Melancon's 9th-inning recovery lifted his grade from a red flag to a not-so-solid D.

Tampa 10, New York 6

Bullpen diary: Logan's command was very shaky and he hasn't come close to the 97–98 velocity that he achieved two weeks ago against the White Sox. He shows just enough potential to keep the Yankees hoping for some degree—any degree!—of consistency.

Melancon was forthwith returned to Scranton. It's obvious that this guy is a terrific pitcher at the Triple-A level but doesn't have the goods to succeed in the bigs.

Game Two vs. the Rays in the Bronx, May 20

Pettitte had trouble keeping the ball in the park, yielded three round-trippers in five innings, and left the Yankees with a 7-4 deficit.

Remember Robinson's 3-2 fastball on the outside corner that struck out Justin Morneau four games back? As advertised, that one clutch pitch seemed to have righted all of his previous wrongs.

Against the Rays, Robertson got ahead of the batters, consistently hit the catcher's glove, and threw several knee-high pitches that barely clipped the outside corner—otherwise known as Hall of Fame pitches since they're virtually unhittable.

In his subsequent two innings, Robertson struck out Upton, Aybar, Reid Brignac, and Crawford. The two guys who managed to make contact—Dioner Navarro and Bartlett—hit easy groundballs. Another A for Robertson, as well as grounds for believing that his resurrection could rescue the battered bullpen.

Park's second appearance after his stay on the DL was not nearly as effective as his numbers might indicate: 2 innings, 27 pitches (18 for strikes), 2 hits (including a HR by Pena), 1 run, no strikeouts, no walks. The reality is that only two of his pitches were alive—a pair of fastballs to Bartlett that moved into the righty's hands and were called strikes. Also, Park's velocity only ranged from 88 to 90, and the first three hitters he faced crushed the ball. That's why Park deserved a D+.

Tampa 8, New York 6

Bullpen diary: The Yanks haven't had a shutdown performance out of their bullpen since Joba and Rivera closed out the second game of the day-night doubleheader eight days ago in Detroit.

With their third consecutive loss, New York is now five games behind Tampa Bay. For sure, they are the walking wounded, with Aceves, Posada, Granderson, and Johnson down and out, but their starting pitching is faltering and the bullpen is unable to bear its unfair share of the load.

Around the league: Trevor Hoffman, one of the greatest closers ever, has blown five of ten save chances so far this year. He is 1-3 with a 13.15 ERA and, worst of all, with 7 HRs allowed. A generation of greats is getting older, Mo included.

May 21–23 @ Citi Field

Vazquez returned to his normal spot in the rotation and had terrific command of all his pitches. Unfortunately, pitchers bat in National League parks, and while bunting a pitch foul prior to laying down an otherwise nifty sacrifice, the index finger on his pitching hand was nicked by the ball. He was removed from the game after throwing seventy pitches (including forty for strikes), allowing a single hit, whiffing six, and leading 2-0.

Robertson was Vazquez's replacement, and Alex Cora greeted him by bashing an opposite-field single. Then, after Jason Bay drove a first-pitch 90-mph fastball into Gardner's glove in deep CF, Girardi had seen enough. Robertson: C.

Damaso Marte faced only one batter, the Mets' prize rookie, LH

Ike Davis, who nubbed a fastball in front of the plate. But Davis was safe when Cervelli's throw was over Teixeira's head. Marte deserves an A nonetheless.

Enter Joba, armed with great command of his fastballs. As usual, he did overthrow several fastballs, but caught David Wright looking at a 95-mph Hall of Fame heater. Then he got Angel Pagan to miss a 3-2 slider that disappeared into the dirt on the far side of the plate.

Rod Barajas battled Joba through nine pitches to lead off the bottom of the 8th, but ultimately failed to connect on a slider. Jeff Francoeur punched a 94-mph fastball to shortstop, and Chris Carter looped a slider into Randy Winn's glove in LF. A return to his A game by Joba.

With the Yankees leading 2-0, and with Rivera having easily disposed of Jose Reyes and Cora, and with Bay on the wrong end of a 1-2 count, it looked as though the game was in the bag. But then Bay slammed a cutter into left-center for a stand-up double. And Davis ripped the first pitch he ever saw from Rivera into CF for an RBI single.

Suddenly, in the person of the ever-dangerous David Wright, the Mets had the potential winning run in the batter's box. But the suspense was short-lived as Wright bounced Mo's initial delivery to Cano to preserve the victory. Mo: D+.

Yankees 2, Mets 1

Save: Rivera (8)

Bullpen diary: The pressure was on Girardi to get his team back on the winning track, especially against their intracity rivals. Which is precisely why he used three pitchers to get three outs in the bottom of the 7th inning. Joba was on one of his rolls and showing some moxie by not giving in to Barajas. Still, Rivera's recent difficulties were extremely troublesome.

Game Two @ Citi Field, May 22

Phil Hughes couldn't keep his fastball away from the middle of the plate, nor was he able to close out troublesome innings. As a result, he was trailing 4–1, with all the Mets' markers scoring with two out, when he was replaced by Park in the bottom of the 6th.

With two out and a runner on first, Park threw a spinning cement-mixer slider that Reyes poked into CF for a single, but Luis Castillo ended the inning by bouncing a first-pitch fastball to Teixeira. Bay led off the bottom of the 7th with a slow ground-hugger, and A-Rod's off-balance throw pulled Teixeira off the bag—an infield single. Davis then popped up and Wright lofted an easy flyball to Swisher in RF. Bay then got a five-step jump and easily stole 2B just before Angel Pagan poked a slow but accurate worm-killer just inside the 3B foul line. It went as an RBI double. But Barajas popped a slider to CF to end the inning.

Park's pitches had lively movement, even if some were poorly situated within the K-zone. And since all of the damage was done by softly hit grounders, Park gets a C+.

Sergio Mitre made his return to the relief corps in the last of the 8th. His delivery was calm and his sinker was bottom-heavy, so it was no surprise that Francoeur popped up. Gary Matthews, Jr., futilely waved at a sinker that had excellent depth. Reyes hit a too-straight 93-mph fastball to CF for a single but was thrown out trying to stretch the hit into a double. A foolish play. Mitre: B.

Mets 5, Yankees 3
Bullpen diary: Park's stuff was outstanding. Mitre looks stronger and more confident after his brief, yet mostly successful, stint as a starter.

Game Three @ Citi Field, May 23
C.C. had no zip on his fastball, plus his location was erratic. After 5 innings, 10 hits, 6 strikeouts, and a pair of homers hit by Jason Bay, C.C. left the Yankees with a 6–0 deficit.

Sergio Mitre took over in a back-to-back appearance and was literally unhittable. Half of the six outs he recorded were elementary groundouts.

But Mitre also hit Bay's front shoulder with a soft curveball that failed to break. Mindful of the possibility that the pitch was retaliation for Bay's twin dingers, the ump behind the plate issued a warning to both teams.

However, pitchers who want to hit hitters do so with fastballs and not lollypop curves. Mitre's best outing of the season rates an A.

Logan was assigned what was apparently mop-up duty. A groundout, a single, and a double play gave Logan an A.

The Yankees created some drama when their bats came alive in the top of the 9th, but A-Rod struck out representing the go-ahead run and the game was history.

Mets 6, Yankees 4

Bullpen diary: It's axiomatic that sinker-ball pitchers are most effective when they're slightly fatigued and unable to overthrow their money pitch. After he threw a scoreless inning the day before, Mitre's sinker was filthy good. Logan also had terrific location with a fastball that topped out at 95 mph. A bang-up job by both relievers.

Around the league: There were fifteen walk-offs this week, including two involving the Braves in amazing fashion. First came on a winning grand slam off the leftfielder's glove—and over the wall—and then the Mets' David Wright's game-ending throwing error to first base.

This day in history: Seventy-five years ago today, on May 24, 1935, the first night game in MLB history was played at Cincinnati's Crosley Field. FDR threw a ceremonial switch at the White House, and the lights went on in Cincinnati. The first night game at Yankee Stadium? May 28, 1946, vs. the Washington Senators.

May 25–27 @ Target Field

A rainstorm (no more Metrodome) caused game one to be suspended after five innings with neither team having scored. The next afternoon, after Jeter cracked a solo HR in the top of the 6th, the Yanks led 1-0 and Burnett was the pitcher of record when Robertson took the ball.

The first batter, Mauer, literally belted a flat curve that struck the belt of Robertson's uniform pants at his right hip. The ball was hit so hard that A-Rod caught the deflection on the fly for the first out of the inning. Robertson shook off the blow and appeared to be okay.

After a walk, a pop-up, and a well-hit double, Jeter ranged deep to his right to field a hot shot off the bat of Delmon Young, and executed a trademark jump-throw to first that ended the inning and saved two runs.

Robertson only lasted for two hitters (and two outs) in the bottom of the 7th, getting sent to the showers when Span looped a single to CF. Because Robertson flirted with danger throughout this stint, and because he tossed too many hanging curves, even though he didn't allow a run his grade is C+.

Joba recorded the final out of the inning on a sharp grounder right at Teixeira, and with the M&M Boys leading off the 8th, Joba tried to muscle up his fastball. But Mauer smacked a 94-mph fastball for a single to LF, and Morneau took a pair of Hall of Fame strikes, 94-mph fastballs that nicked the low-outside corner, and swung and missed a high-inside 94-mph heater. A discreet walk delivered to Kubel was sandwiched between a pair of groundouts, and Joba had successfully relayed a one-run lead to Rivera. Joba: B+.

J.J. Hardy socked a cutter to deep LF. As soon as the bat hit the ball, Rivera was disgusted with himself, believing that he'd just yielded the tying run. But the ball was snared just in front of the wall. A cautiously crafted six-pitch walk to Thome was followed by a game-ending double play. Mo: C+.

New York 1, Minnesota 0

Save: Rivera (9)

Bullpen diary: Robertson was saved by his belt—and by Jeter's outstanding play. Perhaps the reason why Chamberlain wasn't up to snuff right away is that he isn't working hard enough in the bullpen.

Of Rivera's thirteen pitches, only six were strikes.

Roster moves: The Yankees announced that Alfredo Aceves' rehabilitation took a bad turn when he felt a sharp pain in his injured back while participating in a soft-toss session on flat ground. Although Ace was eligible to be reactivated today, it's now feared that he might require season-ending back surgery.

This development compelled a roster move: Logan was sent to Scranton, and Chad Gaudin was re-signed after being waived ten days ago by Oakland. Even though Gaudin was 0-2 with an 8.83 ERA in twelve games with the A's and was just as inept during his spring-training stint in Tampa, the Yankees were aware that at the end of the '09 season Gaudin had pitched well for them—2-0 with a 3.43 ERA in eleven games.

Game Two @ Minnesota, May 26

The regularly scheduled game began about thirty minutes after the completion of the suspended game, and Andy Pettitte's brilliant performance, coupled with a clutch top-of-the–9th HR by Nick Swisher, gave Rivera a 3-2 lead to protect.

However, since Swisher's two-out dinger caught the Yankees by surprise, Mo didn't have enough time to get completely loose before taking over. Girardi was within the rules when he had Pettitte complete his eight warm-up pitches prior to the start of the inning before summoning Mo.

Subsequently, Rivera made eleven pitches in inducing three elementary groundouts, thereby recording two saves in one day's work. Mo: A.

New York 2, Minnesota 2
Save: Rivera (10)
Bullpen diary: Mo's first A in five appearances.

Game Three @ Minnesota, May 27

Vazquez, the erstwhile innings-eater, couldn't locate his breaking pitches and was replaced by Park in the bottom of the 6th with two outs and the Yanks trailing 5-2.

Span hit a dribbler that ducked just under Park's glove and went for an infield single, before Hudson grounded out. Park walked the ever-dangerous Mauer to start the 7th, then Morneau bounced a base hit between Cano and Teixeira. That was enough for Girardi. Even though three of the four hitters he faced got on base, none of them made solid contact, so Park's grade is C-.

Marte was called upon to face Thome, but with fastballs sitting at 92 mph and clipping the outside corner, Thome never managed a good swing and could only produce a foul pop-up. Marte: A.

The next candidate from the bullpen was Chad Gaudin, who hadn't thrown a ball in the heat of real competition in ten days. His recent inactivity was not evident when he struck out Cuddyer with an assortment of lively sliders and late-sailing fastballs. But then Kubel whacked a mediocre fastball into the LF stands for a three-run homer.

For the remainder of his outing, Gaudin was impressive: two strikeouts, a lightly hit infield single, a walk, and a double-play ball off the bat of Mauer, who is arguably the best hitter in the league. Only one truly bad pitch at the worst possible moment reduced Gaudin's grade to C-.

Minnesota 8, New York 2

Bullpen diary: Park's fastball sat at 90 mph, about a foot longer than the 96–97 he showed in the '09 World Series. But since he's still only a few days removed from the DL, the Yankees have no choice but to patiently feed him innings. Marte is regaining the effectiveness he demonstrated in '09 during the Yankees postseason drive to the championship.

Gaudin was forced to throw a fastball to Kubel after several breaking pitches were fouled off. Still, the vast majority of his other offerings (41 in all) had above-average movement. At the same time, it's understandable that his command was shaky. Overall, a promising déjà-vu debut for Gaudin.

May 28–31, Cleveland Indians @ Yankee Stadium

Hughes reprised his early-season success with a solid seven-inning outing in which he struck out seven. The game was tight until Cano blasted a grand slam in the bottom of the 7th to give the Yankees an 8-2 lead, and that allowed Girardi the chance rest the mainstays of his bullpen.

Sergio Mitre's delivery continues to be smooth and repeatable. He threw only nine pitches, all of them bottom-heavy sinkers. In so doing he recorded an impressive strikeout, but even though a pair of up-in-the-zone sinkers were lined to CF, Mitre's 1⅔ innings earned a grade of B+. Park pitched the top of the 9th, hoping that the pressure-free situation would get his head straight while he got more angular movement in his stuff. And for the most part, Park succeeded. His fastball touched 94 mph in whiffing Austin Kearns and Luis Valbuena. Jhonny Peralta got under a late-sailing 91-mph fastball and popped out to Jeter. The only blot on Park's record was a solid single to LF struck by Russell Branyan, a lefty who routinely abuses even the best right-handed pitchers. Give Park an A.

New York 8, Cleveland 2

Of note: Peralta told Murray Chass of the *New York Times* back in '05, with a smile we assume, that the spelling of his first name is correct, and all the other Johnnies are misspellings.

This day in Yankees history: Today marked the fifteenth anniversary of Derek Jeter's call-up to the big time in May 1995. Jeter was with the Columbus Clippers Triple-A team, and when he got the call from the manager to pack his bags, he thought he was being traded. No, not likely for the Yankee first-round draft pick in '92 and the '94 Baseball America Minor League Player of the Year. He flew to Seattle and went 0-for-5 on May 29, 1995, but he and Rivera were sent back down in June. Buck Showalter brought them back up to experience the '95 playoffs, and starting in '96, the rest is mostly glorious Yankees history.

Game Two vs. the Indians in the Bronx, May 29

This game marked a total collapse of the bullpen.

Sabathia didn't have his best stuff, but he left after six innings with a bulging 10-4 lead. Robertson succeeded C.C. and was touched for two runs and only credited with gaining a single out. However, he bent over in obvious pain after delivering a ball to Peralta and had to be removed from the game. Robertson: C.

Sergio Mitre got the hook after throwing three more balls to Peralta, thereby completing the walk. Why was Mitre lifted so quickly? Because, said Girardi, LH Branyan was due up, and he routinely crushes righties. Mitre: D. Damaso Marte retired Branyan on a routine flyball to CF. Marte: A.

Then Joba simply blew the game.

He gave up four consecutive base hits on respective 94-, 95-, and 96-mph fastballs and a waist-high cement mixer of a slider. Although Joba got two strikes on almost every hitter he faced, he couldn't put any of them away until he struck out Shin-Soo Choo to finally end the inning. Joba: F.

(In '09, Shin-Soo became the first Asian player in MLB history to have a 20-20 season—20 home runs and 20 steals. He also has to do his required two-year South Korean military service by 2012; that is, until an exemption he may have earned for helping South Korea win the gold in the Asian Games.)

With the Indians leading 13-10, Gaudin got through the 9th with no damage after giving up a walk and a pair of hard-hit outs. Gaudin: B-.

Cleveland 13, New York 11

Losing Pitcher: Joba (1-3)

Bullpen diary: The initial report on Robertson's back was "a mild sprain." This is the very same early diagnosis that was issued for Aceves. Although Joba was lighting up the radar gun—he also threw a pitch recorded at 97 mph—his disastrous performance was further proof that location is much more important than sheer velocity.

Adding to Joba's woes, he couldn't throw his slider for strikes.
Around the league: Can the year get stranger? Kendrick Morales of
the Angels hit a walk-off grand slam—and broke his leg jumping on
home plate.

Players will have to consider toning it down, though the traffic at
home plate is one of the game's truly joyous moments. It's one thing
that the player greeted at home plate has to remember to toss off his
batting helmet so a teammate doesn't break his hand hitting him on
the head; now the same player has to remember not to leap into the
air and land on a piece of rubber wearing slippery spikes.

Game Three vs. the Indians in the Bronx, May 30

It was imperative that Burnett throw at least eight innings and pass
a lead to Rivera, the only rested pitcher left in the bullpen. And
that's precisely what he did. Burnett was trailing 3–0 after faulty defense gave up two unearned runs, but a dramatic rally in the bottom
of the 7th—featuring a three-run blast by Teixeira—presented the
Yankees with a 5–3 lead. In order to further spare the depleted bullpen, Burnett came out and pitched a truly heroic 8th inning, even
striking out the last two batters he faced. Rivera did his thing to
close out the game: two whiffs and a bouncer back to the mound.
Actually, the comeback ball was accompanied by the broken upper
half of the bat, which Mo neatly jumped over before fielding the
ball. A feat of sheer athleticism. Mo: A.

New York 7, Cleveland 3

Bullpen diary: Rivera's cutter had more life than in his past few appearances. And both of his swing-and-miss strikeouts came on two-
seamers. Looks like Mo is making necessary adjustments in his most
senior season.

Game Four vs. the Indians in the Bronx, May 31

Immediately following the 7th-inning stretch, the Yankees opened
up what had been a narrow 2–1 advantage by scoring six big runs,

highlighted by a grand slam by A-Rod. The rally put an end to Pettitte's day after he had pitched brilliantly. It also gave Girardi still another opportunity to get Park back in some kind of groove. Even though the game was out of reach, Park was reluctant to throw fastballs. Instead he utilized his slider to get five of the six outs he eventually recorded. However, he did tire a bit in the 9th, when he gave a up walk and a pair of singles. Park: B-.

New York 11, Cleveland 2

Bullpen diary: It's quite clear that as he rapidly approaches his thirty-seventh birthday, Park's fastball has lost several miles per hour. Since a slight (but late) tailing action constitutes the only real movement on his fastball, Park is obviously looking to depend more on his slider—the only pitch he throws that has both horizontal and vertical movement.

Around the league: The Dodgers won on a walk-off *balk* by the Diamondbacks' reliever Esmerling Vasquez. The last major league balk-off? The Braves over the Rockies in '08.

Bullpen Scorecard for May

Ivan Nova (1 appearance): 4.0 = A
Javier Vazquez (1): 4.0 = A
Romulo Sanchez (1): 3.75 = A-
Alfredo Aceves (3): 3.5 = B+
Damaso Marte (2): 3.3 = B+
Sergio Mitre (4): 3.1 = B
Joba Chamberlain (11): 3.1 = B
Mariano Rivera (8): 2.4 = C+
Boone Logan (10): 2.4 = C+
Chad Gaudin (2): 1.75 = C-
David Robertson (11): 1.7 = C-
Mark Melancon (1): 1.4 = D+

The total efficiency comes to C+ (2.64), which is precisely 0.10 higher than April's average. The erratic nature of the relievers' efforts is underlined by their accumulating twelve F's. Compare this to only ten F's in April.

⚾ ACCORDING TO the *Daily News*, at around 4 A.M. on Monday, May 31, in a Tampa motel, the Staten Island Yankees' pitching coach, Pat Daneker, called the front desk to say he'd been robbed. By two hookers. Of his 2009 World Series ring. (All key members of the Yankee organization got the rings.)

No one claims that professional athletes are any less or more prone to human foibles than the general populace; they just make the front page of the papers a lot more often.

Memory Lane

A Truly Blown Save

Here's the testimony of a onetime Yankee starting pitcher who wishes to remain anonymous:

"I'd pitched on Friday night and I'd partied with all my heart after my complete-game win. I was still hungover and feeling pretty blotto by the time I reported to the Stadium for Saturday's afternoon game. So I hid from the skipper in the trainer's room as long as I could, gulping down as many cups of black coffee as my already queasy stomach could take. Still, my eyes were bloodshot, my skin had a yellowish tinge, I felt like someone had driven a spike into my forehead, and it seemed that I was perpetually in danger of tossing my cookies. If the skipper saw me in this condition, his hard stare would be enough for me to vomit on his shoes. So, after cringing in the trainer's room for about five innings, and squatting on the porcelain throne for two more, I decided to hide out in the bullpen.

"Now one of the team's veteran relievers had a hard-on for the skipper, but only because he thought the skipper had a hard-on for him. It seems that the pitcher, let's call him Joe, had one or two top-notch years coming out of the Yankees bullpen and racking up a modest but impressive amount of saves. But as Joe's slider began to lose its bite, he was only being used in mop-up situations.

"Joe would sit in the bullpen and bitch about how he was being denied the chance to make the money he deserved. 'Wins and saves,' he'd say. 'That's what pays the big bucks. And here I am wasting the best years of my career only working in blowouts.'

"Anyway, on this particular afternoon, our best reliever had a sore arm, and two other guys had pitched long innings on Thursday night. The only other available relievers were Joe and some raw rookie who couldn't be trusted to wipe his ass after he took a crap. Meanwhile, our starter was in trouble every inning. Walking guys, hitting two or three, giving up line-drive hits, but barely managing to survive because the other guys made some stupid baserunning mistakes. Plus he was the beneficiary of two outstanding fielding plays that resulted in bang-bang double plays. And our lineup was smashing the shit out of the ball, so we were up by a score of ten to five. It should also be noted that if a reliever pitched three innings to close out a winning game, he'd get a save no matter what the final score was.

"Anyway, I was ambling through the tunnels on my way to the bullpen, praying that none of my teammates would hit a homer while I was en route. This was because the fans overhead would then start stomping their feet and screaming at the top of their lungs, and my head would surely explode. Fortunately, we had a very quiet bottom of the seventh.

"I was rounding the last turn and about fifty yards from the bullpen when I heard some big-time gasping and groaning coming from a nook where some maintenance equipment was stored.

"Turned out that Joe was facing me in a kind of half-crouch with his uniform pants down around his ankles. And squatting in front of him was a redheaded groupie that at one time or another had serviced most of the guys on the team up in the Concourse Plaza, a hotel a few blocks away from the Stadium where all of the single guys stayed during the season. She was always hanging around the hotel bar just waiting for the chance to be summoned. We called her 'Room Service Red.' But giving a blow job in the ballpark was something else again.

"Joe smiled when he saw me, and motioned for me to join in the fun. No, thanks.

"When I finally got to the bullpen, the phone from the dugout was ringing. The starting pitcher had already thrown about 120 pitches and was complaining about stiffness in his elbow. Skip wanted Joe to warm up in a hurry and take over in the top of the eighth inning. A save situation! But Joe was nowhere around. Not in the bathroom. Not in the private alcove in the corridor just outside the bullpen where we all snuck out for a smoke. Of course, there was no way I was going to rat on Joe. So the rookie was forced into the game and actually did a good job.

"When the skipper found out why Joe was really AWOL, he was pissed and fined him a hundred bucks, which was big money back in the day. Of course, Joe was then pissed at me for being a snitch and wouldn't talk to me until it was discovered that a member of the grounds crew had come upon him and Red while looking for some tools to repair a broken rake. And he was the one who told the skipper.

"To make matters worse, the rookie had pitched so well that not only did Joe miss the chance to get an easy save, but he was cut the following week.

"I've heard of guys blowing saves, but that was the first time I ever saw a blow job blowing a save."

June 2010

- The Year of the Pitcher takes shape, and the almost-perfect game.
- Interviews with Dave Robertson and bullpen coach Mike Harkey.
- Lady Gaga visits the locker room, and Dave Eiland takes a leave of absence.
- The Pat Venditte Rule.
- Yanks draft more really tall pitchers, and Mo grabs a bat.
- A true story about Yogi, Joltin' Joe, and knuckleballs.

We had a very scientific system for bringing in relief pitchers. We used the first one that answered the phone.

—CHUCK ESTRADA, RANGERS PITCHING COACH, IN A 1974 *BASEBALL DIGEST*

June 1–3, Baltimore Orioles @ Yankee Stadium

In game one, Vazquez had almost total command of all of his pitches and left after seven innings with a 3-1 lead. Here was another test for the grand scheme to use Joba as a bridge to Rivera. Joba responded with the most consistently high-octane fastballs he's shown all season long. He needed only eight fastballs (all of them 96–98 mph) to retire the side on a pair of flyballs and a grounder. Joba's grade: A. Rivera closed the game in good order with a trio of high-school-hop groundouts. Mo: A.

New York 3, Baltimore 1

Save: Rivera (11)

Bullpen diary: Despite the clean innings registered by both Joba and Mo, there were some potentially troublesome signs. The giddyyap on Joba's fastballs produced nary a swing and miss, and the flyout to lead off the inning was hit to the deepest part of CF. That's because none of Joba's offerings showed any discernible movement. Except for the first two pitches to start the 9th, the same was true of Mo.

Indeed, scouts all around the league are buzzing that Rivera isn't quite the force he used to be.

Game Two vs. the Orioles in the Bronx, June 2

Phil Hughes continued to show All-Star stuff with his well-placed fastballs and unexpected curves. With the Yankees up 8-1, Gaudin took over and got into trouble right off the bat when Tejada singled and Markakis doubled. But the threat was ended when Baltimore's 3B coach (and future interim manager), Juan Samuel, waved Tejada to the plate, where he was thrown out. Down by seven runs, this was a foolish decision. After walking Wigginton, Gaudin settled down. Two pop-ups, three groundouts, and a harmless double, and Gaudin was credited with a pair of shutout innings. However, because four of the nine hitters he faced got on base, Gaudin only grades out at C.

New York 9, Baltimore 1

Bullpen diary: Gaudin demonstrated that he might be an acceptable mop-up man.

After an extended stretch against some of the better teams, the Yankees are now beating up on some of the worst teams in the American League. While they are padding their records and certainly enjoying the mismatches while they can, the bullpen still needs to get up to snuff.

It should also be noted that Granderson is back in action in CF, and that Posada has come off the DL to serve as the DH. So the

Yankees' recent difficulties in scoring against above-average pitching need to be rectified by hitting coach Kevin Long.

Around the league: June 2 saw the infamous almost-perfect game, the one Tiger pitcher Armando Galarraga lost out on after the blown safe call at first base. But it was good to see the ump face up to his mistake and the players and fans act in a classy fashion that day and the next.

Game Three vs. the Orioles in the Bronx, June 3

Sabathia held the Orioles in check until he tired, and left after seven innings with a 6-3 lead. His departure created still another opportunity for Joba to pass the baton to Rivera.

While it was true that Joba had a 1-2-3 outing, it took him two batters to pump his velocity up to the 97 mph that he'd reached in his last outing. Even though he cruised through a 1-2-3 inning, two batters made hard-hit-at-'em outs, so Joba only rates an A-.

Mo got himself in trouble by walking Markakis and then hitting Wigginton—on a 3-1 offering! Mo then went to a full count on power-hitting Luke Scott, who had already clouted a homer off C.C. Since Scott represented the potential tying run, the 3-2 offering was the most critical pitch in the game. Rivera proceeded to hump up and throw a 94-mph cutter that was several inches off the outside corner, but Scott bailed Mo out by taking a futile swing for the K. After this drama, the rest of the inning (and game) was anticlimactic: a broken-bat grounder and another whiff. Rivera's grade: C-.

New York 6, Baltimore 3

Save: Rivera (12)

Bullpen diary: Joba's first pitch was a 93-mph fastball, and his tenth and last hit 97. His not being able to come out firing is a recurring problem.

Rivera issued a total of eight walks in '08 and twelve in '09; the base on balls he relinquished today was already his fifth in '10.

Around the league: A Mariners reliever got four strikeouts in the 8th inning today, thanks to a wild pitch on a swinging third strike and a scoot down to first. Surprisingly, this happens more often than we think. It has happened 54 times in MLB history, and greats like Gibson, Drysdale, and Walter Johnson have accomplished the four-Ks-in-one-inning feat. Knuckleballers Wakefield and Niekro (Phil) have done it, not surprisingly. Chuck Finley did it three times, A.J. Burnett did it with the Marlins in '02, and Kerry Wood with the Cubs, also in '02. No Yankee pitcher has ever had this luck/misfortune.

Has it ever happened in the World Series? Once, Orval Overall (yes, that's his name) did it—the last time the Cubs won it all.

June 4–6 @ Rogers Centre

Burnett's fastball had no zip whatsoever, and consequently he had trouble keeping the ball in the park. After giving up three homers to the Blue Jays, who lead the majors in dingers, Burnett handed off a 6-1 deficit to Sergio Mitre in the bottom of the 7th.

Mitre labored over the next two innings, but managed to escape, without undue damage after giving up a walk and a double. Actually, he was saved when Jose Bautista foolishly tried to tag up and advance to 3B on a long flyball from Alex Gonzalez, but was easily thrown out by Marcus Thames. The other four outs registered by Mitre were evenly split between strikeouts and groundballs. Mitre: B.

Toronto 6, New York 1

Bullpen diary: When Mitre pitched from a full windup, his motion was clean and steady, enabling him to get on top of his drop-dead sinker. From a stretch, however, he reverted to that incredibly extraneous toe-tapping. As a result, he wound up slinging his pitches, and his sinker was flat.

Still, after Sergio completed his fourth high-grade performance in his last five appearances, it seems as though Girardi now trusts him more than he does Robertson.

Of note: Before the game it was announced that Dave Eiland had been granted a "leave" to deal with unspecified "family matters." The official announcement made sure to mention that the absence had nothing to do with Eiland's health. Mike Harkey switches from the bullpen to the bench and will act as "interim" pitching coach, while Charlie Wonsowicz, the video coordinator and advance scout, who last pitched for St. John's University, will take Harkey's place in the pen.

MIKE HARKEY

At age forty-three, Mike Harkey still looks like what he used to be: a broad-shouldered, thick-chested, 6'5", 225-pound power pitcher. Back in 1990, as the National League's Rookie of the Year with the Chicago Cubs, Harkey posted a 12-6 record to go with his 3.36 ERA.

"I was always a pitcher," he says, "starting in the Little Leagues, up through the Babe Ruth league, and through my high school career

Mike Harkey and Mo

in San Diego. When the Cubs signed me in 1987, I could throw in the mid-nineties. But in the next couple of years, I had two surgeries on my pitching shoulder. After the first operation, I was down to the low nineties, and eventually I could only get it up there at eighty-nine miles per hour. That's when I had to learn how to pitch."

In all, Harkey achieved a career record of 36-36 with the Cubs, Rockies, A's, Dodgers, and Angels, before finally retiring in 1997.

From 2000 to 2005, Harkey was a pitching coach in the San Diego organization—making stops in Rancho Cucamonga, Fort Wayne, Lake Elsinore, and Mobile. Then in 2006, he was Joe Girardi's bullpen coach in Florida, before becoming the pitching coach for the Triple-A Iowa Cubs in 2007 after the Marlins fired Girardi. In 2008, Girardi brought Harkey with him to the Bronx, also to run the bullpen.

"Before the games," Harkey says, "I'm out in the pen with Dave Eiland watching the starters and maybe some of the relievers who haven't seen much recent action go through their workouts. Dave does most of the instruction out there, and that's when guys work on their mechanics. When the game starts and guys are warming up before entering the action, I may make some very minor tweaks, but my main job is to go over the hitters that are due up."

Harkey is necessarily more involved with overseeing the delivery problems of the younger pitchers.

"In the three years that I've been here," he says, "I've spoken to Mo about his mechanics maybe three times. I mean, he has great balance, a perfect straight line between his release and the catcher's mitt, a totally repeatable delivery, and he always finishes his pitches in perfect fielding position. The only quirk in Mo's mechanics is that he sometimes doesn't complete his follow-through and leaves his cutters a bit flat and up in the zone. But this is a rare occurrence and usually accounts for the one bad stretch that he experiences every season."

By his own admission, the most enjoyable part of Harkey's job description is his throwing batting practice every day. "The sun, the green grass, the crack of the bat—what could be better?"

As such, Harkey subscribes to an updated version of the young Waite Hoyt's memorable testimony on the joys of wearing pinstripes: "It's great to be middle-aged and a Yankee."

Game Two @ Toronto, June 5

A terrific outing by Pettitte (10 strikeouts) was marred by two bad pitches, both of which were smacked for round-trippers.

When Joba took over with two outs in the bottom of the 8th, the score was knotted at 2-all. Joba proceeded to throw seven consecutive sliders—the first of which was hit for a single by Vernon Wells, and the last being a flat spinner down the pipe that was fortunately fouled off by Jose Bautista, the league's leader in homers. Joba then whiffed Bautista with a 97-mph fastball. Joba also breezed through the 9th with two more strikeouts, a harmless single, and a pop-up. Joba's grade: A-.

As the game ventured into extra innings, Damaso Marte succeeded Joba. In quick succession, Marte induced a pop-up, issued a walk, and was saved when Swisher went to the RF wall to snag a long drive by Adam Lind. Even though Marte had retired the two lefties he had faced, Girardi was unnerved by Lind's drive and summoned Robertson to try to keep the game alive. Marte's grade: A-.

One pitch was all Robertson needed to get the dangerous Wells to hit into a force play. But Robertson's stint in the bottom of the 11th was more of a cliffhanger: a walk was erased by a double play. Then came a single followed by Buck smashing a drive that was caught at the wall in LF. Robertson's grade: B+.

Next to take the ball was Park. As the game stretched into the 12th and 13th innings, Park managed three groundouts and three strikeouts, while yielding a single and a pair of walks. Park's grade: B+.

Having run out of relievers, and not wanting to risk a possible extended outing by Rivera, Girardi was forced to send Gaudin in.

Whoops! A walk and a sacrifice bunt preceded Aaron Hill's game-winning single. Gaudin: F.

Toronto 3, New York 1 (14 innings)
Losing Pitcher: Gaudin (0-3)
Bullpen diary: Joba's fastballs ranged from 95 to 98, his slider was erratic, and he whiffed the dangerous Alex Gonzalez to commence the 9th with a curveball! If Marte's slider was outstanding, his fastball was ordinary. Robertson got his twin-killing by jamming Gonzalez with a fastball, but John Buck nearly hit a hanging curve into the LF seats. Park obviously had no faith in his fastball, getting four of his six outs with sliders. Gaudin demonstrated precisely why the Yankees don't trust him in clutch situations. Surely one of the younger arms—Nova or Sanchez—would be a significant improvement.

Game Three @ Toronto, June 6
Vazquez had great stuff, but his command of his change-up was totally awesome. In seven innings he struck out ten and was touched for only one hit—a two-run homer that put him in a 2-0 hole. But the Yankees rallied for four runs in the top of the 8th and Joba was called upon to conserve the 4-2 lead.

Girardi was already in the clubhouse, having been banished after taking issue when the home plate umpire refused to check with the 3B ump and wrongly called Swisher out on a checked swing. Tony Peña assumed the managerial duties. But after witnessing a double, an RBI single, and a hard-hit double-play ball, Peña had seen enough of Joba, whose grade was D-.

However, as Peña walked to the mound he distinctly waved his left hand, a clear indication that he wanted Marte, but it was Rivera who trotted onto the field before another wave from Peña returned him to the bullpen. Peña later claimed he had changed his mind as soon as he left the dugout, ultimately deciding that he wanted Marte to pitch to LH Lind.

Which Marte did, needing only four pitches to whiff Lind on a sharply breaking slider that earned him a straight A.

The home half of the 9th was a five-pitch, grade-A breeze for Mo.

New York 4, Toronto 3
Save: Rivera (13)
Bullpen diary: This marked only Rivera's second clean inning since May 16 in Minnesota.

DRAFT STRATEGY

A complete listing of the Yankee's draft choices made beginning June 7 reveals that sixteen pitchers were selected. The shortest of these were two six-footers, and the rest included two who measured 6'4", two at 6'5", and three who topped the list at 6'6". Bet your boots that the vast majority have power arms.

June 8–10 @ Camden Yards

Hughes was mediocre, but the Yankees' bats were exceptional. So when Robertson trudged up the mound in the 7th, the Yankees had a 12-3 lead. Except for a first-pitch single by Tejada, he was on his game. His fastball only ranged from 90 to 92 mph and didn't show much movement, but he was hitting his spots—mostly the low-outside corner. After getting two strikeouts and a flyball to short CF, Robertson deserved his A.

Gaudin was asked to finish the game, but Mr. Mop-Up got blasted. In his two innings, Gaudin yielded five hits, two walks, and five runs. He was so pathetic that Girardi was forced to order Mo to start his warm-up routine when the first three batters got on base to start the bottom of the 9th. Somehow, though, Gaudin persevered, but not before getting pinned with another F.

New York 12, Baltimore 7
Bullpen diary: Despite his horrific showing, Gaudin officially gets credit for a hold. Why is he still wearing pinstripes?

With Eiland still Absent with Leave, Josh Paul, the manager of the Yankees' farm team in Staten Island, became the latest interim bullpen coach. Charlie Wonsowicz was returned to his dual duties as advance scout/video coordinator, possibly as a result of the Marte/Rivera mix-up in Toronto.

Game Two @ Baltimore, June 9

C.C.'s beating the Orioles is not news, but he did struggle at the outset. Because he repeatedly came up with big pitches in clutch situations, he left after 7 IP with a 4-2 lead.

Enter Joba, who was greeted by Adam Jones smoking a long drive to RF that Kevin Russo snared with a sensational diving catch. This was followed by Matt Wieters rocketing a shot to RF for a stand-up double. But Joba ended the inning on a high note with a whiff and a high bouncer to Cano. Even though he kept Baltimore off the scoreboard, the two hard-hit balls reduced Joba's grade to a pedestrian C+.

Rivera had no trouble whatsoever in the three-up, three-down 9th—ending the game with a strikeout of Tejada, Baltimore's most professional hitter.

Another A for Rivera is an indication that he's getting his game together.

New York 4, Baltimore 2

Save: Rivera (14)

Bullpen diary: Once again, Joba's fastball lacked snap, crackle, or pop. After Wieters' double, Joba started to jump up and down on the mound, trying to get himself energized.

What's he doing in the bullpen when he's supposed to be getting ready to go?

Game Three @ Baltimore, June 10

Burnett hit two batters in the first and never could locate his fastball. If he managed to pitch 6⅔ innings while giving up only four runs, that's only because the Orioles are such a bad team. Marte entered with the Yanks trailing by 4-3, two on and two out, and his second pitch jammed LH Luke Scott and produced a pop-up. Marte: A. Park closed out the 9th on a pair of strikeouts and a pop-up. Park: A.

Baltimore 4, New York 3

Bullpen diary: Lefty hitters are now only 5-28 against Marte—a batting average of .178. Park breezed through the 8th using only twelve pitches, successfully mixing his fastball, slider, curve, and change-up.

June 11–13, Houston Astros @ Yankee Stadium

Another masterful performance by Pettitte. He allowed only four hits in 7⅓ innings, and although the Yankees led 4-2 and he'd thrown only 98 pitches, Jeter flubbed a toss from Cano that botched an easy double play. After a sac bunt, Joba entered the game with runners on second and third and one out. His immediate goal was to whiff Jeff Keppinger in order to prevent a sac fly or hit. But Joba was unable to throw his sliders for a strike, so Keppinger sat on a fastball and lofted a fly to deep RF that easily allowed the runner to tag up and score. Joba did shut the door by striking out the dangerous Lance Berkman on his only slider that caught a piece of the plate.

For striking out the wrong guy, Joba's grade is reduced to B+.

Rivera ended the suspense and the game with a groundout and a brace of strikeouts. Just another day at the office for Mo earned him another A.

New York 4, Houston 3

Save: Rivera (15)

Bullpen diary: Joba's fastball registered 94–95 right away, a sign that he's bearing down from the first pitch. While several of Mo's cutters had the best movement he's shown all season, a couple that were stillborn were fortunately fouled off.

Game Two vs. the Astros in the Bronx, June 12

Except for coughing up a homer on a dead-fish fastball, Vazquez was in control of Houston's less than frightening lineup. He left after seven solid innings with a 9-3 lead.

Since the Astros were so far behind, Robertson was able to get away with throwing virtually all fastballs. Overall, Robertson's outing consisted of a strikeout, one seeing-eye groundball single, one looping single, a hard line drive to RF, and a swinging third strike. Because only the line-drive out was hit hard, Robertson rates a B+.

Chad Gaudin, Mr. Mop-Slop-Up, took over in the 9th. He showed good location in securing two outs—a strikeout and an easy grounder. But Jason Michaels foolishly tried to stretch a single and was thrown out at 2B. Given the gift out, Gaudin's performance rates a B+, his highest grade of the season.

New York 9, Houston 3

Bullpen diary: Instead of trying to get on base in the last two innings, too many of Houston's hitters were focused on swinging for the fences. And even though they could sit on fastballs (which all of Gaudin's nine offerings were), only one ball was hit hard. The Astros are certainly not a thinking man's team.

DAVE ROBERTSON

While Dave Robertson has learned to deal with the media with politeness and honesty, being interviewed still remains somewhat of an ordeal. Indeed, he was standing in front of his dressing alcove while we conversed, and all the while his right hand was busily spinning the heavily padded captain's chair in an endless circle.

"I started off playing tee-ball when I was five," he said, his eyes rapidly flitting from me to the wall behind me. "In high school I was a better hitter than a pitcher, so I batted in the four-hole. But that was because I played on very weak-hitting teams. I didn't become a full-time pitcher until I enrolled at the University of Alabama."

Courtesy of Amanda Rykoff

David Robertson

In his initial season with his hometown Crimson Tide, Robertson put up record-setting numbers as a reliever—including averaging 12.8 strikeouts per 9 IP, holding hitters to a .105 average—and was named to several freshman all-American teams. A year later, he was drafted by the Yankees.

Even as he spoke, Robertson kept his pitching hand busy like a manic croupier who refuses to let the roulette wheel come to rest.

His ascension through the minor leagues was uncommonly swift, with his Yankee debut occurring late in the 2008 season. After undergoing a quick tune-up in Scranton at the start of the 2009 season, he was recalled to the big club and has been a mostly reliable pitcher ever since.

Except, of course, for his early-season troubles this season.

"My front side wasn't following through properly," he said, "and my delivery was pulled off-line. Still in all, I wasn't throwing that many bad pitches. It's just that they were hitting just about everything I threw."

Robertson is well aware that his fastball is usually lifeless. "I tried to develop a two-seamer in spring training in 2008," he says. "Two-seamers are supposed to have some sinking action, but mine was as straight as an arrow. After about four or five games in Trenton [the Yanks' Double-A franchise], I just gave it up."

He felt good about his recent improvement: "I'm completing more of my pitches, although sometimes I'll still short-arm my curve. Coach Eiland is right on top of things and I have faith both in him and in myself that I'll get back to where I'm supposed to be."

Faith is the key word here.

And he works his right hand like a Buddhist monk forever spinning a prayer wheel.

Game Three vs. the Astros in the Bronx, June 13

Hughes had the Astros well in hand and, thanks to Jorge Posada's second grand slam in as many games, the Yankees had a 7-1 lead entering the 6th. But after securing two outs, Hughes fell apart. By the time Damaso Marte arrived at the breach, the Yankees' lead had narrowed to 7-5. Marte got his job done in good form, whiffing LH Michael Bourn on five fastballs and, in the process, earning another A.

The Yanks stretched their lead to 9-5 before Park recorded a groundout, strikeout, and flyout—after Gardner made a running, leaping catch in deep LF. That one long shot reduced Park's grade from an A to B+. Joba was next, and he gave up a groundball single before retiring the side on three flyballs. Both the base hit and the last out were well struck, so Joba's grade is B+.

Mo easily completed the three-game sweep with a bouncer back to the mound and a pair of strikeouts. Another A for Rivera.

New York 9, Houston 5

Bullpen diary: Of Park's ten pitches, only two were fastballs (both at 92 mph), and all of his outs came on sliders. Joba's fastballs (93–94) still lacked any discernible movement, but only two of his eleven offerings were wide of the K-zone.

Monument Row

Ahead by four runs, Rivera didn't enter into a save situation. But the Yanks have a day off tomorrow and Girardi wanted guaranteed closure to the game and the series.

Yankee trivia: Jorge is the first Bronx Bomber to hit grand slams in consecutive games since '37, when catcher Bill Dickey did it.

Dickey wore number 8 for the Yanks, which was retired *after* Yogi wore it, and he got his number retired, too. The number 8, retired twice. Only with a team as rich in history as the Yankees.

Posada's grand slams bring to mind the memory that Chan Ho Park is the only pitcher in major league history to give up grand slams in the *same* inning to the *same* player: Fernando Tatis of the Cards, when Park was with the Dodgers.

Where we stand: Now that the Yankees have fattened up on MLB's weak sisters (11-2 vs. Baltimore, Cleveland, and Houston), their schedule gets much tougher with the Phillies, Mets, Diamondbacks, and Dodgers on the immediate horizon.

Around the Country—and World

The weekend of June 12 and 13 had sports fans feverishly working their remotes and DVRs. For some, the first weekend of the World Cup in South Africa was *the* thing, even if *all* of America was talking about the damn vuvuzelas.

Several of the triumphant Chicago Blackhawks brought the Stanley Cup to the Cubs/White Sox game, and, down three games to one, the Lakers beat the Celtics twice to tighten up the NBA finals.

There was also the College World Series; Stephen Strasburg's second game (which helped sell out a road game); the Weaver brothers pitching against each other; and Tim Wakefield's reaching 3,000 innings pitched in his career, matching only Pettitte and Jamie Moyer as active players to hit that mark.

The Cubs and White Sox pitchers both carried no-hitters into the 7th, the first time that's happened since Yanks vs. White Sox in '80. Pitching is especially dominating this season.

And the Yankees are once again tied for first.

A Scout's Eyewitness Appraisal of Who's Doing What

It's evident that Rivera's velo is a mile or so down from what it once was, and that he's throwing a few more two-seamers. But if his cutter and his command are now rated 70, he still throws good enough to beat anybody. Part of this is because Rivera always has a plan. Two-seamers out, cutters in, with good enough location. Because today's hitters don't adjust—like zeroing in on certain spots when they're ahead in the count and staying away from everything else, or like keeping their hips closed and looking to drive a pitch to the opposite field—Rivera doesn't have to adjust. That's why he's just as effective as ever even with his reduced arsenal.

Joba still has no pitchability and never will, so he has

to totally rely on his stuff. It's surprising that he frequently starts off throwing 91 or even 90 mph. He's pacing himself just like he did when he was starting. Not a very good idea for a late-inning reliever. In fact, it's just plain stupid. But Joba is what he is, and that's just about as good as any other bridge guy in the game.

Sergio Mitre is a valuable player with plus-velocity and a plus-sinker. As long as he can cut the extraneous motion out of his delivery, he has the stuff to be able to go as long as five innings. Mitre's problem, though, is that his career has been blighted with periodical injuries.

Somebody in the Yankees organization must really like Gaudin. His stuff is just okay, but his command is seriously faulty. The more he presses to paint the black, the more he gets hit hard. The only reason why Sanchez and Nova haven't taken his place is that the younger guys need more innings to develop than they'd get up here. The fact that Gaudin's still around also comes down to money.

Robertson has two big flaws. His fastball is straight, and he sometimes tilts his shoulder and doesn't finish his curve. But he's locating much better than he did earlier in the season, when he was getting belted just about every time out. It pays for the Yankees to stay with him because of the success he had last year.

Damaso Marte has a long, stiff arm swing. He's what we call a pie-thrower. His trouble is his inconsistency. He can pound the paint or he can pound the wall in back of the catcher. If Marte doesn't get ahead in the count early, then he's in big trouble. The biggest plus in the Yankees bullpen is the team's starting rotation. With the exception of Burnett (who's always liable to get shelled early), they've got a bunch of horses who can be relied on to pitch at least into the seventh inning.

June 15–17, Philadelphia Phillies @ Yankee Stadium

The reprise of the Yanks-Phils World Series face-off weren't the most exciting games, but some Yankee relievers are beginning to go in distinctly different directions.

In game one, C.C. had one bad inning, but the lineup clobbered Roy Halladay for three HRs and the Bronx Bombers led 8-3 when Robertson mounted the mound in the top of the 8th. Robertson cruised through the inning throwing only fastballs (91–94 mph). The only glitches were a hard line-drive out to CF by Ryan Howard and a seven-pitch walk to Raul Ibañez. For his efforts, Robertson rates A-. Park neatly disposed of the Phils in the 9th, mixing his slider, cutter, and curve, earning an A.

New York 8, Philadelphia 3

Bullpen diary: Before the game, Sergio Mitre injured his left oblique muscle while taking batting practice in preparation for next week's interleague games in Arizona and Los Angeles. The seriousness of the injury was, as always, downplayed, but Mitre was placed on the fifteen-day DL and replaced by Logan.

Since Mitre has shown positive signs in his last few outings, his absence could be critical, especially since Aceves is still down and out. The other candidates for the long role are Robertson (who's best suited for at most two innings), Park (who can work a maximum of three innings in a pinch), and Gaudin (who pitched extremely well against Houston).

Call-up: Logan returns to the bigs after a very successful stint in Scranton—posting a 1.32 ERA in nine games and limiting lefty hitters to 3-26. Here is what Logan said that he learned while in the minors: "You have to attack guys to get them out. I've got to take that approach and bring it up here."

Game Two vs. the Phils in the Bronx, June 16

Unfortunately, the bad Burnett showed up. Unable to survive a not-so-merry-go-round of hits, hit batters, walks, homers, and stolen bases, Burnett was pounded for six runs in 3⅓innings. Even though he inherited runners on second and third, Logan's return was a triumphant one. He delivered an intentional walk to Jayson Werth, but otherwise snuffed the other eight batters he faced. Boone's fastball topped at 95 mph, but five of the outs he registered (including all three of his strikeouts) resulted from darting sliders. An A for Boone.

Gaudin's perfect three innings were even better. Four flyballs (only one of which was hit hard), an infield pop, an easy grounder, and three strikeouts. Gaudin's first A of the season.

Philadelphia 6, New York 3

Bullpen diary: Boone obviously learned his lesson well, since (discounting the intentional pass) twenty-two of his twenty-nine pitches were strikes. Except for one slider that got away, his breaking pitch was sharp and well situated, and his heaters were hot.

Gaudin showed an effective split-fingered pitch that stayed around knee level. His sliders had a nice tilt, and he successfully jammed the Phillies with 91–92 mph fastballs.

Game Three vs. the Phils in the Bronx, June 17

Pettitte didn't have his best stuff, but he battled his way through seven innings after being hurt early by a two-run gopher ball.

Robertson entered the fray down 3-1 seeking to keep the Yanks capable of tying the game with a bloop and a bang. And he did his job, relying mostly on his 92–94 mph fastball and a fall-off-the-table curveball. As such, Robertson's 1-2-3 inning and grade of A marked his fifth consecutive superb outing.

Unfortunately, Joba let the game get out of hand. A first-pitch double, RBI single, and a walk—and the hook. Another F for Joba.

Marte also had a distinctly under-par performance. The walk he delivered to Chase Utley was low-lighted by his fourth pitch hitting the backstop on the fly! After a pair of sac flies and another walk, Marte's laborious twenty-nine-pitch outing was done. Give him a D.

Park technically gave up two hits to the two batters he faced. The first was a standard RBI double and the second was a groundball that struck the runner—officially recorded as a hit for Ben Francisco and an out charged to the runner (Ibañez). The freak play raised Park's erstwhile grade of F to a barely passable D.

Philadelphia 7, New York 1
Bullpen diary: The usually gregarious Chamberlain hid in the trainers' room after the game and refused to face the media. His reaction emphasized the fact that Joba's maturation process remains a work in progress.

June 18–20 vs. the Mets @ Yankee Stadium
Vazquez was brilliant, allowing only two hits and one run in seven innings. But the lineup was comatose, so when Park took over in the top of the 8th, the score was still 1-0.

Park had nothing. His fastball bottomed out at 89 mph and most of his sliders were exercises in suspended animation. A walk, a double, a two-run double, and then a groundout constituted the gory details. Another F marked Park's back-to-back failures.

Logan climbed the hill with the Yankees now facing a 3-0 hole. He squeezed through the 8th without incurring any further damage. But Logan was then hurt by a double, two singles, and a walk that extended the Mets' lead to 4-0. He finally ended the misery by coaxing a double play off the bat of David Wright.

Because five of the eight hitters he faced became base runners, Logan gets a D+.

Mets 4, Yankees 0
Where we stand: Despite suffering their third consecutive loss, the Yanks remain tied with Tampa for first place in the AL East.

Off the field: The most intriguing postgame clubhouse news involved the appearance there of Lady Gaga, dressed in bikini panties and an unbuttoned Yankee jersey that revealed her black bra. Unbeknownst to the team's brass, she had gained entrance into the sanctum sanctorum by sweet-talking several security guards. She then spent approximately thirty minutes chatting with several of the Yankees while simultaneously stroking her breasts.

No wonder Hal Steinbrenner, Brian Cashman, and Joe Girardi were outraged.

Game Two vs. the Mets in the Bronx, June 19

Hughes was touched for three runs, all accounted for by a pair of dingers hit by Jose Reyes. Otherwise, Hughes was flawless and exited after seven innings on the long end of a 5–3 score.

Chamberlain's first pitch, a 96-mph fastball for a called strike to Reyes, announced that he was on target to redeem himself after getting slammed by the Phillies. Except for yielding a double to Angel Pagan, Joba was overpowering—two infield chops and an impressive whiff of Wright on a sharp slider. Joba's grade: A-.

Mo hadn't pitched in six days, but except for some of his early cutters being a mite too high, he easily terminated the game with a strikeout and a brace of weak groundouts. Rivera's fifth straight A.

Yankees 5, Mets 3

Save: Rivera (16)

Bullpen diary: Joba celebrated his termination of Wright with one loud scream and two fist pumps. Rivera's cutter had much more late life than in his most recent stints.

Hughes is now 10-1.

⚾ TWO YEARS ago today, switch-pitcher Pat Venditte of the Staten Island Yankees famously changed his six-fingered pitching glove several times while the Brooklyn Cyclones' switch-hitter changed sides of the plate. The ump finally called an end to the comedy, which can still be enjoyed on YouTube.

On July 3, 2008, the Professional Baseball Umpire Corporation added this to the rulebook:

- The pitcher must visually indicate to the umpire, batter and runner(s) which way he will begin pitching to the batter. Engaging the rubber with the glove on a particular hand is considered a definitive commitment to with which arm he will throw. The batter will then choose which side of the plate he will bat from.
- The pitcher is not permitted to pitch with the other hand until the batter is retired, the batter becomes a runner, the inning ends, the batter is substituted for by a pinch-hitter or the pitcher incurs an injury.
- Any switch (by either the pitcher or the batter) must be clearly indicated to the umpire. There will be no warm-up pitches during the change of arms.
- If an injury occurs the pitcher may change arms but not use that arm again during the remainder of the game.

Game Three vs. the Mets in the Bronx, June 20

C.C. blanked the Mets on only four hits through eight innings. His bid for a complete-game shutout was washed away by a twenty-two-minute rain delay. And on the strength of a grand slammer by Teixeira, Rivera was called upon to lock up the game in a nonsave situation. Using only thirteen pitches, Mo breezed through a painless top of the 9th. Rivera's latest grade of A stretches his string of optimal performances to six.

Yankees 4, Mets 0

Bullpen diary: Rivera has now held the last twenty-one batters he's faced hitless—almost a fractured no-hitter.

After the series: Since Tampa lost this afternoon, the Yankees are alone at the top of the AL East with the best record in MLB.

⚾ ALTHOUGH THE other starters have been humming along since Dave Eiland's indefinite leave was granted on June 4 for indefinite reasons, Burnett seems to be totally discombobulated. Indeed, the sequence of Burnett's three inept starts coincided with Eiland's departure on June 4. Make that four.

June 21–23 @ Chase Field

A.J. was smacked around by the last-place Diamondbacks, giving up six runs on six two-out hits in the bottom of the 1st. He plugged along for another four innings, until he was finally sent to the showers after 5 IP with the Yankees in a deep 7-1 hole. Chad Gaudin was presented with mop-up duties again and continued to get the job done. The only specks on his otherwise clean sweep were a walk, a hit batsman, and a line-drive single spread out over 2 IP—earning Gaudin a B.

The Yanks narrowed the gap to 7-3 by the time Park took over in the bottom of the 7th. He avoided throwing his fastball in the strike zone, but after an impressive 7th he was bombarded in the 8th, with the most explosive damage accomplished by Justin Upton's second homer of the game. Another bummer by Park registers his second straight F.

Arizona 10, New York 4
Bullpen diary: Gaudin's stuff was lively and well located, and his fastball topped at an impressive (for him) 93 mph. Park seems to be trying to make the transition from being a power pitcher to a junkman, with erratic results.

Game Two @ Arizona, June 22
Pettitte boosted his record to 9-2 with still another quality start. He'd cruised through seven innings on the plus side of a 3-2 lead

when the lineup exploded for six runs while he was in the shower and before Chamberlain left the bullpen.

Joba came out firing. His fastballs ranged from 95 to 98 mph, plus he was consistently hitting his spots. After walking the leading lady with a pair of out-of-control sliders, Joba dished out a pop-up sandwiched between a pair of strikeouts. A top-of-the-line A for Joba.

Robertson finished the game in topsy-turvy style. Two whiffs and a sharp liner into Teixeira's glove contrasted with a sharp single and an RBI double. After five superlative outings, this was a huge step back for Robertson, and because three of the five hitters he faced got good wood in the ball, his grade is a mere D-.

New York 9, Arizona 3

Bullpen diary: This was the hardest Chamberlain has thrown all year. His only minus was a couple of spinning sliders. Robertson's curveball was erratic and one of his fastballs was a wild pitch that cost him the run. That he required thirty pitches to complete the inning shows how much he labored. Because of Robertson's maxed-out pitch count, Logan had to warm up in the bullpen just in case.

Game Three @ Arizona, June 23

Vazquez turned in his poorest effort in a while, giving up four runs in five innings. Nor was the cause aided by several baserunning mistakes and the lineup's collective failure to deliver runners in scoring position.

Even so, the score was tied 4-4 when Marte was summoned in the bottom of the 6th. After almost getting stung by a sharp liner to short, Marte walked Chris Young, who promptly stole 2B, advanced to 3B on a balk, and then scored the go-ahead run on a tantalizing groundout that covered as much ground as a well-placed bunt. Another walk and a groundout completed Damaso's erratic performance, leaving him with a D-.

Robertson's work in the 7th featured an infield hit, a twin-killing, and a strikeout. Robertson moved the radar gun up to 94 mph (very high for him) and threw several Hall of Fame pitches that barely clipped the low-outside corner. Accordingly, he achieved an A.

Like Robertson, Joba was called upon to pitch his second game in two days. Several of his fastballs registered 98 mph, but he started off by whiffing the powerful Justin Upton on a nasty slider. In swift order, the D'backs mustered a line-drive single (on a straight-as-a-string 96-mph fastie), a hard-hit grounder that eventuated in a force play, a stolen base, and another walk, before another slider caught Mark Reynolds looking. Joba's grade: B-. With the score still knotted at 4-4, Girardi sent Mo to the hill.

This was significant for several reasons: it was a no-save situation, and given that Mo would prevent any of the D'backs from touching home plate in the 9th, he would also likely get the ball in the 10th, the first time this season that'd he'd be called upon to work two innings.

In any case, the home half of the 9th was a breeze that extended Rivera's flawless string to twenty-four frustrated hitters.

After Granderson smacked a homer to lead off the 10th, Mo needed a miracle to maintain the Yankees' 5-4 lead after yielding a looping single, a line-drive double, and an intentional walk. Bases loaded, none out, with the meat of Arizona's lineup due up.

However, the miracle was granted when Chris Young fouled out to the catcher on a 1-1 cutter; Adam LaRoche (who had already knocked in all of Arizona's five runs) was jammed by a 1-1 cutter and lofted a harmless pop-up to A-Rod; and Mo finished with a flourish by striking out Mark Reynolds.

Even though he was hit relatively hard, Mo's great escape rated an A.

New York 6, Arizona 5 (10 innings)
Winning Pitcher: Rivera (1-1)
Bullpen diary: Joba continued to light up the radar gun, yet even his fastest fastballs lacked noticeable movement—which meant that

he's still eminently hittable unless his blazers are precisely located.

In the 10th inning, Mo's cutter repeatedly reached 93 mph, about 2–3 mph quicker than they were at the beginning of the season and about 3–4 mph quicker than they were for most of last season. Since Rivera needed an uneconomical total of forty pitches to get this particular job done, it's questionable how effective he might be if Girardi is forced to use him in game one of the upcoming Dodgers series.

Mo at the plate: Rivera grabbed a bat for the first time this year in the top of the 10th. His teammates laughed when he swung and missed the first pitch he saw, cheered when he fouled off the next one, and were visibly impressed when he struck a sharp grounder to the second baseman for an easy out. Rivera merely trotted toward first, and the whole episode seemed to lift Mo and the team.

Where we stand: Both Boston and Tampa lost, providing the Yankees with a 2½ game lead in the AL East.

EN ROUTE

As the Yanks traveled to meet the Dodgers, the New York media was lathered up about Joe Torre and the first game against his former team. The Yankee fans'—and the New York media's—love/hate with Joe continued.

It is noteworthy that Joe's Yankee number 6 is the last single-digit pinstripe not retired except for Derek's number 2. The sixteen Yankees uniform numbers retired are the most of any professional sports team.

June 25–27 @ Dodger Stadium

An outstanding effort by C.C. limited the Dodgers to four hits and a solitary run in eight innings. As Mo climbed the mound looking to maintain the 2-1 lead, it remained to be seen how much gas remained in his tank as he faced the 3, 4, and 5 hitters in LA's lineup.

Leading off was the always dangerous and always unpredictable

Manny Ramirez. Although Mo did get away with a flat cutter in Manny's wheelhouse, he fisted Ramirez with a pair of cutters before whiffing him on still another cutter on the outside corner.

Matt Kemp, another home-run threat, was Mo's second strike-out victim, failing to connect on a high-and-tight cutter. Against James Loney, Rivera clipped the outside corner with three cutters that ended the game but initiated vociferous arguments from the Dodgers dugout. Loney would be fined for tossing both his bat and his helmet to protest the ump's last call, and Joe Torre was thumbed from a game that was already over, with another fine to come. For Mo, an A. Eight in a row.

New York 2, Los Angeles 1
Save: Rivera (17)
Bullpen diary: His cutter showed good late movement and he consistently clipped whichever corner of the K-zone he desired. Ol' Man Mo keeps rollin'.

Game Two @ LA, June 26

Another sorry start for Burnett—3+ innings, 6 hits, 6 walks.

With runners on first and second and zero outs in the 4th, Logan managed to coax LH Andre Ethier into flying out, then was super careful with Manny and issued a free pass. Next came an RBI single (with the peripheral bonus of a runner being thrown out at the plate) and an RBI double, before Logan finally got out of the inning. He cruised through the bottom of the 5th, but because of the runs he allowed and the fact that he was the beneficiary of two gift outs— the runner out at the plate and a strikeout of the pitcher—Logan rates a D.

Park succeeded Logan with even less success in his two innings of work. Three solid hits, two walks, two runs allowed, and one line-drive out gave Park a D-.

With the Yankees on the low end of a 9-3 score, Robertson moved his fastball in-out and up-down for profit, giving up only a six-pitch walk on the debit side of his ledger. Even so, a bullet-like line drive to Cano for the final out of the inning lowered Robertson's grade to B+.

Los Angeles 9, New York 4

Bullpen diary: Logan's slider had great movement but was barely under control. Park's fastballs only occasionally reached 90 mph, and his cutters had decent horizontal but no vertical movement.

Conversely, the Dodgers never saw two consecutive pitches at the same eye level from Robertson, yet his control remains subpar; he went 3-2 on two of the four batters he faced.

Starter's dilemma: What to do about Burnett? His humongous salary prohibits a trade. Should the Yankees fake an injury, put him on the DL, and send him to Tampa, where Dr. Contreras can oversee his "recovery"? Should the team be patient with Burnett? For how long? The team's decision makers might also try praying that Dave Eiland returns ASAP.

Game Three @ LA, June 27

Aided by two costly throwing errors by Pettitte, the Dodgers were leading 5-2 when Robertson relieved to start the bottom of the 6th. After giving up a single and a walk, he escaped disaster when Reed Johnson was caught in a rundown. Still, he could only navigate two outs before being replaced by Marte. Robertson: C+.

Marte was lights out, closing the inning by whiffing the ever dangerous Ethier, then hurling a perfect 7th inning that was highlighted by inducing Manny to loft an easy flyball to CF. Four up, four down earned Marte his A.

Joba continued his erratic season by giving up a walk, a single, and an RBI double that extended LA's margin to 6-2. Chamberlain: D.

The Yankees staged a dramatic 9th-inning rally to tie the score, and with a day off on the immediate horizon, Girardi sent for Mo in the same scenario as Arizona just four days ago—on the road and the score knotted in the bottom of the 9th.

And Mo made short work of the Dodgers—a grounder, a flyball, and a whiff. Thanks to a round-tripper by Cano in the top of the 10th, the Yankees now led 8-6 as they took the field to give LA last licks.

In the dugout, Girardi had one question for Mo: "Can you go another inning? Don't lie."

Of course, Girardi's last words were superfluous, but Rivera merely said, "I'm ready."

However, the outlook looked gloomy after Loney bounced an infield single and Mo started Russell Martin's at-bat by throwing three straight balls. However, the Sandman humped up and sealed the come-from-behind win with a groundout and two strikeouts. A gutsy A for a tired Mo.

New York 8, Dodgers 6 (10 innings)

Winning Pitcher: Rivera (2-1)

Bullpen diary: Marte was absolutely sensational. Joba continues to alternate good outings with miserable ones.

Mighty Mo strikes again. Both Martin and Garret Anderson were tossed when they complained that the umpire had goofed in calling each of them out on questionable third strikes—but replays demonstrated that both of the ump's decisions were righteous.

Of note: Just before the game, it was announced that Dave Eiland would be rejoining the team two days hence when the Yankees returned home to play Seattle. Eiland's top priorities will be to fix Burnett and Park, and to get Joba on a steady course.

When asked how quickly he can recognize a flaw in a pitcher's delivery, Eiland snapped his fingers and said, "As quick as that."

June 29–July 1, Seattle Mariners @ Yankee Stadium

Phil Hughes returned to action after being skipped a start to limit his pitch count. But the layoff had to be the reason why he was hit so hard and so often. After struggling through 5 ⅔ innings, Hughes left with the Yankees in a 7-1 hole and was replaced by Logan. After striking out LH Michael Saunders to end the top of the 6th, Boone was in and out of trouble in the 7th. But he managed to strand a runner on 3B with no outs by producing a pop-up and a pair of groundouts. Logan: B. Park then hurled two perfect innings, getting four outs with his 92-mph fastball, one out with his slider, and one on a curveball. His command, the results, and the aura of confidence he projected earned Park his first A in two weeks.

Seattle 7, New York 4

Bullpen diary: Logan showed more guts than stuff. With Eiland back on the job, Park has just about completed the transition from being a fireballer to a softballer who only spots his fastball. Still, one has to wonder what happened during the off-season that subtracted 5 mph off his blazer.

Game Two vs. the Mariners in the Bronx, June 30

Vazquez had a decent outing but couldn't match zeroes with "King" Felix Hernandez, who pitched a complete-game, two-hit shutout.

When Damaso Marte was handed the ball in the top of the 7th, the Mariners enjoyed a modest 3-0 lead. Marte first retired Ichiro Suzuki on a high-bouncer, marking the nineteenth consecutive at-bat in which lefties have gone hitless against the Yankees' most-specialized specialist. However, LH Russell Branyan ended this streak by launching a slider into the RF seats. Marte: F.

Robertson had been warming up to replace Marte, but with the score now 5-0 and with Hernandez so dominant, Girardi hoisted the white flag and called on Gaudin to finish the game; Gaudin registered the final out in the 7th and the first two in the 8th. His sinker was sinking, his change-up was confounding, and Gaudin seemed to be cruising. But then Cano made a bad error, muffing an easy foul pop-up that, instead of ending the inning, gave life to Rob Johnson—who ultimately walked.

The miscue clearly discomforted Gaudin, who coughed up a

homer to Michael Saunders. Gaudin recovered in time to whisk through a scoreless 9th, but his grade: C-.

Seattle 7, New York 0

Bullpen diary: Marte had minimal control of his slider, which is supposed to be his out-pitch; six of the ten he threw were off-target. Gaudin's shaky self-confidence along with his unacceptable and sudden lack of poise did much to undermine his three previous outstanding appearances.

Game Three vs. the Mariners in the Bronx, July 1

Sabathia was brilliant in defending a 2-0 lead until he ran out of gas in the 8th and surrendered the tying runs. But in the bottom of the 8th, A-Rod reached the seats to restore the lead. Rivera's spotless 9th earned him still another A.

New York 4, Seattle 2

Save: Rivera (18)

Bullpen diary: Dustin Moseley, a right-handed reliever, was summoned from Scranton, and Logan was returned to the Yankees Triple-A outlet. Besides the fact that Logan still had an option to spare, the primary reason for this move was that Moseley's contract called for him to become a free agent had he not been on the Yankees roster by July 1.

This day in Yankee history: Jeter memorably goes into the stands against the Red Sox on July 1, 2004, and comes out with cuts on his face. The Yanks win that Sox marathon in the 13th inning.

Where We Stand

The Yankees are in first place in the AL East with a record of 48-30, 1½ games ahead of Boston and two in front of Tampa. While their hitters have fizzled, the team is now being carried by the starting pitchers *and* the bullpenners.

Bullpen Scorecard for June

Rivera (10 appearances): 3.8 = A–
Robertson (9 appearances): 3.28 = B+
Mitre (1): 3.0 = B
Chamberlain (11): 2.7 = B–
Marte (3): 2.69 = B–
Park (9): 2.36 = C+
Logan (4): 2.3 = C+
Gaudin (7): 1.6 = D+

The bullpen's overall grade comes to B+ (3.15), certainly championship caliber. But Joba and Park are both irritatingly erratic, and Robertson is still unsettled, leaving no reliable bridge man to Rivera.

Memory Lane

Yogi, Joe, and Knuckleballers

I can remember a reporter asking me for a quote, and I didn't know what a quote was. I thought it was some kind of soft drink.

—JOE DIMAGGIO

Back in 1984, I was doing a story on knuckleball pitchers for a since-defunct magazine. The only practitioners of this arcane art at the time were Charlie Hough and the brothers Niekro—Phil and Joe. Since Phil was with the Yankees at the time, I wandered into the pregame clubhouse at the Stadium to see what I could see and ask what I could ask.

Yogi Berra was the Yankees manager, at age fifty-nine still bumptious and wise. Imagine my surprise and delight when I saw Yogi standing in the middle of the room, having a lighthearted discussion with Joe DiMaggio. The Yankee Clipper still stood tall and stately at age sixty-nine, but he was also beginning to list with arthritis.

They were talking about the rising cost of baseballs, the absence of the "Scooter" from the Hall of Fame, and the lapsed elegance of the nearby Concourse Plaza Hotel.

Under normal circumstances, DiMaggio was always reluctant to deal with the media, but since he seemed to be in a jovial mood, and since I had a tight deadline, during a slight pause in their conversation I dared to intrude with a question that I hoped would spark a response from Joltin' Joe.

"Mr. DiMaggio, sir? Do you happen to remember the starting rotation of the 1945 Washington Senators? Johnny Niggeling, Mickey Haeffner, Dutch Leonard, and Roger Wolf?"

"How could I forget them?" DiMaggio replied, his interest clearly piqued. "All of them were knuckleballers. We'd see knucklers on a Friday night, followed by Saturday afternoon, and then a doubleheader on Sunday."

Berra hadn't reached the bigs until 1946, yet he puffed on a cigarette and nodded in quick agreement.

"Let's see," DiMaggio wondered. "There was also Nelson Potter with the Browns. Bobo Newsom. Ted Lyons. Did Hank Borowy throw a knuckler?"

"Maybe," Yogi grunted. "Sometimes. Maybe not."

"Almost every team back then had a knuckler," DiMaggio added.

"How did you do against guys like that?" I asked.

"I didn't always make the greatest contact," DiMag answered, "but I had my share of luck."

Luck! From an all-time great who sported a lifetime .325 batting average.

Other hitters whom I had interviewed claimed that facing knuckleballers messed up their swings for weeks at a time. Did this also happen to DiMaggio?

"No," he said. "I faced so many of them that I just took my normal swing. Besides, I used to take a very short step with my left foot when I attacked a pitch so my weight was always back and my timing was always consistent."

At that point DiMaggio began to look around the room for someone to rescue him from me. But before he escaped, I proffered a baseball for him to sign. "For my kid," I said. Since this was years before such autographs went for hundreds of dollars, he silently signed the ball.

But just as DiMaggio turned to exit stage right, Yogi cleared his throat, threw his cigarette butt into a nearby spittoon bucket, and said this: "I know the secret how to hit the knuckler."

DiMaggio turned back to Berra, leaned forward, and even cupped his ear.

"It's simple." Yogi shrugged. "All you gotta do is to only swing at the ones that don't break."

July 2010

- Old-Timers' Day and past Yankee pitching greats.
- The Cliff Lee trade falls through, Joba falters, and Kerry Wood has to shave the beard.
- Within two days of each other, Bob Sheppard and George Steinbrenner pass away, as well as Ralph Houk at the end of July.
- The Yankees' future, as seen during a hot summer night's Triple-A game, with much to be both amused and pleased by—including secret baseball mud.

> *More than any other American sport, baseball creates the magnetic,*
> *addictive illusion that it can almost be understood.*
>
> —TOM BOSWELL

July 2–4, Toronto Blue Jays @ Yankee Stadium

Eiland's brainstorming provided immediate results as Burnett hurled 6⅔ scoreless innings. Unfortunately there continued to be too many holes in the lineup's bats, so the home team was nursing a mere 1-0 lead.

Marte threw only fastballs (seven of them) and forced LH Fred Lewis to end the inning with a pop-up, thereby earning himself an A.

Joba took the ball from Girardi in the top of the 9th and temporarily avoided disaster when Brett Gardner made a leaping catch at the LF wall to turn an extra-base hit into an out. The next hitter walked, but after another long flyball out, Chamberlain was only one out away from handing the game to the best closer ever. However, a pair of singles scored the tying run. Joba: F.

Because the Yankees' heavy hitters—Teixeira, A-Rod, and Cano—were due up in the bottom of the 10th, Girardi gave the ball to Rivera. And Mo did his part, keeping the Jays scoreless.

With the Yankees still unable to dent home plate, Robertson worked the top of the 10th. Throwing nothing but fastballs (91–93 mph), Robertson issued a walk, and was hit hard for two line-drive outs and a well-struck grounder to Cano, but he managed to complete a scoreless inning.

In the top of the 11th, however, Robertson was touched for three singles and an intentional walk. Throw in a sacrifice bunt and the Blue Jays took a 3-1 lead. Robertson's grade: F.

Park was then summoned to keep the game under control. He started off with a clutch strikeout, but then yielded a walk (with the bases loaded), a triple, a hit batsman, and another walk. By the time the dust settled, the game was over. Park's grade: F.

Toronto 6, New York 1 (11 innings)
Losing Pitcher: Robertson (0-3)
Bullpen diary: Joba's failure to hand the baton to Mo hurt the most. In all, Robertson threw twenty consecutive fastballs, but with rookie Jarrett Hoffpauir squaring away and poised to execute a sacrifice, Robertson threw two curves, the easiest pitch to bunt. Even though Park's fastball reached 94 mph, hitters had little trouble making solid contact.

Game Two vs. the Jays in the Bronx, July 3

After a rough 1st inning, Pettitte settled down and cruised through Toronto's lineup, his easy living enabled by the Yanks' lineup tallying eleven runs in the bottom of the 3rd.

Newcomer Dustin Moseley made his Yankee debut in the top of the 7th and was nothing short of sensational. His four-seam fastball wiggled, his two-seamer sank, his slider was sharp, and his change-up had depth. He needed only fifteen pitches to engineer six consecutive outs, earning him an A. Park finished off the Jays on a perfect six-pitch 9th. He grades out at A- only because the third out was a solidly swatted drive that Gardner caught at the CF wall.

New York 11, Toronto 3

Bullpen diary: Moseley is a 6'4", 210-pound Texan, who was 4-4 with a 4.21 ERA in twelve games with Scranton. Moseley seems completely recovered from the forearm and hip problems that curtailed his 2009 season and is auditioning for a middle/long relief role. Since Mitre is about two weeks away from returning to action, Gaudin will certainly be a goner, while Moseley just might be battling Park for the last spot on the staff.

Or perhaps the Yankees are working on some kind of deal to strengthen and stabilize their relief corps.

Game Three vs. the Jays in the Bronx, July 4

Just hours after being officially certified as a first-time All-Star, Hughes was tagged for 3 HRs, and was fortunate to be even at 5-all after logging six lackluster innings.

Marte breezed through the top of the 7th on the wings of two strikeouts and a flyball. An A all the way.

When the Yankees tacked on another run after the 7th-inning stretch, Joba had another chance to preserve a save opportunity for Mo. As ever, Chamberlain's performance was uneven: a line-drive out followed by a smoked single succeeded by a strikeout and a pop-up. Even though he maintained the Yankees' 6-5 lead, Joba gets a B- because two of the four batters he faced made solid contact.

Enter the Sandman to save the game in the 9th. But, hold on! Three groundball singles produced the tying run. Although he eventually struck out John Buck, the two groundouts recorded by Rivera were also hit on the nose. Accordingly, Mo got his third F of the season.

Robertson gave up a single and a walk to commence the top of the 10th but was rescued when Edwin Encarnacion popped an erstwhile sacrifice bunt down the 3B line and became a spectator. When A-Rod let the ball drop, he was able to initiate a 5-6-4 double play. Then Robertson blew a 93-mph fastball past Jose Molina to pull another Houdini.

In the bottom of the 10th, Marcus Thames, fresh off the DL, dropped a two-out pinch-hit single into left-center to make the Yankees winners.

New York 7, Toronto 6 (10 innings)

Winning Pitcher: Robertson (1-3)

Bullpen diary: Marte was razor-sharp with both his fastball and slider. Although Joba's fastballs were clocked from 95 to 98 mph, they had virtually no movement and were poorly situated. Credit his well-placed sliders for getting him out of the inning. Mo's cutters reached a high of 93 mph but were uncharacteristically lifeless. That's because his lead (left) shoulder was opening up a bit too soon.

Of note: The United States is now 235 years old, and George Steinbrenner has reached his eightieth birthday. The red-white-and-blue Boss is a super patriot, so it's no surprise that the main lobby in the new Yankee Stadium is graced with an artificially weathered eight-foot replica of the Statue of Liberty.

The surprise comes around the corner, where a taller, bronze-cast statue of Steinbrenner Himself stands in a more prominent place.

July 5–7 @ Oakland–Alameda County Coliseum

Vazquez had his full repertoire working. The Yankees enjoyed a 3-1 advantage after he allowed only four hits in seven innings. In the 8th, Joba overthrew the only slider he attempted, but his fastball topped out at 97 mph and he was simply overpowering. Two whiffs and a lazy flyball earned him an A. Mo was back on track and easily slammed the door shut in the bottom of the 9th. His lead shoulder was nicely tucked, his cutter was alive, and Mo was restored to the A list.

New York 3, Oakland 1

Save: Rivera (19)

Bullpen diary: Cashman's dream! Seven strong innings from the starter, a successful bridge inning from Joba, and Mo's doing what he's been doing for lo these many years.

DL news: Bad news, however, from Tampa, where Alfredo Aceves experienced serious "discomfort" in the middle of a bullpen session. With another setback, Ace moves closer to career-threatening surgery. This means that Mitre, Moseley, or Gaudin must emerge as a successful long man, with Mitre being the most likely to succeed. Also, if Moseley turns out to be the real deal, Park—and his mega-buck salary—become expendable.

Game Two @ Oakland, July 6

Sabathia cruised to his seventh straight win, dominating the A's with ten strikeouts over 7⅔ innings. Robertson inherited a 6-1 lead and zipped through the last four outs via a groundout, a liner to Teixeira, and a pair of strikeouts. Robertson gets his first A since his outing on June 23.

New York 6, Oakland 1

Bullpen diary: Turns out that Rivera's right knee hurts every time he pushes off the rubber. Plus, he still has some lingering pain in an oblique muscle on his left rib cage. Accordingly, he will skip the All-Star game. As usual, the Yankees downplay this situation.

"It's nothing serious," says Girardi. But it can't be coincidental that Mo's problems became noticeable after he made a two-inning appearance against the Dodgers on June 25. It's expected that Rivera will be limited to three-out situations for the foreseeable future. Mo's distress spells TROUBLE with a capital *T*.

Game Three @ Oakland, July 7

Burnett responded to Dr. Eiland's ministrations with another quality start: 7 innings, 5 hits, and 2 runs. Marte took over in the bottom of the 8th with the Yanks enjoying a 6–2 lead. Only three of Marte's pitches missed the K-zone as he earned his third consecutive A. Joba preserved the victory, but not until after being touched for a line-drive single, then a smash that Teixeira gloved and turned into a double play, followed by a hard-hit grounder to Cano. Because all three hitters he faced hit hot shots, he rated only a B.

New York 6, Oakland 2
Bullpen diary: Although Marte pushed the gun upwards of 88 mph only once, his command was exemplary. Meanwhile, Joba's blazers ranged from 96 to 99 mph, but his location was awful and his pitches were flatlined.

July 8–11 @ Safeco Field

Still another gem fashioned by the ever-young Pettitte—nine strikeouts, five hits, and only a single run allowed in eight innings. Although he left with the score 1–1, the Yankees pushed ahead two runs in the top of the 9th to eventually make Andy a winner. Rivera swallowed his pain and gutted out a twenty-two-pitch inning to put the Mariners to sleep and earn an A.

New York 3, Seattle 1
Save: Rivera (20)
Bullpen diary: Despite the soreness in his right knee and left rib cage, Mo's delivery was as smooth as ever.

RELIABLE REPORTS have surfaced claiming that the Yankees are "on the verge" of trading three high-caliber minor leaguers to Seattle for Cliff Lee. The projected thinking is that the Yankees are getting nervous about Hughes' accumulated pitch count and want him to take Park's place in the bullpen. Or else Hughes will stay in the rotation and Vazquez might be dealt for prospects.

Even though the Yankees claimed that Seattle had agreed to the swap, the Mariners proceeded to shop New York's offer around the league—a decidedly unethical procedure—and wound up sending Cliff Lee to Texas for a package of prospects.

The only good news is that Lee was scheduled to go against the Yanks in game three in Seattle.

Game Two @ Seattle, July 9

Another sterling effort by Hughes—7 innings, 5 Ks, no walks; he left with the Yankees up 5-1. Robertson failed to field a very catchable bouncer through the box that went for a single. That was his only mistake in an economical fourteen-pitch outing that earned him an A-. On the other hand, Park had to sweat through a thirty-two-pitch 9th inning to close out the game, and several line drives reduced his scoreless outing to B-.

New York 6, Seattle 1

Bullpen diary: Robertson relied on his curve much more than he had in previous games. Park also altered his pitching pattern, using more change-ups than usual. Another positive sign was Park's fastball topping out at 95 mph.

Starter's dilemma: Hughes is now 11-2, so the only way his innings can be curtailed is for him to miss an occasional start. However, the last time this was done, Hughes was belted in his return to the rotation.

Game Three @ Seattle, July 10

A brilliant outing by Vazquez was wasted by Joba's 8th-inning meltdown. He entered the game with the Yankees having a fragile 1-0 lead, and his first pitch, a 97-mph fastball, was squibbed off the end of Jack Wilson's bat only to land in front of the hard-charging Granderson for a single. Then came a force-out, a hard-hit single, a wild pitch, and an intentional pass, before Joba missed on a pair of sliders, enabling Jose Lopez to sit on a fastball and power it into the LF seats. The grand slam put the Mariners up 4-1, and that's all she wrote. Joba's seventh F of the season.

Seattle 4, New York 1

Losing Pitcher: Chamberlain (1-4)

Bullpen diary: Although Joba's heater ranged from 96 to 99 mph, his slider was out of whack and his location was awful. Blame his shortcomings on his mechanics, especially his stiff front leg, which prevents him from working low in the strike zone.

Game Four @ Seattle, July 11

After seven commanding innings, Sabathia left on the plus side of a 7-1 margin. Gaudin had his number called for the first time since June 30, and after missing with his initial three pitches it seemed as though he'd need a guide dog to find the plate. But he quickly zeroed in and zipped through a perfect inning to record only his second A. Moseley took over in the 9th and his sinker induced two groundball outs. Then Casey Kotchman blasted a 2-0 fastball for a homer. Moseley's effort rates a B+.

New York 8, Seattle 2

Bullpen diary: With his team down 8-1, the "book" procedure was for Kotchman to take a strike before looking to swing. Moseley likewise expected that his automatic strike would be watched, so he threw a meatball. Kotchman can't be blamed for trying to inflate his anemic .218 batting average, but neither can Moseley be faulted.

Halfway Home

At the All-Star break the Yankees' record of 56-32 is the best in MLB. They lead Tampa by two games and the injury-riddled Bosox by five games.

If their hitting has been spotty, and their bullpen erratic, the Yankees have been carried by their starting rotation. However, Brian Cashman is definitely looking to do something to improve his relief corps.

Despite Joba's roller-coaster first half, Girardi has restated his confidence that Chamberlain will eventually come around and will continue in his 8th-inning role. Robertson has made some improvement (especially with his curveball) but remains undependable. Marte seems to be peaking. Gaudin shows signs that he can effectively eat up meaningless innings. Moseley shows promise. Although Girardi claimed that he liked the way Park threw in his last two outings, he looks to be disposable via a trade, waiver, or faux injury. Mitre is due to be activated when play resumes after the intermission—with a critical three-game series at home against Tampa—so some change is inevitable.

And, even with his nagging injuries, Mo is always Mo.

JULY 11, 2010
RIP BOB SHEPPARD

JULY 13, 2010
RIP GEORGE STEINBRENNER

July 12–15, All-Star Break

Baseball tells us who we are; it is a barometer of our country.

—KEN BURNS

Back in spring training, several scouts gave their considered opinions and evaluations as to who would be the closers for the Yankees' opponents once the season began, and how effective these bullpen aces would be.

Here is a compilation of their professional judgments, followed by the official statistics that several of these pitchers have registered thus far midway in 2010.

G = games pitched; W-L = record; INGS = innings pitched; H = hits; BB = bases on balls; SO = strikeouts; SVS = saves; BL-SVS = blown saves; OPBA = opponents' batting average; OP-OBA = opponents' on-base average (supplied only if there is a meaningful difference with OPBA); ERA = earned run average.

* = on All-Star roster

DAVE AARDSMA, SEATTLE:

His fastball is straight, his slider is average, and his command rates 45. Aardsma is a "pie thrower" who gets by on his funky delivery.

G	W-L	INGS	H	BB	SO	SVS	BL-SVS	OPBA	OPOBA	ERA
30	0–6	27.1	25	13	27	16	.4	.255	.347	5.60

ANDREW BAILEY,* OAKLAND:

His fastball is rated 65 and his slider is "nasty." Bailey's all-important command is 55, which is deemed to be solid-average to above-average. All the scouts agree that Bailey, still only twenty-six and in his second season in the bigs, has the making of a prototypical upper-tier closer.

G	W-L	INGS	H	BB	SO	SVS	BL-SVS	OPBA	ERA
35	0–3	37	27	10	27	18	3	.206	1.70

JONATHAN BROXTON,* DODGERS:

A "grizzly bear" with a nasty slider and a fastball that routinely reaches 98 mph. Broxton's only real problem is his command; 45-rated.

G	W-L	INGS	H	BB	SO	SVS	BL-SVS	OPBA	ERA
39	3–0	38.1	34	7	55	19	2	.234	2.11

OCTAVIO DOTEL, PITTSBURGH:

Is erratic and offers a lifeless fastball. His other two major flaws are his flat-angle delivery and his overall lack of stuff. Should be a 7th-inning pitcher.

G	W-L	INGS	H	BB	SO	SVS	BL-SVCS	OPBA	OP-OBA	ERA
35	2–1	34	29	17	42	19	4	.230	.329	4.41

NEFTALI FELIZ,* TEXAS:

Has a truly great arm, which has encouraged the Rangers to force-feed the youngster.

G	W-L	INGS	H	BB	SO	SVS	BL-SVS	OPBA	OP-OBA	ERA
39	1–2	37	27	13	42	23	2	.197	.286	3.82

BRIAN FUENTES, ANGELS:

Isn't really a closer. Is better suited to be the first lefty out of the bullpen. Throws across his body and his effectiveness depends on hitters not being able to pick up the ball.

G	W-L	INGS	H	BB	SO	SVS	BL-SVS	OPBA	OPOBA	ERA
26	3–1	25	21	10	29	16	4	.219	.299	4.26

MIKE GONZALEZ, BALTIMORE:

An inconsistent lefty with a big leg kick, Gonzalez is always sore—he's currently out with a shoulder injury. Even when healthy, he has poor command (45) and throws too many pitches.

G	W-L	INGS	H	BB	SO	SVS	BL-SVS	OPBA	ERA
3	0–3	2	5	4	3	1	2	.556	18.00

KEVIN GREGG, TORONTO:

A respectable but not bona fide closer. His fastball and slider aren't dominant, and his best pitch is a sinking two-seamer. His command grades at 45–50, and he lacks pinpoint control.

G	W-L	INGS	H	BB	SO	SVS	BL-SVS	OPBA	ERA
34	0–3	34	29	18	37	20	3	.232	3.67

BOBBY JENKS, CHISOX:

His fastball ranges from 93 to 98 and his curve can buckle right-handed hitters. He also comes with a 60-rated change-up. Jenks' command is just okay: 45–50. His inconsistency is his major shortcoming.

G	W-L	INGS	H	BB	SO	SVS	BL-SVS	OPBA	OP-OBA	ERA
35	1–1	32	33	14	39	19	1	.258	.331	3.86

JON RAUCH, MINNESOTA:

Is 6'11" and weighs 290, but isn't a power pitcher. Has above-average fastball, curve, slider, and change-up, and can throw any of these anywhere at any time. Super command and control. He's making up for the loss of Joe Nathan.

G	W-L	INGS	H	BB	SO	SVS	BL-SVS	OPBA	ERA
31	2–1	33	34	4	24	19	4	.264	2.45

JOAKIM SORIA,* KANSAS CITY:

His fastball sits at 92 mph, his change-up is above average, and he uses his curve to strike out both lefty and righty hitters. Has very good but not great stuff. Soria's success is due to his fearlessness in challenging hitters, his ability to hide the ball, and his 70-rated command.

G	W-L	INGS	H	BB	SO	SVS	BL-SVS	OPBA	ERA
34	0–1	34	29	9	43	25	2	.227	2.34

RAFAEL SORIANO, TAMPA:

His fastball ranges from 94 to 96 mph but is often straight. Also throws an above-average splitter and cutter. Has good command but makes too many mistakes up in the strike zone.

G	W-L	INGS	H	BB	SO	SVS	BL-SVS	OPBA	ERA
34	2–0	33.2	7	29	23	29	1	.168	1.60

JOSE VALVERDE,* DETROIT:

A power pitcher with a straight fastball. But is more widely known as a "stage show" because he constantly talks to the ball, shouts, and grimaces. As good as he is, none of the scouts wanted him on their respective teams.

G	W-L	INGS	H	BB	SO	SVS	BL-SVS	OPBA	ERA
39	1–1	39	16	16	36	19	1	.201	0.92

KERRY WOOD, CLEVELAND:

Has a good arm and good stuff. Throws a nifty slider and effective curve, while his fastball ranges from 94 to 97 mph. His command is suspect; only 45. Wood makes lots of mistakes and seems to crumble with a game on the line.

G	W-L	INGS	H	BB	SO	SVS	BL-SVS	OPBA	OP-OBA	ERA
23	1–4	20	21	11	18	8	3	.263	.366	6.30

July 2010 and Old-Timers' Day

You're not in the big leagues until Bob Sheppard has announced your name.
—CARL YASTRZEMSKI

Old-Timers' Day @ Yankee Stadium, July 17

During the ceremonies, much attention was devoted to honoring the respective memories of George Steinbrenner and Bob Sheppard. But when the old-timers were finally introduced, only a few authentic ex-relievers were on hand: Goose Gossage, looking trim and broad-chested with only the whiteness of his trademark Fu Manchu mustache demonstrating that he was fifty-nine years old; Dave Eiland, who made only nine trips from the bullpen during the fifty-four games he played for the Yankees; and Don Johnson, who relieved in seven games for the Yankees over his two seasons (1947, 1950) in the Bronx.

Gossage took the ball as the old-timers' game commenced, and tossed nothing but marshmallows. However, at a similar function just a few years ago, the Goose didn't take kindly to being razzed by his contemporaries for not throwing hard. Gossage responded by striking out the side on nine 85-mph fastballs.

Long before Gossage dominated endgame situations for the Yankees, the Bronx Bombers sported a long history of outstanding relievers.

⚾ ALTHOUGH HE made 12 spot starts in his 50 appearances in 1927, Wilcy Moore was the Yankees' first relief specialist. A thirty-year-old rookie, Moore had broken his pitching (right) arm in 1925 and learned how to throw sidearm. Taking over the pitching chores whenever he was needed, Moore was 19-7 that year, with a league-leading 13 (retroactive) saves. His ERA was 2.28, low enough to top the league's list, but he had only six complete games to his credit and the governing rules stated that a pitcher needed ten CGs to qualify for the ERA title. Overall, Moore hurled 213 innings that season, a total that created debilitating arm problems and essentially made him a one-year wonder.

Back when pitchers batted, Babe Ruth was rightly critical of Moore's pathetic attempts to make contact. Early in 1927, Ruth wagered $300 to Moore's $15 that the pitcher would not hit a homer all season long. "My money's as safe as a church," Ruth boasted. But Moore did smack a four-bagger (the only one of his career) and used the money to buy two mules for his farm—one he named "Babe" and the other "Ruth."

Three years ago, Moore's game-used 1927 road uniform was sold for $43,000. Bids are still taken on a pair of blank checks signed by him.

⚾ JOHNNY MURPHY was a Yankee from 1934 to 1946. After having a two-game cup of coffee in 1932, Murphy was used exclusively as a starter when he made the big club for good, notching a respectable record of 14-10. However, the starting rotation in 1935 featured Lefty "Goofy" Gomez, Red Ruffing, Johnny Broaca (a holdover who went 15-7 that season), and Johnny Allen (who sported a career record of 37-13 and was returning from an injury). Since there was no room in the rotation, manager Joe McCarthy wanted Murphy to become a full-time reliever. Murphy resisted until the Yankees agreed to pay him on a scale commensurate with starters.

The results were dynamic. Murphy had pinpoint control of all his pitches (fastball, curve, and change), and over his career he set records for total saves (107) and wins in relief (73) that were eventually eclipsed when closers became routine in the 1980s. As a result, Murphy was acclaimed as the original "Fireman."

When asked about the reasons for his own success, the party-loving Gomez said this: "Clean living, fast outfielders, and Johnny Murphy."

JOE PAGE appeared in 278 games with the Yankees from 1944 to 1950. Like Murphy, he began his major league career as a starter, but after enjoying only middling success, manager Bucky Harris sent Page to the bullpen in '47. Page felt that his "demotion" to what he felt was "second-string" status was his punishment for flopping as a starter. But after he had an exceptional initial outing from the pen, Page thought his performance would convince Harris to give him another chance to start. When Harris refused, Page began to brood. Page became convinced of his value as a reliever only after Harris said he was "a natural" in this role.

For the 1947 season, Page accumulated seventeen saves (retroactive) and won fourteen games in relief. He won the seventh game of the '47 World Series by limiting the Brooklyn Dodgers to one hit in five innings. That's when baseball pundits began to understand how important a bullpen ace could be.

Armed with a rising fastball and a sharply breaking overhand curve, Page routinely sneered at the erstwhile hitters he faced. But too much alcohol, partying, and womanizing led to too many days when he could barely see home plate well enough to find the strike zone. (In 790 lifetime innings, he whiffed 519 and walked 421.)

Since he hailed from a family of coal miners in Cherry Valley,

Pennsylvania, he was raised with the threat of imminent death. Accordingly, miners were accustomed to living day to day and spending their earnings in a hurry. And that was precisely Page's modus operandi with the Yankees. His teammates thought him irresponsible, but with his movie-star good looks, Page was only concerned with how the ladies regarded him. The Yankees once hired a female detective to trail Page and itemize his excesses, but she quickly fell in love with him and filed only glowing reports.

Page's career and his partying ended abruptly in spring training of 1951, when he tore a muscle in his pitching (left) arm.

⚾ RYNE DUREN's tour with the Yankees lasted from 1958 to 1961. He could throw hard—95 mph—and he wore the proverbial eyeglasses as thick as the bottom of Coke bottles. Indeed, Blind Ryne's uncorrected vision was 20/70 and 20/200. During a minor league game, Duren actually hit the on-deck batter on the fly. No wonder batters were reluctant to dig in at the plate.

While warming up before a game in 1958, Duren was thrown off stride by a hole that the previous pitcher (Bob Turley) had dug in front of the rubber—and his resulting pitch sailed over the catcher's head and thudded into the backstop. Coach Frank Crosetti encouraged Duren to further frighten hitters by occasionally duplicating the same errant warm-up pitch. Soon enough, Duren had evolved a routine: he'd take off and wipe his glasses, squint at the catcher, remove and rewipe his glasses, then hurl a pitch against the backstop.

Duren did walk hitters galore (393 in 589 lifetime innings), but he also struck out 630. In '58, he led the AL in saves with 20 and posted a 2.02 ERA. For his encore, Duren saved 14 in '59 and pitched to a 1.88 ERA. But that same year, he accidentally ran into a fan who had leaped onto the field immediately after the last pitch was delivered; Duren fell and broke his wrist. His career continued for another seven years, but he never recovered his chops.

🔵 Luis Arroyo was a lefty with a dominating screwball who was still another one-season wonder. That season was 1961, when he had a record of 15-5 to go along with his league-best total of 29 saves (most of which benefited Whitey Ford).

In fact, after the season, when Ford received the Cy Young Award at the New York Baseball Writers banquet, he began his acceptance speech by saying, "I had a nine-minute speech prepared, but I'm only going to talk for seven minutes and let Arroyo finish the last two."

Unfortunately, Arroyo also led the league with 65 appearances that season, and his arm never fully recovered. (Arroyo is still alive but was too ill to attend today's Old-Timers' Day.)

🔵 Steve Hamilton was a leansome sidewinding lefty with the Yankees from 1963 to 1970 whose sharp slider and roundhouse curve were anathema to southpaw hitters. But Hamilton was much more than an ultimate lefty specialist.

As a senior at Morehead State, the 6'7" "Hambone" averaged 23 points per game playing basketball. He also became the only Yankee ever to play in the NBA—playing in eighty-two games for the Minneapolis Lakers in 1958–60. Hamilton averaged a modest 4.5 points per game with a career high of 15 against the Knicks in Madison Square Garden. Torn cartilage in his left knee suddenly ended his basketball career, so he simply turned full-time to baseball.

During the Yankees off-seasons, Hamilton taught sociology and was also the assistant basketball coach at his alma mater. Yet Hamilton is perhaps best remembered for developing a blooper pitch during his later years in New York. Modeled on Rip Sewell's "Eephus ball" (which Ted Williams once famously slammed for a home run in an All-Star game), Hamilton called his version the

"Folly Floater"—and it reached a height of at least twenty feet before crossing home plate and landing in the catcher's mitt.

Most hitters simply couldn't resist taking a hack at the pitch. Early in the 1970 season, Detroit's Tony Horton took a mighty swing and could only manage a pop-up that was easily caught. In his embarrassment, Horton then crawled to the Tigers' dugout on all fours.

⚾ AFTER PEDRO RAMOS (1964–66 with the Yanks) retired, he admitted what every hitter he faced always knew—that he threw a spitter. Using what Ramos called his "Cuban palm ball," he recorded 40 saves as a Yankee.

He was equally well-known for bringing a BB gun to the bullpen, where Ramos and his fellow relievers would line up bottles and cans out of sight of the playing field and indulge in highly competitive shooting contests. In fact, during one close game, Ramos ignored the command to start warming up because it was his turn to shoot.

⚾ JIM BOUTON was only a sometimes reliever with the Yankees (1962–68), but he reported still another interesting incident while walking through the subterranean tunnels at the Stadium on his way to the bullpen.

Whitey Ford had pitched and won the day before and there he was . . . conducting a solo celebration among the shadows. Ford was seated at a small table that was covered with a red-and-white checkered tablecloth, and that held a bottle of wine, a glass, and a pizza.

⚾ GOSSAGE'S CAREER as a dreadnought Yankee reliever encompassed two stretches—1983–83 and 1989. While he has nothing but supreme respect for Rivera, Goose also harbors some resentment.

When Gossage was inducted into the Hall of Fame, he was

informed that 53 of his 310 career saves were earned by his getting seven-plus outs. By contrast, Rivera has logged only one such save. The point being that while Gossage needed to have at least three pitches in his repertoire (a blazing fastball, a snapping curve, and a rarely used slider), Rivera usually only pitches a single inning and can therefore succeed with a single pitch.

Indeed, whenever Gossage got credit for a one-inning save, he felt guilty. And his teammates would tease him, saying, "You're going to take that? Does that count?"

However, Gossage (and Rollie Fingers) were the last closers who routinely pitched two or more innings. They were paid to accumulate saves, and to get more saves for the money, those closers who succeeded them are usually limited to one-inning save situations.

⚾ SPARKY LYLE'S career as a Yankee (1972–78) overlapped Gossage's. Lyle tallied virtually all of his 238 career saves via his devastating slider, which confounded both right- and left-handed hitters.

Lyle was also an infamous prankster who was fond of sitting on any cakes (and shitting on at least one) that were brought into the clubhouse to celebrate a teammate's birthday. He also caused heart attacks throughout the Yankees organization when he showed up at one spring training with his left arm and left leg encased in casts.

"Some people say you have to be crazy to be a relief pitcher," Lyle claimed, "but I was crazy before I ever became one."

⚾ MO'S IMMEDIATE predecessor was John Wetteland. During the 1995 and 1996 seasons, Rivera functioned as Wetteland's setup man. And Wetteland did a hell of a job, using a sizzling 97-mph fastball to tally 74 saves over the course of those two seasons.

Wetteland grew up outside of San Francisco and confessed to having a multitude of sins as a young man—drinking, drugging, and rocking. His over-the-top intensity continued into his stint with the Montreal Expos, where (in 1993) he broke a toe when he kicked a pitcher's screen in training camp. But shortly thereafter he found Jesus and has lived cleanly ever since, even going so far as to invite indigent people to share his New Mexico home.

The Yankees deemed that Rivera was ready to assume the closer's role and failed to offer Wetteland a contract when he became a free agent after the 1996 season—saving $6 million in the deal.

Mo, of course, succeeded Wetteland as both a lights-out closer and a sincerely sincere practitioner of "New Testament imperatives."

⚾ ON JULY 14, the Yankees announced that the team would wear a Bob Sheppard patch featuring an old-fashioned microphone on their left sleeves and Steinbrenner's initials, *GMS*, on the front of their uniforms for the rest of the season.

Tonight, the PA booth was empty and no announcements were made.

July 16–18, Tampa Bay Rays @ Yankee Stadium

Sabathia's seven-inning performance was uneven, and he took to the showers trailing 4-3. However, on the strength of excellent relief work by Robertson and Rivera and clutch hitting by Swisher (a game-tying HR in the 8th and a game-winning single in the 9th), the Yankees prevailed in appropriately dramatic fashion.

Robertson was absolutely brilliant, whiffing Aybar, Kapler, and Bartlett on curveballs, and therefore deserving of his eleventh A of the season.

Rivera came on in the top of the 9th with the score knotted at 4-all and proceeded to jam Upton with a nasty cutter that shattered the bat. Unfortunately, both the barrel of the bat and the ball were sent flying straight at A-Rod, who decided that discretion was the better part of valor and ducked the splintered shaft before vainly attempting to snare the soft liner. The upshot was a single for Upton, who promptly got picked off first.

Mo then retired Crawford on a soft flyball before striking out Longoria to end the game. Another A for Rivera.

New York 5, Tampa Bay 4

Winning Pitcher: Rivera (3-1)

Bullpen diary: Robertson's arsenal now includes a curveball with a few mph subtracted off; it ranges from 79 to 81, or 3–5 mph slower than before. The increased difference in velocity between his adjusted curve and his fastball had the three hitters he faced seriously off stride.

The four-day rest has put some life back in Mo's cutters. He was also masterful in working both sides of the plate to lefties and righties alike.

As HE crossed home plate after swatting his HR, Swisher pulled on his jersey and planted a kiss on the Steinbrenner memorial patch the Yankees will wear above their hearts for the rest of the season.

Around the league: The sport press is abuzz about the no-hitters and perfect games already this season. Scoring is down in general, and of course, the leading theory is no steroids.

But there is just as much evidence pointing to MLB teams focusing much more on pitcher development in the minors, and those pitchers are now blossoming in the majors.

The other reason has been the emphasis on speed in the field, and the morning highlights are as much about dazzling stops in the infield and diving catches in the outfield as they are of home runs.

Game Two vs. the Rays in the Bronx, July 17

Burnett got slammed by the Rays, then after the top of the 2nd he retreated to the clubhouse and slammed his hands into a door. Unfortunately, he made two-handed contact with the plastic lineup-card holders pasted to the door and suffered several moderate lacerations. After facing two hitters in the top of the 3rd, Burnett's bleeding hands forced him out of the game.

At first Burnett claimed that he had injured himself when he tripped in the clubhouse. But he later fessed up and apologized to all concerned.

In any event, the Yankees were trailing by only 4–2 when Moseley took over. Although he yielded a single and issued a walk, Moseley kept the game in hand by inducing a groundout and a double play. He likewise wiggled out of a jam in the top of the 4th, but his Houdini act ended in the top of the 5th when he gave up a walk, two singles, and a three-run HR to Brignac that stretched Tampa Bay's lead to 8–2.

While it's true that Moseley's three innings overextended him, he was still the instrument that enabled the Rays to blow the game open. In so doing, Moseley was tagged with an F.

Chad Gaudin got pounded for five hits and two runs, but he ate up four innings and finished out the game. The ultimate mop-up man, Gaudin's perseverance deserved a C-.

Tampa Bay 10, New York 5

Bullpen diary: Damaso Marte was placed on the injured list with an inflammation in his left shoulder. This was the same injury that put Marte out of commission for 3½ months last season.

Accordingly, Boone Logan was once again recalled from Scranton.

Sergio Mitre was back in the dugout and ready to go. But since he pitched three innings yesterday at Scranton, he'll remain inactive until he can pitch again—most likely Tuesday when the Angels visit the Bronx.

With Mitre's return assured (and barring a trade), somebody will have to be exiled. If today's game constituted a pitch-off between Moseley and Gaudin, the latter was clearly the winner. Moseley's sinker was flat, and he labored in every inning, while Gaudin was much sharper and showed superior command.

Game Three vs. the Rays in the Bronx, July 18

Déjà vu. Like Burnett before him, Pettitte had to be lifted in the 3rd inning. However, Andy's departure was caused by his straining a left groin muscle while making a sensational diving play on a bunt by Carl Crawford—a situation that will probably require Pettitte to miss at least one start and quite probably a few more.

The Yanks trailed 3-2, with two on and two out, when Girardi made an astute move. For sure, his bullpen was short, yet he brought in Robertson to hopefully keep the game close. Although he had some difficulty locating his curve, Robertson fulfilled his skipper's expectations by producing a pop-up and a harmless outfield fly.

After the Yankees tied the score at 3-3, Robertson cruised through the top of the 4th—the key pitch being a 3-2 curve that struck out the homer-happy Carlos Peña. For keeping the game under control, Robertson was awarded an A.

Enter Park, whose fastball reached 94 mph and whose curve danced away from the Rays' bats. Park's A was his first in a month.

Boone Logan made his re-return an effective one. His fastball sat at 95 and topped at 98 mph, and he struck out Crawford with a rapidly vanishing curveball. Although Logan did cough up a meaningless HR to Kapler, he earned a solid B.

The Yankees now led 10-4, and the plan was for Joba to pitch the 8th and 9th and demonstrate that the rumors claiming that Robertson was on the verge of replacing him as the bridge to Mo were premature.

Chamberlain's fastball ranged from 95 to 98, yet his slider was his best pitch. Indeed, his swerves provided the finishing touch on all three of his strikeouts and were also responsible for a pair of flyball outs.

But after Joba had thrown thirty pitches on a hot, humid afternoon—with his last offering getting smacked by Matt Joyce for an RBI double—Girardi called Mo's number in still another nonsave situation. This was an extravagance made possible by tomorrow's off day.

Joba got a B- but didn't help his cause: to maintain his privileged role.

All that Mo needed was one pitch to coax a pop-up from Brignac that ended the game and the series. Another A for Rivera.

New York 9, Tampa Bay 5
Winning Pitcher: Park (2-1)
Bullpen diary: With Pettitte's injury opening up a spot for Mitre, both Moseley and Gaudin appear to be safe—unless the Yankees decide to give another chance to Jonathan Albaladejo, who has been handcuffing the Triple-A hitters with Scranton (31 saves and 0.96 ERA).

Has Robertson truly surpassed Chamberlain? Joba's batting average against with two out and a runner on base is a ghastly .378. Could Joba be trade bait? Since Pettitte was diagnosed with a Grade 1 strain and is indeed headed for the DL, will Mitre take Pettitte's next scheduled start? Since Mitre is, at best, a five-to-six-inning pitcher, there will be more pressure than ever on the bullpen. Also, since Burnett has likewise turned into a short-inning starter, what happens to the plans to limit Hughes' innings?

The only sure bet is that Brian Cashman will be spending the next few days working the phones.

CHAN HO PARK

This South Korean–born pitcher knows why he frequently gets into trouble when he can't get a leadoff hitter out. "I lose my focus and rush my delivery with a runner on base," he says. "Especially if he's a threat to steal a base. It's one mechanical problem that I always have to think about. Another one is to keep my arm speed constant when I'm throwing different pitches so that I don't tip off what they are. Sometimes all the thinking I have to do can be distracting."

Another constant distraction is the frequency with which he winds up on the injured list. He was originally signed by the Los Angeles Dodgers as a nondrafted free agent in 1994, and has been a part- and full-time major leaguer ever since then. During this time he's spent over 350 days out of action because of pulled hamstrings (twice), a blister on the middle finger of his pitching hand, lower-back strains (twice), an intestinal virus, and intestinal bleeding. However, only recently recovered from his latest hamstring pull, he feels "one hundred percent."

All of these various miseries make the thirty-seven-year-old Chan Ho fondly recall that far-off time and place when his body was young and strong.

"We don't have tee-ball or Little League teams in Korea," he says. "Instead, each of the bigger cities and some of the small ones have teams that play each other. Seoul had three teams, but there was only one in Kongju, where I come from."

Chan Ho began his baseball career as a ten-year-old third baseman: "I was a pretty good hitter, but the best thing I could do was to so easily make the long throw from third to first. Because of my arm, I was turned into a pitcher when I was fourteen."

Chan Ho believes that the training procedures for young ballplayers in South Korea are superior to those in America. "We had more coaching from a younger age," he says, "a more organized program, and much better conditioning. I was in great shape when I was selected to the national team when I was eighteen."

Serving in the armed forces is mandatory in South Korea, and Chan Ho completed his military commitment in 1999 when he was with the Dodgers. "Boot camp was really serious," he says, "because we were trained to kill. If we made a mistake on a battlefield, we'd either die or get somebody else killed. The experience made me mentally and physically tough, and also made me aware of the importance of teamwork. When I returned to play for the Dodgers, I was in the best condition of my life and I had my best season ever."

Indeed, in 2000, as a full-time starter, Park went 18-10, with a 3.27 ERA and 217 strikeouts in 226 innings. Having thereby established himself as a top-notch major leaguer, Chan Ho took full advantage of his eventual free agent status—subsequently signing lucrative contracts with Texas, the Mets, Dodgers, Phillies, and last winter with the Yankees.

Through it all, Chan Ho has learned to do most of his thinking in English. "Especially when I'm in the States," he says. "But when there are baseball terms involved I first think of them in Korean and then translate them into English."

July 20–21, Los Angeles Angels @ Yankee Stadium

Just when the Yankees needed Hughes to give the weary bullpen a rest, he got shelled and was replaced after 6-plus innings trailing 6-2.

Jonathan Albaladejo was indeed recalled from Scranton to replace Pettitte, and the Yanks were hoping that his third go-round with the big club would prove to be the charm. He threw more four-seamers than he had in the past, but two of the three curves he unleashed were smoked—one for a single and one for an out. He did register a strikeout with the only change-up he threw, and gave up two solid hits and a walk in $1\frac{2}{3}$ innings. The only run charged to his record came when his free pass scored on a subsequent homer allowed by Park.

Still, the young man showed some poise and even his misses were close ones, so he earned a C+.

Except for that one poorly located fastball, Park actually did a commendable job—it being the only safety he permitted in his $1\frac{1}{3}$ inning stint. Park's grade: B-.

Gaudin pitched the top of the 9th and did nothing to convince Girardi that his services should be retained when Mitre comes off the DL over the weekend. Gaudin's stats: two walks, two hits, two runs—and another F.

Los Angeles 10, New York 2
Bullpen diary: Since Albaladejo habitually worked only a single inning at a time in Scranton, the extra eighteen pitches he threw in his second inning of work today was somewhat of an overload.

Last season, Park allowed zero homers in fifty-six innings—the HR hit off him today was his seventh in thirty innings this season.

Game Two vs. the Angels in the Bronx, July 21

Vazquez sailed through four innings and was staked to a 6-0 lead when he was suddenly shipwrecked in the top of the 5th. By the time the storm subsided, the Yanks' lead was only 6-5. In the 6th, Robertson loaded the bases with two outs, but he wriggled out of the jam when Howie Kendrick hit a rocket into Swisher's glove in RF. Another narrow escape and a C-.

Logan was next and disposed of the two lefties he faced—a K and a flyball out—but had a hanging slider smacked for a single. For his effort, Logan rated B-.

Chamberlain gave up a walk and an infield hit before terminating the Angels in the 7th. When the Yanks produced four runs in the bottom of the 8th—on dramatic homers by two recent call-ups, Juan Miranda and Colin Curtis (who actually had to pinch-hit for Gardner with an 0-2 count after Brett was ejected)—the hometown heroes upped their lead to 10-4. The two strikeouts Joba rang up were no consolation for the brace of hits and the Angels' sixth run, which further sullied his unsatisfactory record. A C- for Joba.

Mo zipped through an easy thirteen-pitch 9th inning to put the game in the books and earn another A.

New York 10, Angels 6

Bullpen diary: Robertson threw six curves, only one of which was a strike. Logan's velocity was geared up to 95 mph. Chamberlain paid the price for his 93–96 mph fastballs getting too much of the plate.
Obituary: Ralph Houk died yesterday at the age of ninety. Houk served in World War II, reaching the rank of major, and upon returning home, he made it as backup catcher for the Yanks and played sporadically for eight seasons. Known as a player's manager, he earned his place in Bomber fans' hearts with the 1961 World Championship. After being swept by the Dodgers in the '63 World Series, the Yankees went into their long decline in the CBS/Horace Clarke years. Houk went on to manage the Tigers for three years in the '70s and the Red Sox from 1981 to 1984.

July 22–25, Kansas City Royals @ Yankee Stadium

How erratic was Sabathia? How about 11 hits, 9 strikeouts, and 4 runs in 6⅓ IP. Robertson entered with two on and the Yankees clinging to a 6-4 lead. But he easily got out of the jam, earning another A.

Chamberlain was threatened by two infield chops that went for base hits, a bad call when a runner was erroneously called safe on the front end of a double steal, and a walk—but he escaped unscathed when the dangerous Jose Guillen bounced a 95-mph heater to Cano. Because he wasn't hit hard, Chamberlain deserves a solid B.

The Yankees blew the game open with four runs in the bottom of the 8th. Since the potential save situation was no longer in effect, the mop-up job fell to Park. There was no pressure on him, but his recording two groundouts, a deep flyball out, and a curve bounced through the middle for a single earned him an A-.

New York 10, Kansas City 4

Bullpen diary: Aside from Joba's inability to repeat his delivery, he also seems reluctant to discomfort right-handed hitters by pitching them inside. After another sharp performance by Robertson, how long before he inherits the 8th-inning role?

The trade deadline is only nine days away.

Game Two vs. the Royals in the Bronx, July 23

Burnett's return to excellence was cut short after he'd thrown five shutout innings when the game was interrupted by an eighty-five-minute rain delay. Gaudin took over when the skies cleared, with the Yankees ahead 4-0. His job was to eat up as many innings as possible to rest an already weary bullpen—especially with Mitre scheduled to start in Pettitte's place tomorrow and not expected to pitch deep into the game.

Gaudin did have difficulty domesticating his sliders, but he procured two outs using his secondary pitch, his cutter. Otherwise, over his three-inning stint, Gaudin got four groundouts, one pop-up, and four flyouts. Two balls were hit hard—both going for doubles—and he also was hurt by a pair of groundball singles. Blame the poor location of his 90–91 mph fastballs for every hard-hit ball. Still, gobbling up three innings at the expense of only one run earns Gaudin a B+.

Albaladejo neatly finished the game with two strikeouts and a grounder. Instead of totally relying on his sinker as he had in his previous appearances, he mixed in several rising four-seam fastballs. For his sterling effort, Albie rated an A.

New York 7, Kansas City 1

Bullpen diary: Despite their losing record, the Royals are actually a good-hitting team, so Gaudin's work was impressive. Perhaps impressive enough to keep him around for a while. Mitre was activated from the DL immediately after the game and roster room was created by sending Albaladejo back to Scranton. Even though he pitched well this time around, Albaladejo was caught in a numbers game.

Still, his future as a fixture in the Yankees bullpen looks bright.

Game Three vs. the Royals in the Bronx, July 24

Mitre was treated rudely on his return. The appropriate action on his sinker was a sometimes thing, and too many were situated too high in the strike zone. He did produce eleven groundouts in his 4⅓ innings, but also several long hits. Mitre left trailing 7-2.

The weather was brutal in the Bronx—a hot, humid afternoon with the mercury topping off at 100 degrees. Moseley was faced with the task of sweating out as many innings as possible. Turned out, he pitched one-hit ball for 4⅔ innings, getting half of his outs on grounders and four on infield pops. Not one of his pitches was hit with authority, guaranteeing Moseley an A.

Kansas City 7, New York 4

Bullpen diary: The bad news: Mitre's dismal start. The good news: Pettitte's groin strain is feeling so good that he predicts he'll be back on the mound within 2–3 weeks, not the 4–6 weeks that had been the initial medical prognosis. That means the Yankees will only have to start Mitre another 3–4 times. However, Moseley most likely not only saved his job, but might also be under serious consideration to supplant Mitre as Pettitte's temporary substitute.

No apparent movement on the trading front.

Game Four vs. the Royals in the Bronx, July 25

The fourth game of the KC series would see a once-in-a-lifetime play.

Still another disappointing start by Hughes. Indeed, he's been off his feed since his start was skipped just before the All-Star break. Still, the Yankees led 5-3 after 5 1/3 innings when the heavens opened once more. This time the rain delay lasted for two hours and thirty-two minutes.

Logan pitched with unusual efficiency for the subsequent 1 2/3 innings. His fastball topped at 95 mph, and 12 of his 17 offerings were strikes. Logan's grade: A.

The Yankees' lead was extended to 7-3 by the time Joba climbed the pitcher's hill to commence the top of the 8th. But he immediately got himself in trouble when he walked the ninth-place hitter and then was touched for a two-run HR. Chamberlain escaped further damage by recording a groundball out, a strikeout (on a slider), and a hard-hit liner to RF. Grade: still another F.

The Yankees broke the game open in the bottom of the 8th. But in the bottom of the frame, with Rick Ankiel on third, Park's cutter to Brayan Peña hit the dirt and bounced away from Posada. The Yankees' veteran backstop flipped off his mask and tried to toss it out of the way, but the mask landed on top of the ball.

According to an arcane rule, this constituted an error on the catcher and Ankiel was allowed to score from third base. Girardi came out to discuss it, but the rule is for real.

Park finally ended the Royals' (and his) misery by getting a skyball to CF. Since he really wasn't hit hard and the only run he permitted came on Posada's miscue, Park's grade: B-.

New York 12, Kansas City 6

Bullpen diary: Joba's continued failures have blossomed into a problem of major proportions. Barring an unexpected trade, it's almost a certainty that Girardi will be forced to move Robertson into the 8th-inning setup role.

According to a veteran advance scout, "Both Chamberlain's front leg and his overall delivery are much stiffer than they have ever been. His arm slot is also a tick lower, and his slider shows no consistency whatsoever. That means that hitters can simply sit on his fastball, which tends to be up in the strike zone anyway. The Yanks thought that Park would provide insurance to cover any bumps in Chamberlain's season, but there are less than ten weeks before the playoffs and Joba is putting the bullpen and the entire season in jeopardy. Something's got to be done, and it's got to be done yesterday."

⚾ AT THE Hall of Fame ceremonies in Cooperstown, John Fogerty's song "Centerfield" was inducted, the first song or musician to be included in the hallowed halls. We can only hope Terry Cashman is next.

July 26–29 @ Progressive Field

Vazquez gave the Yankees what they so desperately needed—depth from a starter. After walking the leadoff hitter in the bottom of the 7th, Vazquez went to the clubhouse with the Yankees sitting atop a 3-2 lead. Instead of automatically calling for Joba, Girardi summoned Robertson to pitch, and he quickly induced a double-play grounder. This constituted Robertson's eighth consecutive appearance without yielding a run and his seventh A since June 1. Logan closed the inning by striking out the tough LH Shin-Soo

Choo with a 95-mph heater, earning another A. Mo's cutter wasn't cutting, so he went almost exclusively with his sinking two-seamer. After being touched for a Texas League single, he closed the game with three weak groundouts. Rivera's grade: A.

New York 3, Cleveland 2
Save: Rivera (21)
Bullpen diary: After the game, Girardi said that "match-ups" would determine whether he used Chamberlain or Robertson in setup situations. The skipper emphasized his hope and belief that Joba would soon recapture the rapture. Meanwhile, the Yankees have rejected including Chamberlain in several trade discussions. Logan's control is much better in this incarnation with the Yankees. Rivera once again demonstrated his ability to make in-game adjustments.

Girardi also announced that Mitre would be returning to bullpen duty and Moseley would be starting in the concluding game of the Cleveland series. Mitre's awful start in Kansas City coupled with Moseley's sensational relief stint certainly influenced this decision.
Around the league: Tampa's Matt Garza threw the fifth no-hitter of the season tonight.

Game Two @ Cleveland, July 27
C.C. was sabotaged by costly errors made by Cervelli and Cano and was trailing 4-0 after throwing 120 pitches over seven innings. Meanwhile, for the sixth time this season, the lineup was once again shut down by a youngster making his initial major appearance. This time their tormentor was Josh Tomlin, who mostly baffled them with change-ups. Park breezed through the bottom of the 8th, thereby getting an A.

Cleveland 4, New York 1
Bullpen diary: Park needed only seven pitches: curves, changes, sliders, and a lone fastball that was belted for the only hit he relinquished.

Game Three @ Cleveland, July 28

Burnett's curve was snapping, his fastball was spot-on, and he continued his resurrection by tossing a string of 6⅓ scoreless innings. After he'd thrown 114 pitches, he was replaced by Joba. With the Yankees having an 8-0 death-grip on the game, this was a perfect opportunity to exercise Chamberlain with nothing at stake.

And Joba made quick work of the Indians by inducing a pair of semi-deep flyballs to RF. His fastball was clocked from 95 to 97 mph, yet both outs came on sliders. Joba's graded out at an A, his first in four weeks covering five appearances. Mitre finished up the game with a minimum of drama and was credited with an A.

New York 8, Cleveland 0

Bullpen diary: According to Eiland, the problem with Joba is that his front (left) shoulder was opening up, which caused his hand to drag. This sequence gave hitters a longer look at the ball, which is why even his hottest fastballs have been scalded. Eiland's diagnosis is to close Chamberlain's shoulder by shortening his stride—which certainly didn't happen in this particular outing.

Mitre got two of his three Ks on off-speed pitches, but his two-seamer was dipping to perfection. Yet after being replaced in the starting rotation by Moseley, Mitre wasn't very happy. He felt that his one start wasn't enough of a chance to show what he could do. But with the Rays only two games behind and the dog days of August just ahead, there's no time to keep everybody happy. In any event, better to have a guy who wants to pitch under pressure than one who doesn't.

Game Four @ Cleveland, July 29

Moseley survived a shaky opening frame and used his top-to-bottom curve and well-placed 89–91 mph fastball (his slider was mostly a waste pitch) to allow one run and four hits over the course of his six-inning stint. He left with a 2-1 edge before a seven-run explosion by the Yankees in the top of the 7th put the game, and Moseley's win, on ice.

In a tune-up for the forthcoming Tampa Bay series, Robertson relied on his fastball to set down the Indians on a grounder and a pair of whiffs. Grade: A.

Park came on in the bottom of the 8th with the Yankees now up 11-1. His mop-up job went smoothly through the first five hitters he faced—two strikeouts (one in the first-ever confrontation with Park's countryman Shin-Soo Choo), two weakly struck grounders, and a casual flyball to RF. But with only one more out needed to secure the victory, Park fell apart.

A pair of four-pitch walks, a single, an error by Marcus Thames (playing 3B for the first time in his major league career), a wild pitch, and another walk plated three runs for Cleveland—before a warning-track drive to deep RF was run down by Swisher. Park's grade: D+, the first unsatisfactory grade he's had since an F on July 2.

New York 11, Cleveland 4

Bullpen diary: Here's why traditional statistics are often misleading: despite Chamberlain's erratic performances he is credited with twenty "holds," which ranks him fourth in the majors.

🔵 THE TRADING deadline is 4 p.m. ET on July 31. Because Moseley has accepted and even surpassed the challenge of starting, the bullpen's needs are paramount.

- Assuming that Robertson is now the bridge to Mo, and with Joba consistently inconsistent, the 7th-inning role still needs shoring up.
- Somehow the Yanks must find the best way to rid themselves of Park, who would then have to be replaced.
- Another lefty is required to either back up or replace the historically unreliable Logan.

- Gaudin is totally expendable, and will most likely be gone when Pettitte returns from the DL.

The next stop is Tampa Bay, where the Yankees hope to extend their two-game lead.

Around the league: Marlins outfielder Chris Coghlan will miss 6–8 weeks for surgery on a damaged knee he twisted while applying the postgame shaving-cream face pie to Wes Helms after a walk-off hit against the Braves.

July 30–August 1 @ Tropicana Field

Two swings generated all the runs in the opening game of this critical series: Swisher's two-run blast in the 1st and Matt Joyce's three-run round-tripper off Hughes in the bottom of the 6th.

Joba took over in the bottom of the 7th and zipped through his two innings looking like the pitcher the Yankees had expected (and hoped) he'd be: three strikeouts (including getting Longoria on four consecutive sliders), a pop-up, and two uncomplicated groundouts. His fastball pushed the gun to 96 mph, his command was excellent, and his slider had terrific bite. Joba's grade: A

Tampa Bay 3, New York 2

Bullpen diary: Chamberlain succeeded in slowing down his delivery and keeping his front shoulder tucked, thereby allowing him to get over his stiff front leg in a smooth and timely fashion, as well as hiding the ball from the hitters for a fraction of a second longer. The problem of what in baseball lingo is his "straight as a string" fastball still needs to be addressed. Eventually Joba will have to develop a cutter or a sinking two-seamer, but Eiland insists that his mechanics have to be properly tuned before his repertoire can expand.

With the loss, the Yankees are only one game ahead of the Rays.

TRADES

After the game, the Yankees announced a pair of deals designed to boost their hitting: cash for outfielder and right-handed hitter Austin Kearns, plus Mark Melancon and a low-level infielder for Lance Berkman.

Just before the deadline the following afternoon, Kerry Wood became a Yankee in exchange for cash or a player to be named later, depending on Wood's ability to remain healthy. Given his fourteen stints on the DL throughout his career (including two this season), it's a good bet that money will be exchanged at season's end.

The immediate plan is for Wood to push Joba even further down the pecking order, and hopefully to take over the bridge role and enable Robertson to return to his 7th-inning slot. As scouts have previously noted, Wood still has good stuff that includes a crooked slider, an effective curve, and a fastball that ranges from 94 to 97 mph. Only his propensity for suffering a variety of injuries, for making mistakes up in the strike zone, and for his lack of command (45-rated) are suspect. More troublesome, scouts repeat, is Wood's tendency to crumble with a game on the line.

Eiland, however, says that Wood can be cured of all his problems by raising his arm angle.

Game Two @ Tampa, July 31

Vazquez pitched in and out of trouble throughout his 6⅓ innings, and was fortunate to bequeath a 4-4 tie to Logan. After he faced two lefties, threw three pitches, and got the last two outs of the bottom of the 7th, Logan's effectiveness and efficiency resulted in an A. Robertson came on for the bottom of the 8th and quickly disposed of the heart of the Rays batting order to earn an A.

Cano blasted a clutch solo HR in the top of the 9th to give the Yankees a 5-4 advantage, and as usual, Rivera put the lock on still another game, with the only mark against him being a broken-bat bloop single. Mo's grade: A.

New York 5, Tampa Bay 4
Winning Pitcher: Robertson (2-3)
Save: Rivera (22)

Bullpen diary: Why do hitters swing and miss Robertson's 90–92 mph fastballs and cream Joba's 97-mph missiles, especially since neither's number-one pitch has any discernible movement? Only because Dave's overhand delivery enables him to hide the ball better, thereby giving the hitters less reaction time.

Robertson required only twelve pitches to quietly set down the Rays—ten fastballs and two nasty curves that were both swung at and missed. While Robertson was at work, Chamberlain was sitting in the bullpen feverishly biting his fingernails.

Mo's cutter was a bit more active than it had been in his last appearance, and he even managed to pump one up to 93 mph.

Roster moves: To make room for Wood, Chan Ho Park was "designated for assignment," which means he has ten days to decide whether to report to Scranton or to declare himself a free agent and therefore abrogate his contract and forgo beaucoup bucks.

Game Three @ Tampa, August 1

Sabathia was victimized by some shoddy fielding (including his own tardiness in covering 1B), the abject failure of the lineup, and a couple of bad calls by the umps—that is, a foul grounder hit by Swisher becoming a rally-killing out and a fourth ball becoming a third strike.

With the Yanks trailing 3-0, Kerry Wood made his pinstriped debut with two outs in the bottom of the 7th—whereupon he punched out Longoria with a wicked 3-2 curve. Wood was only one day removed from the DL (for a blister) and his rust showed in the 8th. He labored through two walks, a single, and two strikeouts before Girardi took the ball from him after Wood had earned C-.

Gaudin entered with the bases loaded and promptly whiffed Brignac. His location was impressive, as was the 93-mph heater that ended the inning, thereby richly earning him an A.

Kerry Wood

Tampa Bay 3, New York 0

Bullpen diary: Wood's fastball topped at 95 mph and was alive. But when his pitches missed the strike zone, they missed by feet, not inches. It sure did appear as though Wood still has the stuff to be a positive factor.

It should be noted that Wood looks a little less fearsome—and about ten years younger—with his beard shaved off.

After the Series

By taking two of three, the Rays are now only one game behind the Yankees.

Bullpen Scorecard for July

Damaso Marte (3 appearances): 4.0 = A
Sergio Mitre (2): 3.8 = A-

Boone Logan (5): 3.6 = A–
Jonathan Albaladejo (3): 3.4 = B+
Mariano Rivera (6): 3.3 = B+
Dave Robertson (11): 3.2 = B+
Dustin Moseley (4): 2.8 = B–
Chan Ho Park (9): 2.7 = B–
Chad Gaudin (4): 2.3 = C+
Kerry Wood (1): 1.75 = C–

F's: Chamberlain, 3; one each Robertson, Rivera, Park, Moseley, and Gaudin.

Total grade: B+ (3.25).

Pretty good, except that many of the high grades were earned in mop-up duty, and virtually all of the F grades lost games.

A Hot August Night, Triple-A Ball, and Yankee Hopefuls

Let's have some fun out here! This game's fun, OK? Fun goddamnit. And don't hold the ball so hard, OK? It's an egg. Hold it like an egg.
—CRASH DAVIS, IN *BULL DURHAM*

A muggy day and night found me in the rejuvenated twin cities of Scranton and Wilkes-Barre, Pennsylvania, surrounded by rolling hills, deep valleys—and the joys of minor league baseball. For just ten dollars and with free parking, a baseball fan can sit and watch future stars play just a few feet away. In such an intimate setting the beautiful and clear *whump* of the ball in the catcher's mitt is like music.

I had chosen this date a month ago, based mostly on tonight's match-up against the Red Sox—of Pawtucket. A rivalry is a rivalry, and the game would not disappoint time-wise; a four-hour marathon lay ahead. I lucked out with the news a week before my trip that Alfredo Aceves would get a rehab start this night. Also in uniform for the home-standing Scranton Yankees were ten players who had already spent some time this season with the big club: outfielders Chad Huffman, Greg Golson, and Colin Curtis (he of the pinch-hit homer in the Bronx), catcher Chad Moeller, and infielders Kevin Russo and Juan Miranda. More pertinent to the subject at hand, pitchers Jonathan Albaladejo, Ivan Nova, and Romulo

Sanchez were on the squad. The tenth player was Aceves, taking the mound in his first real game after nearly three months spent rehabilitating his back.

With the sole exception of Moeller—whose primary duty was to tutor Jesus Montero, the stud of the Yankees farm system—all of the above were on the New York Yankees' forty-man roster.

Before the game, in the quite modern PNC Field home locker room, I spoke to a few of the available relief pitchers.

Ivan Nova was in Scranton's starting rotation, but he'd been very impressive with the Big Yankees during an extended relief stint in Detroit in early May.

"Man, was I nervous in the bullpen," Nova said. "I never saw so many cameras flashing in my life. But Mo gave me a cup of coffee and he settled me down."

Like every other pitcher in Scranton, Nova was fully aware of the hot spots in his delivery. "What I have to do," he explained, "is

Courtesy of Carl Lennertz

PNC Park in Scranton/Wilkes-Barre; Scranton Yankees vs. Pawtucket Red Sox

plant my front foot about six feet from the rubber when I let the ball go. If my stride is too long, then I'm pitching over the top of my body and my pitches are too high. If it's too short, then my arm slot gets low, and my breaking pitches are flat. I used to make a mark on the mound, but that was too distracting. It has to be automatic. But if a runner's on first and he's a threat to steal, then I can be okay with a five-foot stride out of a stretch."

Nova was also eager to list his other problem areas: "My front foot has to be pointed straight at the plate. I also have a slow arm, so they're always trying to quicken up my delivery. What happens, though, is my arm gets quicker but my body is still slow and I'm wild."

Nova has an easy smile and a friendly disposition. "But you know what the best thing I'm learning how to do here? How to relax between starts."

⚾EVEN THOUGH JASON Hirsh was a starting pitcher, I spoke to him because the Yankees had used him liberally in relief in the early part of spring training (5 strikeouts in 3 2/3 scoreless innings) and because he was a major league veteran (Colorado and Houston) who had suffered several serious injuries. At a towering but muscular 6'8"—even in full uniform with Nike bath slippers on his feet—he is even taller than the prototypical Yankee pitcher. He is also extremely polite, and he smiled when he looked up at my 6'9". "You're a tall drink of water," he said with a big smile.

Over the course of his injury-plagued career, a sprained ankle was his most minor mishap, while a line drive that struck him in the left shin was the worst. "I was with the Astros early in 2007," he recalled, "and although my leg hurt like crazy after it got hit, I tried to ignore the pain and keep going." In fact, Hirsh showed his mettle by pitching another six innings and helping Houston to an important win.

In his halcyon days, Hirsh commanded a dazzling array of

weapons: a sinker that ranged from 91 to 94 mph, an upper-echelon 94–96 mph fastball, a slick slider, and a rapidly improving change-up. Hirsh had been honored as the Pitcher of the Year in the Double-A Texas League and the Triple-A Pacific Coast League, and was generally deemed to be a can't-miss prospect. But during his cycle of injuries and recuperations, Hirsh never fully regained his form. That's why his lifetime MLB record is only 8-11 with a 5.32 ERA.

And his most recent injury is still hampering his effectiveness. "I was in spring training with the Astros back in 2008," Hirsh said, "and I felt a little bite in my shoulder when I threw a change-up. Now, I had always thrown change-ups, so there was nothing unusual about this, and since I'm always meticulous about warming up properly, this came out of nowhere. I tried to work my way through the pain, but it kept on getting worse. Eventually it was diagnosed as a severely strained rotator cuff. I was lucky that the medical staff decided against surgery, but I was told that I needed a full season's rest to fully recover."

Naturally, the time off was very stressful. "I thought that I'd never throw hard again. And when I did start throwing again a year later, I had a mental block about using my change-up. After I was finally pain-free, I felt great. I was convinced that my fastball was up to one hundred miles per hour, but the gun registered only eighty-five."

Feeling he had great potential as well as big-game experience, the Yankees obtained Hirsh from Colorado for a player to be named later in July 2009, but he believed that he's been approaching his pre-injury form only over the course of the last few weeks. "Being in rehab so long and so often hasn't affected my mechanics," he reported, "nor has it banished the concerns I've always had in my delivery. I still have to be careful to keep my arm angle from dropping, and also to maintain my balance when I bring my left knee over the rubber during my windup. Actually, though, I'm still a couple of miles per hour short of my best, but I think my pitches are moving more than they ever did, especially my two-seamer."

At the time of my visit, Hirsh had just been named the International League's Pitcher of the Week (August 2–8) for a pair of dynamic, high-strikeout victories. "I'm heartened," he said, "because I'm feeling better and better as the season progresses. I've been a pro for eight seasons, but I'm still only twenty-six, so I feel that it's only a matter of time before I get back into the bigs."

⚾ AFTER THE afternoon of clubhouse interviews and watching BP and pitching warm-ups on the field, it was game time. PNC Field holds 10,200, but on a Tuesday night, with no breeze and the humidity level reaching a fastball's number on the radar gun, it was less than half full with a family and date-night crowd.

As I first saw at the Yankees minor league complex in spring training, none of the Scranton players sported any facial hair, and they all wore high-stirrup socks, per Yankee guidelines. Moreover, they stood in a perfectly straight line along the grass cutout in front of the 3B dugout while a local contest winner sang the national anthem. In contrast, the Red Sox minor leaguers lounged in haphazard style immediately in front of the dugout rail while the crowd sang along.

Aceves started the game and was understandably ineffective. He also faced all lefties. The only sinker he threw against Josh Reddick bounced in the dirt. Otherwise, Ace's cutters sliced the corners, and a change-up produced a pop fly to CF. Against Bubba Bell, the only pitch Aceves located near the plate was clouted just foul over the RF fence. Otherwise, he missed with a pair of 88-mph fastballs, a slider that broke too much, and a sloppy change-up. For a pitcher whose strength was his pinpoint control, the five-pitch walk was disconcerting. But Aceves partially redeemed himself by striking out Daniel Nava on three cutters. Bell easily stole second on the fourth pitch to Jarrod Saltalamacchia. Once again, Aceves had poor command of all of his pitches, and wound up issuing a six-pitch walk.

With nineteen pitches in the books (only ten of them strikes), Aceves was done.

On the negative side of the ledger, his pitches lacked snap, his control was off, and his arm strength was at least 3 mph below par. On the positive side, his back didn't hurt. Since the Yanklings were about to undertake a road trip, Aceves was scheduled to throw two innings three days hence in Trenton, the Yankees' Double-A affiliate.

⚾ IT STRUCK me during this game that a scuffed baseball stays in the game longer in the minors, not surprisingly. The home plate ump regularly rolled balls over in his hand, keeping most of them in use.

It's actually his job to dirty up the brand-new shiny batch of five or six dozen balls before each game. The same "secret" compound is used in both the majors and minors, secret in that the company that provides the dirt doesn't reveal where in the nearby Delaware River the mud is from. In fact, the owner of Lena Blackburne Baseball Rubbing Mud says if he sees someone lurking around the designated spot, he comes back the next day.

⚾ HERE IN the minor leagues, things are fun and innocent. Young, exuberant employees of the local TV station run between-innings festivities: relay races, middle-aged men competing in hula contests, and musical chairs and tug-of-wars pitting youngsters against a pear-shaped blue mascot, Champion, who always manages to lose in a silly but appealing slapstick fashion. Cute kids wearing Groucho noses telling corny jokes. "What kind of clothes does a lawyer wear? Lawsuits!"

Wholesome stuff that made me laugh in spite of myself, even in a sweltering press box with no A/C. The regular guys brought their own fans. The ice-water cooler was the center of activity, especially during the at-times lethargic game. It was so hot, bugs would check out the press box and then leave.

I was told later that I missed seeing the frozen T-shirt contest held at previous games. Two fans are each given a rolled-up frozen tee, and the first one to crack it open and get it on over his head wins. Turns out it takes over two minutes to do this, though likely less tonight, and I would've paid to have one to put on the back of my neck—unwrapped, frozen.

THE YANKEES bullpen was situated down the LF line and partially obscured from the press box. But I could still make out several interesting goings-on out there.

One unidentifiable pitcher was holding the end of a small white towel and, with the complete simulation of a windup and hard throw from the stretch, snapped it forward and down. This is an odd-looking but standard exercise that both loosens and strengthens the proper wrist action necessary to throw darting sliders and curves.

Fortunately for another player, the bullpen is under an overhang and out of sight from the dugout.

Kei Igawa and his translator were practicing their respective field-goal techniques by kicking a yellow Nerf football into a screen. Igawa, remember, is the Japanese pitcher who received a $20 million contract and then proved to be a total bust. While the Yankees try to convince another team to take him as part of any and all proposed trades, Igawa refuses to learn English, cashes his biweekly checks, occasionally pitches, and waits for a better opportunity on either side of the Pacific Ocean.

Igawa's attitude certainly doesn't jibe with his habit of formally bowing before he steps onto the field for pregame warm-up. This to show his respect for the game, something that he thinks American players lack.

JONATHAN ALBALADEJO, or "Albie," has been having a banner year as Scranton's closer. Having already recorded 37 saves, he was being touted as the International League's MVP and had also been extremely impressive in his two brief stints with the Yankees.

"It's funny how things work out," he said. "During spring training my two-seamer simply wasn't working. It had always been my money pitch, but suddenly it had no sink, no velocity, and I couldn't spot it. I mean, it used to have such great movement that I could just throw it down the middle and let it move under the hitter's swings. My delivery was the same as always. My arm action was consistent. I didn't know what to do, so I started throwing a four-seamer and, for some reason, I was successful. I could hit my spots with increased velocity and it actually had some sinking action. Then about a month ago, my two-seamer just as suddenly came around. Now I've got two different fastballs that I can use, and it makes a big difference."

One of the downsides of Albie's trips to the majors was his inability to hold runners close because of his relatively slow delivery. "I've worked on that," he said. "I now bring my hands up slower than I used to, but I don't lift my leg as much, and I use a slide step with runners on base. Despite cutting down on my motion, the ball is jumping and I can still pitch to spots. Also, my curve and my slider are still plus pitches."

So what were the keys to his mechanics? "My lead foot has to be on line with home plate," he explained. "I also have to key on my overall balance, something that starts with separating my hands exactly when my front leg starts going down. I have a long arm action, so if my hands separate early, my arm is late, my front shoulder opens, and I'm wild high. Opening my shoulder is a continuing problem. I can have my feet straight and have perfect hand separation and sometimes my shoulder opens. This is very tough for me to fix during a ball game. I'd say that about once a month, all of my body parts are working perfectly."

Albie was also learning how to read hitters' swings. "This is especially important in the bigs because of how good the hitters are," he explained. "Is a guy upper-cutting the ball? Is he looking to pull everything or is he going with the pitch? Is his swing long or short? There are several keys here. The way a hitter swings at a pitch determines what the next pitch should be."

The local temperature hovered around 95 degrees and, since Albie had pitched 1⅓ innings the night before, he expected to be unavailable except in emergency. "But, hey," he said, "I'd been going only an inning at a time before my last trip to the big ball club, and they had me go thirty pitches in one and two-thirds innings in Anaheim. And I still had enough gas in my tank to pitch to another couple of hitters. The bottom line is that I'd go ten innings if that's what they needed me to do."

⚾ The Scranton bats were pretty quiet tonight, until Montero hit a homer in the 8th to tie the game at 4-4. With a colleague in the press box sarcastically saying that these guys were ready for the bigs based solely on the pace at which they were playing, the game dragged into extra innings and a fourth hour. Scranton's manager, Dave Miley, decided to go with his ace reliever to start the 10th, and Albaladejo responded with a shaky but effective performance: a five-pitch walk, a balk, a hard liner into the shortstop's glove, a stolen base, a swinging third strike on a nifty curve, then a well-hit flyout to RF. Fifteen pitches in all, with his four-seam fastballs sitting at 91 and topping at 93 mph. However, the hot, muggy night clearly took its toll on Albie.

After the Yankees were scoreless in the bottom of the 10th, the press box denizens were surprised when Albie was sent out to start the 11th. And the results were unfortunate for the hometown heroes. His first pitch was banged for a single by Josh Reddick. Then came the play that ultimately lost the game—a hard short-hop blast right at third baseman Eduardo Nuñez, who adroitly gloved the ball on an obvious short hop but then sat passively on the ground thinking that he'd snared the liner on the fly. When finally aroused by the shouts of his teammates, Nuñez made a high throw to first and the runner was credited with a base hit. A foul pop to LF earned the second out, but Jarrod Saltalamacchia turned a looping curveball into a bullet to left-center for a double that scored the go-ahead run.

Albie was visibly exhausted as Lars Anderson ripped a 92-mph fastball for another single to make the score 6-4. After a total of thirty-five pitches, Albaladejo was done.

Albie was replaced by Sanchez, who had the best pure stuff on the team—a 97-mph fastball with excellent movement, a devastating slider, and an improving change-up. His only problem was his inability to repeat his delivery.

Sanchez was on the cover of the official program for tonight's game, and the pregame press packet noted his stats so far this year: fourteen games started in twenty-eight total appearances, a record of 8-8, with a 4.18 ERA and no saves.

"I have to concentrate on keeping my hips straight," he'd told me before the game with a lilting Spanish accent. "I also get in trouble when I'm too quick to home. This lowers my arm slot and makes the ball tail off the plate and into right-handed hitters. My front leg is okay, but my back leg sometimes bends too much, then the ball is high. But all of this I can correct by myself during a game."

Sanchez also insists that his command is better than ever. "I can hit spots with two out of every three pitches I make," he said. "And I'm also better at mixing up my pitches. Out of every ten pitches, I'll throw five fastballs, three sliders, and two curves."

But can he throw them for strikes?

"Yes," he said. "Any of them for a strike, even if the count is 2-and-0."

Given every scout's concern about his wildness both in and out of the strike zone, I had every reason to be dubious about Sanchez's claims to almost perfect command.

SANCHEZ HAD bad luck from the get-go, when a high-bouncing infield hit put runners on first and third with Jack Hanrahan due up. A 94-mph fastball was wide; another one nipped the outside corner. A slider missed, as did still another 94-mph heater. Meanwhile, there was nothing smooth about Sanchez's delivery—he showed even more effort than Joba.

But on a full count, Hanrahan swung at and missed a slider.

A 3-2 slider! Sanchez was right all along!

Alas, in the bottom of the 11th, the Yanks got a run back, but Chad Moeller ended the game by whiffing with the tying run on second.

Pawtucket 6, Scranton 5

Losing Pitcher: Albaladejo (2-2)

Bullpen diary: In the postgame clubhouse, I waited for a scheduled interview with Scott Aldred, the pitching coach, but he reneged. No problem. After all, who wants to talk to a nosy reporter after a tough loss in which his best pitcher was overextended? I also wanted to talk to Moeller some about the pitchers' mechanics. He wasn't in the mood, either.

As I approached my car in the parking lot, I saw a knot of folks one row over. Then, looming out of the shadows, Jason Hirsh approached me with a big smile on his face.

"Since your last name's Rosen," he said, "could you possibly be Jewish?"

In truth, the answer to that seemingly simple question is complicated. My parents called themselves gastronomical Jews and never went to shul. Plus, I had taken Buddhist vows many years ago. But I said, "Yes."

"So am I," he said brightly, and he proudly rattled off the names of all the Jewish players currently active in MLB: Kevin Youkilis, Ian Kinsler, Ryan Braun, Gabe Kapler, Jason Marquis, John Grabow, Craig Breslow, and Scott Schoeneweis.

"In fact," he continued, "there was one game that I pitched for Houston when my catcher was Brad Ausmus. That was only the second time in major league history when a team fielded an all-Jewish battery. The other time was Koufax pitching to Norm Sherry with the Dodgers in 1959." (I checked later and found that there were several times that Norm caught his brother Larry while they were both with the LA Dodgers from 1959 to 1962.)

Courtesy of Martin Abramowitz and Jewish Major Leaguers, Inc.

Hirsch and Ausmus baseball cards

Hirsh also carried his laptop with him at all times. "By the way," he said, "I looked up all of your books online. They all sound fascinating."

On the spot, Jason Hirsh replaced Gene Woodling as my all-time favorite baseball player. I wish only success for this fine young man. After all, the only famous Jewish Yankee to date was Ron Blomberg, whose main claim to fame is having the bat he used as the first-ever MLB designated hitter encased in Cooperstown.

⚾ THE TRIP to Scranton had a good vibe to it, and I felt this was somewhere I'd like to return to annually. With the coal mines long gone, this area has found new sources of income: a vibrant music and arts scene, several universities, local skiing, as well as being a gateway to all of the Poconos, the setting for the TV hit *The Office*, and the new home for four years now of a pinstriped franchise. Yankee brass were smart to move their Triple-A jewel from Ohio to here, a growing area just three hours from New York, close enough for Yankee fans, here in Phillies and Pirates country, to get to the Bronx easily; and just as important, for Yankees brass to get out here by car to view future Yankees stars.

Maybe Paul O'Neill tipped them off to the pleasures of northeast Pennsylvania. He is fondly remembered here (and nowhere in town more than Scranton baseball central, Diskin's Pub). The Scranton/Wilkes-Barre Yankees, winners of the '08 title in the International League (and runners-up to Durham last year), hope to become permanent fixtures at the top, just like their big brothers are in the Bronx.

August 2010

- The Irish Hall of Fame, and the shot heard 'round the world.
- A talk with Alfredo Aceves.
- Jays, Bosox, Chisox, Royals, Tigers.
- Pettitte out, but Jeter and Tex set records.

Hitters aren't stupid, but sometimes I think they believe they are smarter than they are.

—BOB GIBSON

August 2–4, Toronto Blue Jays @ Yankee Stadium

Burnett started off the home stand by extending his scoreless-innings streak to 12⅓ before Vernon Wells poked an opposite-field HR. Then A.J. simply got shelled in the 5th inning to the tune of six extra-base hits and seven runs, putting the Yankees in an 8-2 hole. Mitre was the first candidate to stop the carnage, but he gave up a double before lucking into a bullet that landed in Gardner's glove in LF. Mitre then closed the door and earned a C+. Robertson was impressive in closing out the Jays in the top of the 7th: His fastball routinely bit the corners and he even pumped the gun up to 93 mph. Grade: A.

Logan battled his way through the top of the 8th. After a whiff, a walk, and a flyout, he hung tough while LH Fred Lewis fouled off six consecutive pitches before grounding to short. Logan's grade:

A-. The 9th gave Joba another chance to show that he's learned his lessons. His fastball touched 97 mph even as he semi-deliberately walked Bautista. Otherwise, Chamberlain struck out two and got a groundout. Joba's grade: A.

Toronto 8, New York 6

Bullpen diary: Robertson threw a couple of cutters for profit, a new pitch for him. Logan was behind either 2-0 or 3-0 on every hitter except Jose Molina. Could it be that Chamberlain's increased concentration and bullpen preparation have been influenced by the arrival of Wood?

Meanwhile, A-Rod seems to be getting frustrated as HR number 600 continues to elude him.

Where we stand: With the loss and Tampa Bay's win, the two teams are now tied for the division lead.

Game Two vs. the Jays in the Bronx, August 3

Moseley pitched a barely creditable 7⅓ innings considering that his sinker was poorly located and was flat too often. The Jays' Ricky Romero went the distance for the Jays and continued the pattern of hurlers whose out-pitch is a change-up always giving the Yankee hitters trouble.

Kerry Wood took over with the Yankees on the short end of a 5-2 score. After his fourth pitch—an 88-mph cutter right down Broadway—was launched into the LF stands by Aaron Hill, Wood struck out two Jays with 93-mph fastballs. Wood's grade: D+. Mitre was the next victim—a double, a HR, and, when three batters swung for the fences, three groundouts. Mitre gets another F.

Toronto 8, New York 2

Bullpen diary: Mitre looked like he was throwing batting practice.

Where we stand: Tampa Bay beat Minnesota, so the Yankees fell into second place in the AL East, a game behind the Rays. The good news was that they still had control of the wildcard slot—although a poor performance in the forthcoming weekend series with the Red Sox might let the door swing open.

Game Three vs. the Jays in the Bronx, August 4

After having completed 100 pitches in 5⅓, Hughes led 5-1—the big blow being A-Rod's 600th HR, which gave the Yankees an early 2-0 margin.

A fastball got away from Logan and struck LH Adam Lind on the shoulder, but the lefty settled down after that to earn an A.

Joba pitched the 7th with mixed results. A line-drive single off a 96-mph fastball was followed by a line drive at Jeter on a 95-mph heater. Otherwise, his sliders produced a bouncer back to the mound as well as a pop-up. Since half the batters he faced made solid contact, Chamberlain's shutout inning only rates a B.

The leadoff hitter in the top of the 8th was Bautista, and while Robertson was thankful that the majors' leading HR slugger was up with the bases empty, he was still careful to keep the ball low and away. Too careful. Bautista eventually worked a seven-pitch walk. Fortunately, Robertson continued his roll with a flyout and a pair of strikeouts, so his A was no surprise.

The Yankees' 5-1 lead eliminated a possible save situation. But Mo hadn't pitched in three games and tomorrow is a day off, so Rivera was sent into the action just to keep his arm loose. After two groundouts, a hit batter (on a cutter that slipped Mo's grip), and a looper back to the mound, Rivera had tossed ten pitches and the victory was secured.

New York 5, Toronto 1

Bullpen diary: Chan Ho Park was claimed off waivers by Pittsburgh.

Where we stand: In one "swell foop" (as Inspector Clouseau used to say), the Yankees broke a three-game losing streak and A-Rod could now relax. Bring on the Bosox!

THE IRISH AMERICAN HALL OF FAME

On August 6, Brian Cashman was honored in the third class of Irish-American baseball players and people attached to the game inducted at Foley's Pub at 18 West Thirty-third Street, across the street from the Empire State Building. Also inducted today: Tim McCarver, Mets announcer Bob Murphy, Bill James, and Mike "King" Kelly. (Kelly was a two-time batting champion in the late 1800s for the Cubs. Baseball historians credit Kelly with developing the hit-and-run, the hook slide, and the catcher's backing up of first base. Kelly was elected posthumously to Cooperstown in 1945.)

The Irish American Hall of Fame was created in 2008 by amateur baseball historian Shaun Clancy. The first class, "The Starting Nine," was comprised of Tug McGraw, Yankee announcer and former catcher John Flaherty, sportswriter Jeff Horrigan, New York Mets groundskeeper Pete Flynn, Mark McGwire (this might be the only Hall he gets into), Sean Casey, Kevin Costner (for his work in *Field of Dreams* and *Bull Durham*), Connie Mack, and longtime official scorer and columnist Red Foley, for whom the bar is named. The 2009 inductees: Walter O'Malley, Steve Garvey, veteran umpire Jim Joyce (yup, that Jim Joyce), Vin Scully, and Ed Lucas, a blind reporter who has covered the Yankees and Mets for more than forty years. Oh, and a fellow named Paul O'Neill.

August 6–9, Boston Red Sox @ Yankee Stadium

Vazquez's fastball was a slowpoke 88 mph, but he was also doomed when Cervelli dropped a pop-up in front of the plate that led to three unearned runs. He was yanked after 5⅓ innings with the Yankees' deficit at 6-3.

Chamberlain's appearance in the top of the 6th was further proof that he has been ousted from the bridge role. Nevertheless, he used 96-mph blazers and crackling sliders to easily retire the two hitters he faced. Joba rated an A.

Wood came on to work the next two innings. In the 7th, all

four hitters smashed line drives, but three of these were at-'em balls. Wood's encore was worth a C-.

Logan came on to close the inning by inducing Ellsbury to break his bat in looping a soft liner to A-Rod. Logan: A.

Chad Gaudin had a relatively easy time navigating his way through the top of the 9th, the only glitch being an infield single credited to Ortiz when Cano unnecessarily rushed his throw. Gaudin's grade: A, his first since July 11.

Boston 6, New York 3

Bullpen diary: For the time being, Joba has become a utility reliever. Wood's stretch of 1⅔ innings was his longest of the season. While his fastball sat at 92 mph and reached 94 mph only twice, Wood's curve was impressive. Gaudin's success was due his ability to keep the ball low in the K-zone.

Where we stand: The loss was the Yankees' fifth in their last seven games. Since Tampa Bay was also slumping, losing three of four, New York has regained first place by a mere half game. However, the Bosox climbed to within five games of the lead in the AL East.

In recent games, the bullpen's efforts have been mostly outstanding. But blame the Yankees' slump on sloppy fielding, the absence of clutch hitting, and, in a reversal of what had been the case thus far, poor starting pitching.

Help, however, appeared to be on the way: Pettitte was on the mend and could rejoin the rotation in ten days. Aceves' remarkably unexpected recuperation was likewise making strides—not only was any possible doomsday scenario of back surgery abandoned, but Ace was scheduled to pitch on August 9 in Scranton.

Game Two vs. the Red Sox in the Bronx, August 7

Sabathia silenced the Bosox bats and handed the game to Rivera in the 9th with a savable 5-2 lead. Victor Martinez smacked a hard grounder just inside the 1B line that Teixeira snared with a backhanded dive and converted into the out. Then came a solid shot to right and a deep smash to center, both of which were caught. B+.

New York 5, Boston 2
Save: Rivera (23)
Bullpen diary: Although his nine pitches produced three quick outs, Rivera's cutters didn't fool anybody.
Where we stand: The Rays lost again, so the Yankees upped their respective leads to 1½ games over Tampa Bay and six over Boston. With Burnett pitching in game three and Moseley in game four, the Yankees will be hard-pressed to manage a split in the series.

Game Three vs. the Red Sox in the Bronx, August 8

Burnett was scratched because of back spasms and was replaced by Moseley. Pitching on his usual four days' rest, Dustin responded to the most important start of his career with $6^{1}/_{3}$ superb innings. Meanwhile, the lineup was battering Josh Beckett, including the single that pushed Jeter past Babe Ruth on the all-time Yanks hit list.

When Joba climbed the mound, there was one out, runners on first and third, and the Yankees comfortably ahead 7-1. He was stung by a seeing-eye RBI single off the bat of Mike Lowell. Then, after retiring Ellsbury on a routine fly to LF, Chamberlain walked Scutaro on a full-count slider after getting ahead 1-2. With the bases loaded and Ortiz due up, Joba gave way to Boone Logan after earning a C-. Logan went to a full count before snuffing Ortiz on a grounder. In the top of the 8th Logan set the Bosox down without incident. A brilliant performance by Logan for a well-earned A.

Robertson began the 9th and was greeted by Ramiro Peña's booting of a semi-difficult grounder that the official scorer erroneously judged to be an error. (Pena was in for the bruised A-Rod, who'd been struck in the shin by a line drive by Berkman during the pregame batting/fielding rituals the day before.) Then came a tap to the box, a flyout to deep LF, and a walk. Robertson's grade: B+.

Girardi summoned Mo in the second consecutive no-save situation, and he secured the game with one pitch that Scutaro grounded
to Cano. Another A for Mo.

New York 7, Boston 2

Bullpen diary: Lefty Logan and righty Robertson now have identical
streaks of facing nineteen batters without being touched for a hit.
Logan has also emerged as a much more reliable lefty specialist than
Marte had been.

⚾ TEIXEIRA HOMERED, giving him 25 HRs in each of his first
eight seasons, tying him with Eddie Matthews, Albert Pujols, and
Darryl Strawberry for that honor. Not the Babe? Ah, his pitching
years. Aaron, Killebrew, Fox, Mays? They did have eight or more
years of 25-plus homers, just not to start their careers.

Game Four vs. the Red Sox in the Bronx, August 9

Hughes was hurt by a throwing error by Posada but was lucky to
survive six quality innings only down 2-0.

Wood grunted his way through the next three outs—a hit batter,
a walk, three stolen bases, all balanced by a flyout, a diving catch by
Kearns in RF, and a strikeout of Martinez on a sharp curveball. For
Wood, B-.

Logan came in to start the 8th and earned his fourth consecutive A by getting Ortiz on a flyball to CF. Chamberlain then finished the top of the 8th with only two pitches that produced a
grounder and a pop-up. But after Teixeira had halved Boston's lead
to 2-1, Joba struggled to survive with a clean slate in the top of
the 9th. After chalking up two quick outs, Joba walked Ellsbury
(who stole 2B when Posada bounced his throw on a pitchout for
his fourth steal of the game), then was saved when Peña made a
diving stop in the hole to turn a potential run-scoring hit into an
out. Joba's grade: A-.

Boston 2, New York 1

Bullpen diary: Boston's relievers, Jon Lester and Jonathan Papelbon, turned the lineup's lumber into twigs. The Yankees failed to score when they loaded the bases with no outs in the 7th, and when they also had 1B and 2B occupied with one out in the 8th. Plus the tying run expired on 2B with one out in the 9th.

Where we stand: A golden opportunity to bury the Bosox under an eight-game lead was lost.

⚾ BEFORE TRAVELING to Texas, Teixeira hurried to be with his wife in time for her expected delivery. It was anticipated that Teixeira wouldn't rejoin the ball club until August 12 in KC. Also, Cano had a severe cold and was capable only of pinch-hitting.

August 10–11 @ Rangers Ballpark

Burnett bounced back to open the series with a solid seven innings, leaving after 112 pitches with the score knotted at 3-all. Logan's job was to retire Josh Hamilton, which he did on a nifty curveball that the slugger missed by at least six inches. Logan's grade: A.

Robertson breezed through the remainder of the 8th, then he walked David Murphy. A sacrifice put the winning run on 2B, then came a flyout to CF and an intentional pass to Mitch Moreland, before Elvis Andrus swung at a 93-mph fastball and hit a humpbacked liner to RF to end the inning and the threat. For his clutch work, Robertson deserved an A-.

Rivera got into trouble right off the bat when Michael Young beat out a nubber to deep short, and Hamilton followed with a weak but well-placed grounder through the right side. A-Rod then made a sensational diving stop-and-throw to nip Guerrero and temporarily save the game. With runners at 2B and 3B, Mo dealt an intentional walk to Cruz. Bases loaded, two outs, the game on the line. Mo has been there and escaped many times. But after missing on three straight cutters, Mo cashed in his automatic strike and got David Murphy to foul off a 90-mph cutter—but then flinched when Murphy drilled the next pitch into LF for the gamer. F for Mo.

Texas 4, New York 3 (10 innings)
Losing Pitcher: Rivera (3-2)
Bullpen diary: Logan's A was his fifth in a row. Robertson's poise and grit were encouraging. Mo's cutter was flat, and his two-seamer misbehaved. Still, he wasn't exactly hit hard by the Rangers, who managed to reprise the immortal advice of Wee Willie Keeler by "hitting them where they ain't."

Once more, the Yankees were doomed by the lack of clutch hitting. **Where we stand:** Their lead over Tampa Bay shrank to a half game, and Boston is now five games back. These games in Texas assumed increased importance, since the Yankees' opponents in the opening round of the playoffs could very well be the Rangers.

Game Two @ Texas, August 11
Vazquez's fastball averaged a mere 88 mph, which meant that his command had to be perfect—and it was not. Nor was Javier helped by still another fielding faux pas by Posada—this one a botched rundown. With one out in the top of the 5th, Nelson Cruz on 2B, and Texas enjoying a 6-1 lead, a margin that seemed insurmountable since Cliff Lee was on the hill, Mitre came in and got an extra out when, for some silly reason, Cruz tried to tag up and get to 3B on a medium flyball to Swisher in RF—and was thrown out by at least five feet.

Even though he hadn't pitched in eight days, Mitre's sinker was teasing the strike zone before taking a dive, and he breezed through the bottom of the 6th to ensure an A.

By the time Wood climbed the mound in the bottom of the 7th, the Yankees had closed the gap to 6-4. Wood survived a pair of singles by inducing a harmless flyball and then a double play. Nor did he have much trouble taming the Rangers in the bottom of the 8th—two whiffs and a pop-up earned Wood a B+.

The Yankees took the lead in the top of the 9th fueled by clutch hits by Jeter and Thames, so Rivera was asked to preserve the win.

But Elvis Andrus started the home half of the 9th by socking a triple; here we go again. However, Mo's cutter dipped to the occasion. Kearns made a nifty shoestring catch in RF, Josh Hamilton (baseball's leading hitter at .358) bounced back to Mo, and Guerrero grounded to A-Rod to conclude a remarkable comeback.

New York 7, Texas 6
Winning Pitcher: Wood (1-0 with Yankees)
Save: Rivera (24)
Bullpen diary: Now that Wood was getting more comfortable in his pinstripes, Eiland had started tweaking his delivery: raising his release point and moving his hand a bit farther from his head.
Where we stand: The Red Sox won and the Rays lost; Yanks up by a half game in the AL East.

⚾ CURTIS GRANDERSON is working to rebuild his swing from scratch, and save his season, with the help of Kevin Long.

⚾ IN THE next series, either the radar gun in KC was off or the Yankee relievers like working in hot, humid weather. In any case, the bullpen would carry the entire pitching staff.

August 12–15 @ Kauffman Stadium
Sabathia didn't have his A-1 breaking stuff, but he was still throwing bee-bees—98 mph in the 9th—and with one out standing between him and a complete game victory, he was victimized by a pair of duck farts that fell for base hits. Robertson came on to protect the Yankees' 4-1 lead, but Willie Bloomquist proceeded to rip a two-bagger on a 94-mph fastball that drove in two runs. Ex-Yankee Wilson Betemit followed by beating out a broken-bat dribbler in the

hole between 1B and 2B. That brought up Jason Kendall, a well-respected contact hitter, with the tying run on 3B and the winning run on 1B. Kendall certainly lived up to his reputation, fouling off four pitches and working the count to 2-2.

Then Robertson snapped off what was perhaps the best curve he'd thrown all season. Kendall's swing contacted nothing but hot, muggy air, and the game was done and won. Robertson's grade: B.

New York 4, Kansas City 3
Save: Robertson (1)

Bullpen diary: Having worked the two previous nights in Texas, Rivera had the game off. Robertson is now just below Mo in the bullpen pecking order.

Around the league: Nolan Ryan and his business partners got approval to buy the Rangers. In his playing days, besides Ryan's seven no-hitters, he also holds the record for the most no-nos broken up in the 7th inning or later: 24.

Francisco "K-Rod" Rodriguez, the Mets closer, he of the safety goggles and exaggerated pointing to the heavens after a win, had a total postgame meltdown, and it remains to be seen whether the season save record holder will ever pitch in the majors again.

Game Two @ KC, August 13

After two rain delays totaling almost three hours, Moseley lacked the spot-on command that's absolutely essential for him to succeed. When the skies cleared for good, the Royals led 4-3, there was one on and one out in the bottom of the 5th, and Gaudin had the ball. The results of the next $1\frac{2}{3}$ innings were surprising.

After issuing a walk, Gaudin struck out three in a row and got a pop-up and a groundout. His fastball topped at a season-high 95 mph, and the bottom repeatedly fell out of his two-seamer, earning Gaudin back-to-back A's.

Wood followed in the 7th and managed a pair of routine ground-outs, one on a slider and the other on a curve. Like Gaudin, Wood had extra oomph on his heater—topping out at 97 mph—earning his first A. Logan completed the inning when Betemit grounded to Cano. Then the tall, rangy southpaw extended his streak of consecutive hitless at-bats by lefty batters to nineteen by striking out Kila Ka'aihue and Alex Gordon. Logan's A was his sixth in a row.

Chamberlain closed out the bullpen's excellent work by coaxing a flyball. All three of the pitches Joba threw were clocked at 99 mph. Grade: A.

Kansas City 4, New York 3

Bullpen diary: Aceves used 26 pitches in hurling two perfect innings in Double-A Trenton. If he's effective and pain-free after a three-inning outing next week, the Yankees will have to make an interesting decision. Would Aceves replace Mitre or Gaudin? Or would Ace simply keep laboring in the minors until the major league rosters expand on September 1?

Where we stand: The Yankees lost no ground, since both Tampa Bay (minus two games) and Boston (minus six) lost.

Game Three @ KC, August 14

Hughes had a so-so performance, giving up three runs in six innings and leaving with a 6-3 lead. But the story of the game was the Yankees' dinger derby—two 400-foot-plus homers clouted by A-Rod, plus one each by Posada and Granderson. Joba pitched a clean 7th in another pressure-free situation. Working off his fastballs, which ranged from 96 to 99 mph, Joba achieved another A. Logan had his hitless-against streak broken when LH Ka'aihue smashed a 93-mph fastball for a single. Logan then needed seven pitches to induce Alex Gordon to pop a flyball to LF. Because he labored more than he had in his most recent appearances, and because the Royals batted .500 in his limited mound time, Logan gets a D. Robertson completed the bottom of the 8th with a groundball out and a strikeout (on another unhittable curve). Moreover, he even threw a season-high 95-mph fastball. Robertson's grade: A. By the time Mitre entered the game, the Yankees had stretched their lead to 8-3. Mitre cruised his way to an A.

New York 8, Kansas City 3

Bullpen diary: Joba is responding in remarkable fashion in situations where the game is not at stake. After his early-season woes, Robertson's restoration to excellence is due to Eiland's coaching. Whereas Robertson's hips and lead-foot plant have previously been slightly angled toward 3B, he's now totally on line with all of his body parts.

Game Four @ KC, August 15

Burnett pitched an outstanding complete game. Unfortunately, it only consisted of eight innings, because the Yankees were shut out on two hits by Bryan Bullington, with 9th-inning help from Joakim Soria. The Yankees were now 4-8 when faced with a pitcher they hadn't previously encountered.

Kansas City 1, New York 0

Bullpen diary: Since being plucked off the waiver list by Pittsburgh, Chan Ho Park has pitched four innings in four games, giving up eleven hits and five runs, and pitching to an ERA of 11.25. Since he's been gone, Chamberlain, Gaudin, Mitre, Logan, and Robertson have stepped up. It's called addition by subtraction.

Pennant race: NY in first, plus-one over TB, plus-six over Boston.

August 16–19, Detroit Tigers @ Yankee Stadium

Detroit's visit to the Bronx saw a number of serendipitous connections between different events over many years.

The Tigers were back in town for the first time with the popular Johnny Damon. He got hugs from many Yankees in pregame warm-ups, and got a standing O from the fans at his first at-bat. Classy.

The Tigers are also wearing the initials *EH* on their jerseys, just as the Yanks have Bob Sheppard's initials and a microphone on their sleeves and a *GMS* over the hearts. The Tigers' initials are for Ernie

Harwell, their longtime beloved announcer, who passed away in the spring.

Only trivia buffs remember that Harwell was actually announcing for the New York Giants on TV in 1951, but it was Russ Hodges on the radio who is celebrated, in sync with the TV footage, for his famous "The Giants have won the pennant! The Giants have won the pennant!" as Bobby Thomson's homer sailed out of the Polo Grounds.

And, earlier that evening, Bobby Thomson passed away at the age of eighty-six.

This past Friday was the thirteenth, and very few players choose to wear number 13. A-Rod defies superstition. Who else in MLB history? Ralph Branca, who changed his number the next year.

In the series opener, Vazquez had to throw 106 pitches in his four-inning stint and was fortunate to be trailing by only 2-0. Sergio Mitre took over and squeezed through a scoreless top of the 5th despite an error by Jeter and the issuance of a walk. Except for being touched by a looping base hit by Austin Jackson, Mitre posted another zero on the scoreboard in the 6th. Plus he retired the two hitters he faced in the 7th. Half of the eight outs Mitre registered came on grounders, proof of the heaviness of his two-seamer. An outstanding effort by Mitre earned an A.

Kerry Wood easily disposed of Ryan Raburn to end the 7th but struggled to escape the 8th unscathed—his problem being lack of control, that is, a six-pitch walk immediately succeeded by a nine-pitch walk. But he quieted the Tigers by getting a pair of strikeouts on a diving curveball and then a sizzling 94-mph fastball. An A- for Wood.

Chamberlain managed two strikeouts and a pop-up in the 9th, but also gave up a home run to Miguel Cabrera, one of the best yet most unsung right-handed hitters in the AL. In fact, the dinger came on a well-placed low-and-outside slider that Cabrera strong-armed into the RF seats. Joba's grade: C.

Detroit 3, New York 1

Bullpen diary: That's three consecutive A's for Mitre, who's making his bid to remain on the roster when Pettitte/Aceves/Marte return.

The remarkable improvement in Wood was, once again, due to Eiland's ministrations. Wood's arm slot has been moved up and his hand has been relocated a few inches farther away from his head. These adjustments have put more life into Wood's pitches.

Joba's fastballs rated from 92 to 94 mph, with a single 95-mph heater to whiff Raburn. Because of his reduced velocity, nine of his nineteen offerings were sliders.

Game Two vs. the Tigers in the Bronx, August 17

C.C. was stung by a pair of solo homers, but pitched well enough to get the Yankees well set for a much-needed W. The Yankees led 6-2 when Dave Robertson climbed the hill. After yielding a sharp single, he got a pop-up and a deep flyout with two 93-mph fastballs, and then an inning-ending whiff of Peralta on a nasty curve. Grade: A-. Mainly because he hasn't worked since August 11 in Texas, Mo pitched the 9th in another nonsave situation. His cutter was in prime form, and he continued his pattern of using his two-seamer against righties. For Mo, his first A in almost three weeks.

New York 6, Detroit 2

Bullpen diary: Over the last twenty games, the relief corps has held hitters to a minuscule .171 batting average.

Rehab update: In Trenton today, Aceves gave up one hit, one run and no walks, and struck out four in dealing thirty-five pitches over the course of 2⅓ innings. Is he ready to return to the Bronx? If so, who leaves?

Pennant race: Yanks share first with the Rays; Boston 5½ back.

Game Three vs. the Tigers in the Bronx, August 18

Moseley had trouble keeping his pitches in the ballpark. After being spanked for three homers in five innings, he was fortunate to be trailing by only 7-4. Joba came in and his third pitch was a hanging slider that was smacked for a double. From there he survived a hard-hit liner that Granderson caught at his shoe tops, and escaped with no runs allowed. Joba's grade: B.

In the top of the 7th, Logan completed a strikeout sandwich that enclosed a sharply hit single and a bunt single. After a D effort, Logan also got the hook.

Wood made a mistake with the first hitter he faced—Austin Jackson. After he overpowered the rookie with two fastballs, Wood threw a curve that was smacked into LF for a single. Fortunately Wood then punched out the next two hitters with lively cutters, thereby earning a B+. With New York now up 9-4, Gaudin failed to register an out in the top of the 8th—a hit batter, a single, and a walk—so his F was well deserved. Robertson let an inherited base runner score on a long sacrifice fly, then kept the game under control with a pair of easy groundouts. Dave's grade: A.

Rivera nailed down the victory with a three-up, three-down 9th. In still another nonsave appearance, Mo also added to his unofficial record of bats broken by his cutter. And his twenty-ninth A of the season.

New York 9, Detroit 5

Bullpen diary: Is it goodbye to Gaudin and hello to Aceves? Robertson has not been scored on in 17 2/3 innings. Mo continued to routinely crowd right-handed hitters with two-seamers; this tactic also prevents them from sitting on his cutters.

Pennant race: No change in AL East standings as all three contending teams won.

Game Four vs. the Tigers in the Bronx, August 19

The Yankees broke up a tight game with a nine-run explosion in the bottom of the 6th. With the lead now 11-2, Hughes was done for the day, thereby saving an inning or two off his not-so-secret inning limit.

Mitre's job was to finish the game and rest the bullpen, since

Rivera, Logan, Wood, Gaudin, Robertson, and Chamberlain had all pitched the previous night. However, after punching out Damon, Mitre was touched for a HR, 1B, and 2B. After another K came an RBI single that made the score 11-4.

Two more hits in the 8th added another run to Detroit's total, but Mitre survived when he induced a double-play grounder to end the inning. Likewise, a twin-killing in the 9th enabled Mitre to complete his mop-up duties without putting the game at risk—which is the only reason why his grade was C-.

New York 11, Detroit 5
Save: Mitre (1)

Bullpen diary: Mitre was short-arming his sinker, and his most effective pitch was his change-up. He gets a save because he pitched the last three innings of a win, which is absurd considering that he was hit hard and allowed six hits and three runs. Although both Logan and Wood were asked to warm up, the only thing that Mitre saved was the bullpen.

Pennant race: With both Tampa Bay and Boston losing, the Yankees' leads are now one game over the Rays and 6½ over the Bosox.

August 20–22, Seattle Mariners @ Yankee Stadium

Ichiro led off the first game with a HR off Vazquez, and three-plus innings later, the Mariners had two more HRs. That was it for Vazquez, who was lucky the game was tied at 4-all when he departed.

Gaudin came up big—three scoreless one-hit innings—and allowed the new endgame rotation to finish the game. That's a total of five shutout innings for him in about seventeen hours. Good enough for Gaudin to rate an A. Logan then pitched an uneventful 7th. He graded an A- because two of the three outs were hit hard. The Yanks now led 7-4 and Robertson was summoned to relay the lead to Rivera. But Robertson had trouble controlling his fastball, so Mo was summoned with two out and two on to end the inning. Robertson's grade: B-.

This marked the first time this season that Rivera was asked to complete a four-out save, something that Girardi said he was extremely reluctant to do. Since Michael Saunders represented the potential tying run, his meek pop-out meant that Mo had a save going, no matter how many runs the Yankees would score in the bottom of the 8th. And they did; five of them. In the top of the 9th, Ichiro poked an opposite-field single to LF, took 2B on defensive indifference, and scored on a bloop. Otherwise, the best the Mariners could muster were two grounders and a called third strike. Rivera's grade: B.

New York 9, Seattle 5
Winning Pitcher: Logan (1-0)
Save: Rivera (25)
Bullpen diary: A remarkable turnaround by Gaudin. His fastball had a wiggle and his command was right on. Logan's fastball topped at a mere 92 mph, but he only needed eight pitches to retire the Mariners (seven of which were strikes). Even though Robertson's location was a bit off, he increased his consecutive scoreless innings to 18⅓. Rivera threw twenty-seven pitches, which made his availability for tomorrow afternoon's game doubtful.

⚾ A-ROD WAS hobbling with a sore calf, so Eduardo Nuñez was called up from Scranton. He fielded 3B flawlessly, and it was his opposite-field single that knocked in the lead run in the bottom of the 7th. This was Nuñez's initial major league hit, and when the ball was returned to him, he kissed it before handing it over to the first-base coach.

AROUND THE COUNTRY
A weekend of more firsts. In the other sport where a ball is hit with a stick, the first-ever Indian-born player won a PGA tournament. Arjun Atwal also became the first Monday qualifier to win on the

tour in twenty-four years. In the sport that involves going fast and turning left-left-left, Kyle Busch was the first NASCAR driver ever to win all three of the weekend's races.

A TV special on tonight profiled the first woman in baseball history to pitch professionally in three countries (Japan, the United States, and Canada). Playing mostly in the west coast Golden League, Japanese knuckleballer Eri Yoshida is also the first female pro pitcher since Ila Borders retired ten years ago. As for famous women players of the past, there's the famous story of seventeen-year-old Jackie Mitchell, who struck out Ruth and Gehrig in an exhibition game in 1931. Notably, the Negro Leagues had three female players: Toni Stone (who got a hit off Satchel Paige), Connie Morgan, and pitcher Mamie Johnson.

The Little League World Series is in full swing. Who of this lot of youngsters will make it to the bigs down the road?

Game Two vs. the Mariners in the Bronx, August 21

Burnett had no curve and no command: 12 hits, 6 runs, 122 pitches, and a deep 6-0 hole against Felix Hernandez, who owns the Yankees.

With a day game on the morrow, Girardi called Gaudin's number, seeking to save his core relievers. Operating in a pressureless situation, Chad was magnificent. His location was A-OK, and the only runner he allowed was Jack Wilson, who was nailed by an errant fastball. An A for Gaudin.

Seattle 6, New York 0

Bullpen diary: Burnett's bush-league performances have been increasingly costly. Even worse, he swore that there was nothing amiss with his delivery. He's just been "off." Why was this so hard to believe, especially since his front shoulder was routinely pointing toward first base as he released each pitch?

Game Three vs. the Mariners in the Bronx, August 22

C.C. was once again totally dominant, pitching six shutout innings, while the lineup was bludgeoning the Mariners pitchers. However, a fifty-seven-minute rain delay necessitated his being replaced when play resumed. Since Gaudin had pitched five innings over the past two days, and Mitre had to be held in reserve to protect against rookie Ivan Nova having an early exit tomorrow in Toronto, Girardi was forced to use two of his short-list relievers in a lopsided game.

The movement on Wood's cutter and curve more than compensated for the lack of velocity on his fastball—that rarely exceeded 92 mph. And he cruised through 1 ⅔ innings until he was victimized by a looping single and a nubber along the 3B line that stayed fair. Wood's grade: A-. Joba finished the game, but not without two of the five hitters he faced hitting the ball on the screws. That's why, despite his fastball topping at 94 mph, he deserved only a C+.

New York 10, Seattle 0

Bullpen diary: Joba did have trouble with his footing after the rain. Yet the two liners were hit on 94-mph fastballs, and a 93-mph pitch was hit hard but foul. More evidence that the hitters were getting good looks at his pitches.

After the series: With the win, the Yankees are now thirty games above .500 for the first time this season.

August 23–25 @ Rogers Centre

In a pressure-packed debut, Ivan Nova did himself—and the organization—proud, yielding only two runs in 5⅓ innings. Both of the Blue Jays' runs, however, came via a HR by Jose Bautista, his major-league-leading 39th. During Bautista's next at-bat, Nova threw a "message" pitch over his head—business as usual in the bigs. But Bautista took exception, the dugouts and bullpens emptied, and there was lots of milling about. And that's when Nova got the hook.

Logan came in to end the 6th inning in fine style but, with the score 2-2, he walked the leadoff hitter (a lefty!) to start the 7th. This was a cardinal sin and moved Girardi to call on Chamberlain.

Logan's grade: C+. Joba forgave his teammate's transgression by inducing three quick flyouts, for which he earned an A.

Robertson began the bottom of the 9th with a strikeout. Up next was Bautista. After nipping the inside corner with a 92-mph fastball, Robertson focused on the target Cervelli was setting up on the outside corner. Unfortunately Robertson missed the spot and another 92-mph pitch came in waist-high and inside—Bautista's wheelhouse. And Bautista walloped it high and far into the second deck in LF. Bautista then strolled casually around the bases, enjoying his game-winning revenge. Robertson was so unnerved he walked the next hitter, but recovered his poise to whiff the last two. Although he wound up striking out the side, Robertson ended up with an F.

Toronto 3, New York 2

Losing Pitcher: Robertson (2-4)

Bullpen diary: Even though Joba's fastball ranged from 94 to 96 mph, all of the hitters made some kind of contact every time they swung. Robertson missed his spot by about a foot.

Nova showed enough to warrant another start, possibly at the expense of Vazquez.

Pennant race: The Yankees' loss was compounded when both Tampa Bay and Boston won, placing them in a tie with the Rays and reducing their wildcard lead over the Red Sox to 5½ games.

Game Two @ Toronto, August 24

Moseley had a quality start and the Yanks cracked 5 HRs in an over-the-wall-to-wall laugher. The Yanks were leading 11-2 when Gaudin returned to his mop-up role in the top of the 7th. He struggled through the next two innings, giving up three hits, two walks, four line-drive outs, and three runs. His grade: D-. Wood pitched a clean 9th, topping at 95 mph and surprising Vernon Wells with a slider on a 3-2 count even though the Yankees were six runs ahead. Wood: A.

New York 11, Toronto 5

Bullpen diary: Girardi announced that Nova would be starting on Sunday in Chicago and that Vazquez would be in the bullpen. Girardi added that the situation would be "reevaluated" after Nova's start.

Game Three @ Toronto, August 25

Hughes was downright awful. He threw 102 pitches in his 3 ⅔-inning stint, and although he got two strikes on nineteen hitters, twelve of them reached base. He left behind 5-2 and with the bases loaded. Enter Vazquez, disgruntled as he was, who was nothing less than magnificent. Except for a homer by Hill, Vazquez was completely in control. His velocity was up to 91 mph and his hitherto moribund fastballs showed exemplary late life. Moreover, his change-up was unhittable, and his slider was sharp. Vazquez retired the last ten hitters he faced and earned an A.

Toronto 6, New York 3

Bullpen diary: Vazquez saved the bullpen, and with a day off tomorrow, everybody in the relief corps should be well rested. Hughes looked weary—perhaps his next turn will be skipped in favor of Vazquez.

Rehab update: Marte suffered a setback in his rehab, raising the probability that his season is defunct. However, since he replaced Marte, Logan has held lefty hitters to a .077 average (2-26).

Pennant race: Boston split a doubleheader, so everything is as it was atop the AL East: New York and Tampa Bay tied, and Boston 5½ back.

ALFREDO ACEVES

Alfredo Aceves' father, Alfredo, Sr., was a power-hitting first baseman in the highly competitive Mexican League. He once clouted 48 homers in a 100-game season. Naturally, Senior had every reason to expect that his son would also develop into a potent hitter.

Alfredo Aceves

"I was eleven years old," says Aceves, "and playing the outfield on a team in a pretty good junior league. I wasn't much of a hitter, but I did have some power. Anyway, everything changed during one game that I'll never forget. My best friend was at bat, I was on deck, and the pitcher was a guy named Chimonco, who was throwing gas. The situation called for a bunt, so my friend squared to the pitch, but the ball glanced off his bat and hit him right in the face. There was blood all over the place. After that, there was no way I was going to be serious about being a hitter."

For the next four years, Aceves played basketball, soccer, and volleyball. Anything but baseball; until he reluctantly got back into the batter's box as a high school freshman.

"No, no," his coach said. "You're bailing out on every close pitch and you'll never be a hitter. What you do have is a strong arm. From now on, you've got to be a pitcher."

This sounded like a terrific idea, especially since high schools in Mexico used the DH so pitchers never picked up a bat.

"When I was just seventeen," says Aceves, "my fastball was clocked at seventy-six miles per hour. Fifteen days later, the gun had me at seventy-nine. And fifteen days after that, I was up to eighty-one. Throwing that hard so young was a big deal, so we had a little party in my house to celebrate."

Three years later, Aceves' fastball registered in the low 90s and he signed with the Toronto organization. After he played in ten games in a rookie league (going 2-1 with a 3.10 ERA), Toronto traded him to Yucatan in the Mexican League.

That's when he connected with Fernando Garcia, a scout with the Atlanta organization. "Fernando began working with me," Aceves remembers. "He put me through all kind of exercises. Lifting my legs. Pivoting my hips. Running until I was exhausted, and doing lots of pitching."

One day, when Aceves had just started throwing in earnest, Garcia said this: "I've got to go, but I want you to keep on pitching until you get tired. When you get home, put ice on your elbow."

So Aceves kept throwing and throwing until he could hardly reach the catcher's mitt. But when he got home he discovered that there was no ice available.

"I didn't know what to do," he says. "I looked all around trying to find something, some kind of substitute. What I wound up using instead of ice was a box of Wheaties."

The Breakfast of Champions.

For the next six seasons, Aceves pitched for Yucatan and then Monterey, sometimes as a long man but mostly as a starter. "There was no such thing as a pitch count in Mexico," he says. "You just pitched until you got tired and then hoped there was enough ice cubes around to put on your arm. Sometimes there wasn't."

The Yankees eventually signed Aceves in 2008, and after

various stopovers in Trenton and Scranton, he's been with the big team ever since.

"Things are very different up here," he says.

"There's all the ice I ever need."

August 27–29 @ U.S. Cellular Field

The Sox's hitters treated Burnett as though he was throwing BP. By the time Mitre restored a semblance of order, the Yankees trailed 9-2. Mitre, though, did a superlative job. His two-seamer was good enough to produce twelve infield outs over his 4 2/3 inning appearance. Grade: A

Chicago 9, New York 4

Bullpen diary: Mitre's four-seamer had terrific left-to-right movement, and his curve was responsible for four outs.

Starter's dilemma: With Burnett showing nothing and both Vazquez and Mitre coming off lengthy lockdown relief appearances, could either one take Burnett's next scheduled start? The only downside of this possibility is that Burnett still has three more years on his contract (making him too expensive to be traded), and a demotion to the bullpen could ruin his self-confidence in perpetuity. Things will become clearer after Nova pitches on Sunday.

Where we stand: The Yankees were sloppy in the field and clutchless at bat. And with Sabathia being their one and only dependable starter, it isn't surprising that the team's record thus far in August is a dismal 12-13. The Red Sox beat the Rays, moving within 4½ games of the AL East's coleaders.

Rehab update: Pettitte had a modestly encouraging bullpen session, but Aceves was bombed for three runs in 1 2/3 innings in Double-A Trenton.

Game Two @ Chicago, August 28

Over the first few innings, Sabathia didn't have much when the ace of the rotation needed to have everything. But he did settle down and the lineup bailed him out by producing eleven runs during his seven-inning stint. When Chamberlain took over in the bottom of the 8th, the Yankees' lead was 11–5. But Joba didn't last long. An infield hit and a strikeout were followed by a solid two-baser that put two runners in scoring position, and put Chamberlain in the dugout. His grade: F. Logan was summoned to pitch to LH Mark Teahen, who grounded a slider to Cano but enabled the White Sox to narrow the gap to 11–6. A double by Gordon Beckham subtracted still another run from the Yankees' once formidable lead. Logan then retired Juan Pierre on a routine fly to LF. Logan did handle the two lefties he faced, but only rated a C-.

With the score now 12–7, Robertson was tasked to put the Chisox out of their misery. Instead he created some misery for Girardi. *Bang!* A home run. *Bang!* A triple. *Bang!* A line-drive single that made the score 12–9 and sent Robertson to the showers carrying his second consecutive F.

With the Yankees sitting precariously on a three-run lead, a save situation had evolved, but after Mo cleaned the bases with a double-play ball, he gave up a single and walked Andruw Jones before Teahen rocketed a liner straight at Cano. Rivera: C+.

New York 12, Chicago 9
Save: Rivera (26)
Bullpen diary: Even though Joba pushed the gun to 99 mph, his fastballs were still too straight and too easily tracked. Logan was clocked at 96 mph but was hurt when a hanging slider was bashed for two bases by Beckham. Robertson reverted to his early-season form, mislocating his fastballs and spinning his curves. Mo hadn't pitched in seven days and his lack of control demonstrated his rust.
Pennant race: Tampa Bay beat Boston to stay even with New York and push the Bosox 5½ games behind them both.

Game Three @ Chicago, August 29
Young Ivan Nova's second start was even more effective than his first had been. Using 88 pitches over 5 ⅔ innings, his fastball touched 97

mph, his curves and change-ups clipped the corners, he registered 9 Ks, and he left with a 2-1 lead.

For the rest of the game, Girardi worked his bullpen as if the Yankees were playing in the World Series.

Logan was victimized when Pierzynski hit a squibbler to 3B. Although Nuñez had plenty of time to make the play, he hurried his throw and pulled Swisher (subbing for the injured Teixeira) off the bag. Instead of Nuñez being charged with an error, the hometown official scorer credited Pierzynski with a bogus base hit. A quick hook and a B on his tally sheet.

Wood came on to issue a walk that loaded the bases, but got a groundout to end the inning. In the bottom of the 7th, Wood got two quick outs, but when he walked the forty-two-year-old Omar Vizquel, Girardi made another move. Wood's grade: B+. Enter Chamberlain, who got Alex Rios to loft a 99-mph fastball to CF.

Nunez bobbled an easy grounder to open the bottom of the 9th, and Konerko was replaced by a pinch runner who was thrown out by Cervelli trying to steal on the very next pitch. A lined single was rendered meaningless when Joba completed the inning with a whiff and a grounder. Joba's grade: A-.

With Rivera on the mound in the home half of the 9th, Ozzie Guillen went against the book by pinch-hitting a right-handed hitter for the scheduled lefty. Guillen's idea was to avoid maximizing Mo's cutter, which jammed lefties. But the strategy went for naught as Carlos Quentin tapped an easy bouncer to Jeter.

However, after getting ahead of Beckham 1-2, Mo walked him on nine pitches—only the ninth base-on-balls he issued all season long. A force play produced the second out and brought Vizquel into the batter's box.

Together, Rivera and Vizquel accounted for eighty-two years of major league experience. Mo won the battle of the old-timers on his first pitch by inducing a pop-up that ended the tightly fought game. Another A for Mo.

New York 2, Chicago 1

Save: Rivera (27)

Bullpen diary: There was something about the air quality or wind current, or else a malfunction of the radar gun in Chicago, that added a few miles per hour to fastballs. Logan threw 99 mph the last time the Yankees were in town and was clocked at 96 today. Wood likewise hit the 96-mph mark. And several of Chamberlain's number ones registered 99 mph, while one blazer reached 100 mph! Even Rivera touched 94 mph.

Pennant race—and a MLB record: For the eighth straight day, New York and Tampa continued to be tied atop the AL East, a modern-day record for the length of a first-place tie this late in the season.

Boston was now 6½ lengths back, and their wildcard hopes were rapidly fading. Boston's spark plug Dustin Pedroia will now be out for the year after surgery on a broken foot.

August 30–September 2, Oakland A's @ Yankee Stadium

Moseley opened the series with a dud. Both his command and his control were off; he was pounded for four runs and was responsible for two runners when he was yanked after only 4⅓ innings. But the Yankees had two reasons to be thankful: they still led 6-4, and Vazquez was magnificent out of the bullpen. Over 4+ IP, Vazquez struck out six and was tagged for two hits and one run. Of the fourteen contact outs he recorded, half were groundouts. All of which earned Vazquez an A.

New York 9, Oakland 5

Winning Pitcher: Vazquez (10-9)

Bullpen diary: Vazquez was now 2-0 in three appearances in relief. Once again, Eiland deserves the credit for tweaking Vazquez's delivery—slightly raising his arm angle, which keeps his front side closed longer and, most important, moving his left leg more across his body when his leg lift initiates his delivery. Whereas this leg lift had been straight up, Vazquez now was able to generate more whole-body momentum, which resulted in increased velocity and better location. Vazquez's back foot was also moved from the 1B side to the middle of the rubber. This adjustment gave him better balance and a better angle on the strike zone.

Sooner rather than later, Vazquez will have to replace either Moseley or Burnett in the rotation.

Game Two vs. the A's in the Bronx, August 31

Hughes huffed and puffed his way through five perilous innings. He walked five and his pitch count was unacceptably high (98), but he did get some important outs and was fortunate that the Yankees' bats were alive. Gaudin was handed the ball to commence the top of the 6th with the Bronx Bombers enjoying a 9–2 lead. Except for a first-pitch lollypop that wound up in the RF stands, Gaudin was in complete control. His two-seamer was dropping out of sight, his cutter had late life, and his fastball topped at 93 mph. Best of all was Gaudin's control—10 balls vs. 28 strikes. Gaudin: A.

Robertson worked the 9th, just to get him some stress-free work after two successive horrific outs. His curve was snappish and his fastball was low in the K-zone, earning him an A.

New York 9, Oakland 3

Bullpen diary: Kudos once more to Eiland—this time for slightly raising Gaudin's arm angle and tightening his delivery. For the nth time this season, the bullpen rescued a faltering starter.

Double-A update: Switch-pitcher Pat Venditte got promoted to Trenton from the Tampa farm team.

Pennant race: With Tampa losing to Baltimore, the Yanks now lead the division by a game over the Rays, and eight over the Sox.

Around the league: KC beat the Rangers on an Alexi Ogando wild-pitch walk-off tonight.

Game Three vs. the A's in the Bronx, September 1

Was this Burnett's last chance to demonstrate that he belonged in the rotation? If so, 6 innings, 3 runs, 8 strikeouts, up 4–3 was decent enough to earn him another start. Chamberlain was erratic in the top of the 7th, yielding a pair of solid singles. But he did keep the A's from denting home plate, and nine of his ten offerings were strikes, so his grade was C+.

Logan started the top of the 8th by whiffing LH Jack Cust on a slider before being pulled. An A for Logan for doing his job. Wood raised the radar gun to 94 mph, but his cutter and curve were responsible for the two outs he produced. However, with two of the four hitters he faced getting on base, Wood earned no more than a C+.

As ever, the 9th inning belonged to Mo. As ever, he was zeroed in on the strike zone, producing two grounders before another infield dribbler resulted in a single. The runner promptly stole 2B, and with the tying run in scoring position, Kurt Suzuki missed the last pitch of the game, a 93-mph two-seamer. Grade: A.

New York 4, Oakland 3

Save: Rivera (28)

Bullpen diary: Where would the Yankees be without Logan routinely stifling lefty hitters, Wood's usually hot hand, and, of course, the Sandman?

Around the league: Cuban left-handed sensation Aroldis Chapman made his MLB debut with the Reds, and was clocked at 103 mph. Impressive.

Game Four vs. the A's in the Bronx, September 2

All season long, Sabathia has been the Yankees' stopper. This time, the opposition could only manage one paltry hit over the eight shutout innings he hurled.

Jonathan Albaladejo was recalled from Scranton yesterday when the major league rosters officially expanded to forty and, on his third turn with the Yankees, he was sent to the mound to preserve a 5-0 lead. The young man's nervousness was evident when his second pitch struck Suzuki in the back. But Albie then settled down and retired the next three hitters. Albie's grade: A-.

New York 5, Oakland 0

Bullpen diary: Albie mixed his four-seamer (clocking from 91 to 93 mph) and his two-seamer (sitting at 91 mph) to great effect.

C.C. and the Cy Young?: Sabathia is now undefeated in his last twenty-one starts in Yankee Stadium, the longest such streak for a Yankee since Whitey Ford in 1961.

Pennant race: After sweeping the four-game series, the Yankees are 84-50, 1½ games ahead of the idle Rays, and eight in front of Boston.

August Bullpen Scorecard

Javier Vazquez (2 appearances): 4.0 = A
Jonathan Albaladejo (3): 3.6 = A-
Boone Logan (14): 3.2 = B+
Mariano Rivera (9): 3.1 = B+
Kerry Wood (11): 3.0 = B
Chad Gaudin (7): 2.96 = B-
Joba Chamberlain (13): 2.90 = B-
Sergio Mitre (7): 2.85 = B-
David Robertson (13): 2.80 = B-
Dustin Moseley (1): 0 = F
TOTAL: 2.89 = B-.

A superlative stretch by the men in the pen.

Indeed, the relief corps was a primary reason why the Yankees remained in contention with the Rays for the top spot in the AL East.

Scouting Report Looking Toward September

Here's the testimony of an advance scout as the season rounds the clubhouse turn and races toward the finish line:

Kerry Wood has saved the Yankees bullpen. His fastball no longer can giddyap to 97 and he uses his 92-to-94 fastballs as spot pitches. Hit a corner. Brush a guy back from the plate. Rarely use what velocity he has left to seriously challenge a hitter. He's an experienced pitcher who has made the transition to using his curve and his cutter as his out-pitches. I'm also impressed with his poise and effectiveness in clutch situations.

Robertson's improvement over the course of the season is a function of his command. His fastball is still in the 91–93 range, but he's keeping it low in the strike-zone. And his curve is magnificent. Plus, he throws both of his pitches with an identical delivery. And coming over the top as he does keeps hitters from tracking his pitches.

Chamberlain is still shaky. Guys are getting good wood on his 94–95 fastballs because they lack movement and are easy to track. For Joba to really be lights out, he still needs to overpower hitters at 97–98, and he has to have great movement and great location with his slider.

Gaudin has come around and become very valuable because he can go two days in a row and also go in long relief. His stuff has always been good, and he doesn't demand a mega-million-dollar contract, which is why he's always had a job. Gaudin's problem has always been maintaining consistency in his command. And this is where he's made great strides.

Actually, the bullpen has done an A-1 job. And nobody can match their lineup. It's the starting rotation that's the problem. That's why it's absolutely imperative that they get

Andy Pettitte back ASAP. Because they have a wild card spot just about sewn up, they can afford to sacrifice a game or two to start Pettitte and stretch him so he can build up his arm strength. They have three weeks to do this, which, barring a physical setback, is time enough.

Without a healthy Pettitte the Yankees have very little chance of repeating.

Memory Lane

Johnny Mize's Bat

When the man with the stick hits the ball into the audience, is that good?
—EVA GABOR

I was twelve years old back in 1953, so it took me several months to save up enough money to buy a baseball bat. Imagine my disappointment when the clerk in the only sporting goods store within walking distance of my neighborhood said there was no such thing as a Gene Woodling model.

What?

My all-time Yankee hero didn't have a personalized bat on the market?

But I couldn't stand the thought of continuing to use whatever bats the other players had brought to our daily games of choose-up baseball in Crotona Park.

Don't hit the ball on the label, Charley, or you'll crack the bat and you'll have to buy me a new one.

No, you can't use it, Charley, because each bat only has a certain number of base hits in it and I don't want to waste any on you.

I simply had to have a bat of my own.

What to do?

Okay, since my second-favorite Yankee was Johnny Mize, and

since there was only one Mize model left on the rack, I figured I'd better grab it before someone else did. So I carefully placed five crinkled dollar bills on the counter and walked off with my trophy.

But Mize was 6'2" and a solid 230 pounds, with hands as strong as vise-grips, while I was 5'9" and a boyishly flabby 160 pounds, with hands as weak as a scarecrow's. Meanwhile, Mize's bat was as long and heavy as a war club. Even worse, there was no discernible knob at the end.

I practiced my home-run swing as I walked home, and each whiff threatened to send the bat flying into the passing crowd. But, hey, it was my bat. And the Big Cat was almost my main hero.

During our subsequent sandlot games, I stubbornly refused to choke up on the bat lest I somehow disrespect the power-hitting Mize. In addition, I stubbornly maintained my approximation of Woodling's corkscrew stance, one that unfortunately required extraordinary bat speed.

No wonder I was so helpless at the plate. And that's the only reason why I turned to pitching.

I CHANCED to encounter Mize some thirty-three years later. I was Phil Jackson's assistant with the Albany Patroons of the Continental Basketball Association, and we were in Louisville, Kentucky, to play the Catbirds. There chanced to be a baseball card extravaganza at the same hotel and we spent several enjoyable hours hobnobbing at the bar with the likes of Enos Slaughter, Catfish Hunter, Billy Martin—and the Big Cat himself.

Mize wasn't in good health and could walk only with the aid of a cane—a huge length of wood that was easily as large as his bat. I didn't say a word and was totally content to sit and listen to these guys share some of their experiences. Mize seemed like a nice man, but he didn't say much, either.

Fast-forward another few years to when I joined the Kingston,

New York, YMCA to rehab my surgical knee. As part of my preparation, I purchased a combination lock to secure my belongings in the locker room while I hit the Nautilus machines.

To my sheer delight, here was—and still is—the computer-generated combination of the lock: the respective uniform numbers of Mickey Mantle, Johnny Mize, and Gene Woodling.

7-36-14.

The god of computers must be a Yankee fan.

September–October 2010

- Mo gets a (new) grip and George gets a (really big) plaque.
- The bullpen of the future takes shape?
- A fountain of talent in Trenton.
- Showdowns with the Rays, Rangers, and Red Sox.
- Eiland's index cards, and two starters get pulled one out short of a win on successive days (and one of them is not happy about it).

The other teams could make trouble for us if they win.
—YOGI BERRA

September 3–5, Toronto Blue Jays @ Yankee Stadium

Few of Ivan Nova's pitches were obedient, his velocity was down to 91–91 mph, and he was charged with six hits in his 4 2/3 innings, one out short of being credited for a win if the Yanks held their lead.

There were two on, two out, and the Yankees nursing a precarious 5–3 lead when Logan was asked to end Toronto's threat as LH Lyle Overbay stepped into the batter's box. No surprise when Logan whiffed him on a steady diet of sliders. Nor were any onlookers shocked when the Yankees added two runs to their lead in the bottom of the 5th. Logan then began the 6th with a walk and a flyball—in so doing, he was a bit wild (seven balls vs. six strikes), so Girardi yanked him in favor of Robertson. Logan earned a B-.

A curveball prompted a force play for the second out of the inning, but Robertson suddenly lost command of all of his pitches. After walking Jose Molina, Robertson was behind 2-1 to weak-hitting Mike McCoy when Eiland paid a visit to the mound. Eiland's advice was for Robertson to forgo his misbehaving curve; Robertson then proceeded to pump two fastballs past McCoy to end the inning. But Robertson's wild streak continued in the 7th. After a strikeout he issued two consecutive walks. Exit Robertson with a grade of D, and enter Wood.

Utilizing a crackling curve, a late-breaking cutter, and a fastball that ranged from 92 to 94 mph, Wood set down five in a row. Wood's grade: A.

Even though the Yanks maintained a 7-3 margin, Mo once more was asked to work in a nonsave situation, broke his umpteenth bat, and easily earned another A.

New York 7, Toronto 3

Winning Pitcher: Wood (2-0 as a Yankee)

Bullpen diary: Although Logan was technically the pitcher of record, the official scorer flexed his discretionary right to award the win to the most effective reliever.

It seemed that Girardi has once again lost faith in Robertson, so the young right-hander is operating on a short leash. Indeed, Wood has become the pre–Mo stopper.

This was the Yankees' seventh consecutive victory.

Game Two vs. the Jays in the Bronx, September 4

In his return to the rotation, Vazquez's fastball never topped 89 mph, and he resorted to his change-ups and his curves to survive—which he barely did. After 4 2/3 innings, the Yankees were up 5-3 and Vazquez was unceremoniously yanked with two on and two out. Only one out short of becoming the pitcher of record, Vazquez threw his hands up in disgust when he saw Girardi leave the dugout.

His replacement was Moseley, who promptly coughed up a

game-tying double to Overbay before a groundout ended the inning. Moseley: F.

Logan took over in the top of the 7th, retiring the two lefties he faced and also inducing a soft flyball to RF from a right-handed batter. But when LH DeWayne Wise led off the 8th with a single, Chamberlain was summoned. Logan's grade: B-.

Joba's turn on the mound resulted in a highly eventful inning.

He began by plunking Aaron Hill with a high-and-tight 95-mph fastball, thereby missing Cervelli's low-and-away target by about three feet. Bautista was next up, and was called out on a 3-2 slider that was at least six inches outside—and his righteous protest resulted in the major leagues' HR leader getting thumbed out of the game. A grounder resulted in an easy force-out, but Teixeira had to catch the ensuing throw by diving to the dirt, stretching as far as he could, yet still keeping his toe on the bag. A spectacular play that completed the double play as well as Chamberlain's workday. Joba's grade: B.

After Marcus Thames clubbed a two-run HR, Wood set the Jays down 1-2-3, thereby earning an A. Rivera was nicked for a two-out single, but otherwise breezed through the 9th to preserve the win and secure another A.

New York 7, Toronto 3
Winning Pitcher: Chamberlain (2-4)

Save: Rivera (29)

Bullpen diary: Vazquez was steamed over Girardi's pulling him without giving him a chance to claim the win. But the two HRs he gave up tied him for the dubious distinction of getting knocked for the most round-trippers (29) in the AL.

In his first relief appearance since July 24, Moseley's sinker was flat. Logan's fastball was mediocre (92–93 mph), but his slider was sharp. Joba's left shoulder was flying open, resulting in his fastballs being too high in the strike zone.

Wood has become the mainstay of the late relievers. With the

Yankees, his ERA is a microscopic 0.64 and he's holding hitters to a .189 batting average.

By crowding right-handed hitters with his a snappy two-seamer, Rivera forces them to be inside-conscious and unable to sit on his outer-corner cutters.

⚾ GIRARDI SHOWED he was serious about the division title having precedence over players' feelings when he pulled both Nova and Vazquez one out short of a win.

According to the Elias Sports Bureau, it was the first time in many years that a manager pulled pitchers in the lead after $4\frac{2}{3}$ innings on consecutive days. The other manager with such a short rope? Lou Piniella.

Pennant race: Both Tampa and Boston lost, stretching the Yankees' respective leads to 2½ games over the Rays and ten over the Red Sox.

Game Three vs. the Jays in the Bronx, September 5

Hughes showed some improvement location-wise, but was banged for three HRs that accounted for the five runs he allowed. Mitre took the ball to commence the top of the 7th with the visitors ahead 5-2. He hadn't pitched in eight days and the inactivity was costly. Two singles, two walks (one with the bases loaded) was the price he paid before getting a double play to prevent a total disaster. Mitre was clearly more comfortable as he pitched a clean 8th, but after two sharply hit singles and a line drive that Teixeira's diving catch and tag turned into a double play, Mitre was done for the day, taking a D+ to the shower. Albaladejo finished up with a strikeout, although his first pitch struck Bautista in the back. Albie's grade: B.

Toronto 7, New York 3

Bullpen diary: From the stretch, Mitre's right leg was twitching and his left foot was bouncing—a return to his bad habits.

Albie's fastball was lifeless and also down to 91–92 mph, several clicks lower than he had previously shown. Also, this was the second straight time that he plunked the first hitter he confronted. Was he still nervous?

Pennant race: Although NY's eight-game winning streak was terminated, both Tampa and Boston also obliged by losing.

September 6–8, Baltimore Orioles @ Yankee Stadium

Next up: Baltimore and Buck Showalter's improving O's. Under the ex-Yankee manager, the O's were no longer pushovers.

Even a decidedly mediocre performance by Burnett was deemed to be an improvement. Burnett's seven innings were a miasma of walks, hits, wild pitches, and a pair of two-out RBI singles that had the Yankees on the short end of a 4-3 score. Logan then came on to face three straight lefty hitters with mixed results: a whiff on a slider, then a chopper that went for an infield hit followed by a seven-pitch walk, and concluding with a flyout off the bat of a righty. For his erratic performance, Logan's grade was C+. Robertson came on to finish the game and, except for getting stung by a sharply hit single, he cruised through 1⅓ painless innings. Robertson's grade: A-.

Baltimore 4, New York 3
Bullpen diary: Logan was plagued with the same unsteady control that got him sent to Scranton earlier in the season.

Game Two vs. the Orioles in the Bronx, September 7
A rare clunker by C.C. at home. The hefty lefty left after being smacked for nine hits and six runs in 6⅓ innings. Meanwhile, the lineup had to scratch and scrabble to score two runs. Wood finished the top of the 7th with a flourish, striking out both hitters he faced, thereby earning an A. Gaudin also finished up in style—five up and five down—likewise earning an A.

Baltimore 6, New York 3

Bullpen diary: Wood only threw one fastball for a strike, getting his snuffs on a slider and a curve. Gaudin had great location and a clever mix of pitches, and was pounding the strike zone.

Pennant race: Yanks a game and a half up on the Rays.

Around the league: Trevor Hoffman got save 600.

Game Three vs. the Orioles in the Bronx, September 8

Nova bounced back to have a distinguished outing. His only mistake was throwing a meatball on an "automatic-take" count of 3-0 to Matt Wieters, who gave the youngster a surprise by depositing the pitch in the LF stands. After six noble innings, Nova was lifted trailing 2-1. Robertson cruised through the top of the 7th, mixing his 93-mph fastball and his well-situated bender to gain two strikeouts and an easy bounce-out. However, after Ty Wigginton creamed a fastball to very deep CF that Gardner managed to run down, Robertson's day was over. Grade: A. Logan then proceeded to whiff two lefties to end the inning and gain his A. In the 9th, Joba had his season's-best combination of command and sheer stuff and gained a well-deserved A.

In the bottom of the 9th, Swisher belted a dramatic two-run, walk-off HR to make Joba and the Yankees winners. (Nick did the same thing last year on September 8.)

New York 3, Baltimore 2

Winning Pitcher: Chamberlain (3–4)

Bullpen diary: Logan was now unscored upon in his last 22 appearances covering 15 innings.

Pennant race: Yanks now up 2½ on the Rays.

September 10–12 @ Rangers Field

Still another stinker by Vazquez—6 hits, 4 runs in 5+ innings. With the Yankees leading 5-4 and a runner on 1B, the quick hook proved once more that Girardi has no faith in Vazquez. Logan came in to walk LH Mitch Moreland, reason enough for his F. Robertson followed, yielding a sacrifice bunt, an RBI groundout, and a grounder. Dave's grade: A. Wood pitched a clean 7th, but a pair of line drives that were caught on the warning track reduced his grade to A-.

For the first time since July 10 in Seattle, Chamberlain was asked to preserve a one-run lead in the 8th inning and hand the game over to Rivera. But Joba's first pitch was a hanging slider that Nelson Cruz walloped into the RF stands to tie the score. Relying chiefly on his 95–96 mph fastballs, Joba then retired the side. But the damage was done and he hoisted still another F.

Since the decision had already been made to skip Hughes' next start and he was scheduled for a bullpen session today, the erstwhile starter was called upon to stifle the Rangers in the bottom of the 9th. Which he did. A strikeout, a grounder, and a clout to left that was caught against the wall combined to give Hughes an A-.

Rivera then got through the 10th and 11th with ease. Rivera's grade: A.

Instead of using Albaladejo, Girardi went with Gaudin—and a 1-2-3 12th validated his decision. Unfortunately, Gaudin's first pitch in the 13th was a lazy fastball that Cruz lost in the seats to end the game.

Texas 6, New York 5 (13 innings)

Losing Pitcher: Gaudin (0–4)

Bullpen diary: Girardi continued to use the only lefty in his bullpen relatively early in the game. The last time Hughes skipped a start, he was ineffective through his next several returns to the rotation. Inserting him into a temporary relief role was designed to enable Hughes to keep his edge.

Rivera threw five balls and nineteen strikes. What else is new? But will he be available tomorrow? And will there be any negative repercussions down the line from extending Mo to two ultimately useless innings?

Being on such a short leash continued to upset Vazquez. "I don't have to prove myself," he said. But he does.

Rehab update: The plan is to give Pettitte one more minor league (or simulated game) start, and then have him return to the rotation in Baltimore (September 19). Pettitte would then have three major league starts before the money season commences.

Pennant race: Yanks are down to a game-and-a-half lead over the Rays.

Game Two @ Texas, September 11

Burnett showed much improvement, especially in locating his curve. But the game was interrupted after four innings by a rainstorm that didn't subside for fifty-nine minutes and ended Burnett's night. Gaudin took over in the bottom of the 5th with the score 2-2. Gaudin faced three hitters only because Guerrero was thrown out trying to stretch a single into a double. The Rangers began the bottom of the 6th with another pair of base hits, before Logan was summoned to the mound and Gaudin left with an F. Logan whiffed Moreland, then was replaced by Robertson after delivering a five-pitch walk that loaded the bases. Logan's grade: C-. Robertson was ineffective, getting touched for a sac fly that put Texas ahead 3-2, then an RBI single before a hot shot to Cano finally ended the inning.

The Yankees retaliated with a run in the top of the 7th but blew a chance to break the game open when Posada bounced into an inning-ending DP with bases loaded.

Robertson then gave up a walk, two singles, and a run in the home half of the 7th; bad enough to be levied an F.

The Yankees took the lead, 6-5, and Wood came on in the 8th to shut the Rangers down and hand the game over to Rivera, which he did except for a single. Grade: A-.

Then Mo proceeded to blow the save and the game. The trouble began when he walked Guerrero to start the bottom of the 9th—with the fourth ball thrown high, outside, and several feet removed from the strike zone—a sure sign that Mo wasn't on his game. This was underlined when Cruz blasted a single and Kinsler knotted the score with a double. An intentional walk was followed by an infield fly, and Rivera was a double play away from extending the game into extra innings. But Mo's next pitch struck Jeff Francoeur's shoulder and the game was over. Grade: F.

A walk-off HBP was a first in Mo's otherwise long and glorious career.

Texas 7, New York 6

Losing Pitcher: Rivera (3-3)

Bullpen diary: Rivera had thrown twenty-three pitches last night, and his arm lacked the resilience it had when he was in his thirties.

Pennant race: Rays win; Yanks just a half game up.

Game Three @ Texas, September 12

A superb job by Moseley was wasted when the frazzled bullpen forced Girardi to try to squeeze an extra inning out of him. The scored was 1-1 after six, and the arm-weary Moseley managed two outs, but also coughed up three runs in the bottom of the 7th. Albaladejo struggled through the following 1 2/3 innings, but no runs were charged to him. His grade: C-.

Texas 4, New York 1

Bullpen diary: For several weeks now the bullpen has carried the burden of brief outings by Burnett, Vazquez, and Hughes. However, coupled with a profound absence of clutch hitting, the relievers are finally spent. As a result, the Yankees' latest loss was their third in a row, and sixth in their last seven games.

Pennant race: Yanks stay a half game up on the Rays.

Yankees trivia: The New Jersey Hall of Fame has inducted three classes of famous Jerseyites, from Thomas Edison to Rosa Parks, Bruce Springsteen to Bon Jovi, Buzz Aldrin to Frank Sinatra, and of course, Yogi Berra to Phil Rizzuto. A new building holding photos and memorabilia has opened in Asbury Park.

September 13–15 @ Tropicana Field

In the first face-off of the most important series of the season thus far, Sabathia and David Price matched goose eggs for eight innings. The game remained scoreless when Wood climbed the hill in the bottom of the 9th. Cleverly mixing curves and 95-mph fastballs, Wood struck out two. His sixteenth consecutive scoreless appearance rated an A.

Logan began the 10th by whiffing Pena on a slider. Grade: A.

Gaudin was fortunate when he struck out Matt Joyce to begin his stint and Brad Hawpe to end it on 93-mph fastballs in the dirt. In between, he issued three walks. However, Gaudin's total of thirty nail-biting pitches somehow managed to keep the Rays from scoring, thereby earning him a C-.

In the bottom of the 11th, Mitre's sixth offering to pinch-hitting Reid Brignac landed in the LF seats and left the Yankees with their first four-game losing streak. Mitre's grade: F.

Tampa Bay 1, New York 0 (11 innings)
Losing Pitcher: Mitre (0-3)
Bullpen diary: Why did Girardi go with the lesser lights of his bullpen in such an important game?

Because before each game, Eiland hands Girardi an index card listing the status of the relievers.

Those pitchers who are unavailable because they've worked two games in a row (or who were up and throwing for long stretches in the bullpen) are marked with red stars. Accordingly, Albaladejo, Chamberlain, and Robertson were slated to have the day off. In addition, Girardi wanted to hopefully save Mo for a save situation and avoid using him in another two-inning outing. And although Vazquez was in the bullpen for the second straight game, Girardi simply didn't trust him.

This is what Eiland had to say about using Gaudin and Mitre (who had only made two appearances since August 27): "Maybe you lose the battle but win the war. This was certainly a big game, but it wasn't do-or-die."

Pennant race: Yanks now a half game back. The lineup has produced one run in the last twenty-one innings.

Game Two @ Tampa, September 14

Nova blew a 6-0 lead with a disastrous 5th, during which he totally lost command of his fastball. Logan was called upon to quell the rally, but was scorched by a three-run HR off the bat of Aybar, and the Rays ended the inning with a 7-6 lead. Logan bounced back to pitch a clean 6th, yet his performance still rated a D.

Joba breezed through the 7th, gunning his fastball up to 98 mph and earning an A. Wood's fastball topped at a season-high 96 mph as he shut down Tampa Bay in the 8th with the score now 7-7. Robertson had difficulty locating his curve, so Zobrist sat on his fastball and clouted a sizzling tweener to deep right-center—the probable triple turned into an inning-ending out by Granderson's sensational diving catch. Robertson's grade: B.

After Posada blasted a round-tripper to give the Yanks an 8-7 lead, Rivera took the ball. After the speedy Crawford beat out a broken-bat infield single, Mo threw over to 1B a total of four times. Longoria then smacked a drive that Granderson caught in front of the CF wall, but Crawford stole 2B during Joyce's at-bat. Joyce then hit a flyball close to the foul line in medium RF, and Crawford was erased trying to tag up and advance to 3B on a sensational throw by Greg Golson. The foolish play by Crawford ended the game.

Because he was the beneficiary of a bonus out, Rivera's grade was reduced to B-.

New York 8, Tampa Bay 7 (10 innings)
Winning Pitcher: Robertson (3-4)
Save: Rivera (30)
Bullpen diary: A terrific comeback by Joba after getting smacked around in Texas. During the three-game hiatus, he continued

working with Eiland to keep his front shoulder closed. Another overpowering performance by Wood; his fastballs were blasts from the past. After delivering a walk-off HBP in his last appearance (in Texas), Mo looked somewhat shaky. But a win is a win is a win.

Game Three @ Tampa Bay, September 15

With a 7th-inning HR by Granderson having staked the Yankees to a 3-2 lead, Hughes quickly flushed an otherwise solid start by delivering a second two-run gopher ball to Dan Johnson. Joba's 96–97 mph aces mowed down all four hitters he faced, but his A was wasted.

Tampa Bay 4, New York 3

Bullpen diary: Wood and Logan were red-starred, but with Scranton's season over, the Yankees added Royce Ring (a curveballing lefty) to the roster. One wonders why Ring wasn't summoned to pitch to Johnson, especially after he had already taken Hughes deep once. Why elevate Ring if not to use him in an appropriate situation?

Pennant race: Yanks a half game back.

Rehab update: The only good news is that Pettitte had a solid five-inning turn for Double-A Trenton and is scheduled to start in four days.

A TRENTON MOMENT

Several locations come to mind when considering the most fiery hotbeds of baseball: the Bronx, Brooklyn, Williamsport, St. Louis, Fenway Park, Los Angeles, Japan, Puerto Rico, Cuba, and San Pedro de Macoris, in the Dominican Republic.

But one center of both passion and excellence is usually overlooked: Trenton, New Jersey.

Since 2003, the Trenton Thunder have been the Yankees' Double-A farm team, and on the passion side of the ledger, the

2006 Thunder became the first team in minor league baseball history to draw over 400,000 fans for twelve consecutive seasons at the Double-A level or below. Over the past thirteen seasons, the Thunder has attracted more than 5.4 million paying customers.

As for excellence, past Thunder rosters read like a who's who of current Yankee success. The list of Thunder veterans who appeared in Yankee uniforms during the 2010 season is impressive: Phil Hughes, David Robertson, Brett Gardner, Joba Chamberlain, Robinson Cano, Francisco Cervelli, Ivan Nova, and Alfredo Aceves.

Trenton is also where Yankee stars go, via the GWB and I-95, to get in a rehab game: Andy Pettitte this year, and in past years Jeter, Matsui, Bernie Williams, Clemens, and Kevin Brown.

Before the Yankees took over the operation, Trenton was a farm team of the Tigers and then the Red Sox. Accordingly, some other notable alumni include Kevin Youkilis, David Eckstein, Nomar Garciaparra, Carl Pavano, Tony Clark, and Trot Nixon.

Looking to the future, Trenton is stocked with future Bronx players. Late in 2010, *Baseball America* magazine announced its prospect rankings, and for the AL East, eight of the top ten prospects played in Trenton in the last two years, and some have already moved up to Triple-A Scranton and even had a few games at the Stadium: catchers Jesus Montero and Austin Romine, third baseman Brandon Laird, infielder Eduardo Nuñez, and several pitchers: Andrew Brackman, Dellin Betances, Manny Banuelos, and Hector Noesi. After spring training, most of these players will go back to Trenton to get in playing time, but look for them to be in the Bronx before long.

In the past, this pool of talent would be considered primarily trade material to get big-league-ready players from other teams, but it looks for now like the Yankees are looking to build from within, although some of these guys will still certainly be traded at some point, especially as their positions higher up the ladder are held down by the likes of Cano and Teixeira. But the rest is or will be open, especially in starting and relief pitching slots.

⚾ TRENTON'S SUCCESS at the gate and the plate isn't bad for an industrial city of about one hundred thousand souls who are mainly employed in producing parachutes, cigars, paint, tile, woolens, and car parts, as well as various steel and plastic products.

And whereas the cost of field-level seats purchased the day of a game in Yankee Stadium ranges from $150 to $325, equivalent seats at the Mercer County Waterfront Park (situated a long home run from the Delaware River and Philadelphia) can be had for a mere eleven bucks.

If all Triple-A players and venues have major league pretensions, Double-A baseball is a celebration of hard-core hustle and humility, as well as being a frugal fan's delight.

September 17–19 @ Camden Yards

Burnett managed seven acceptable innings in which he allowed two solo HRs and was trailing 3-1. Robertson had a clean bottom of the 8th. His 93-mph fastball was a tick higher than normal and he registered all three outs with his curve. Grade: A. In the top of the 9th, the Yankees had two on, two out, and a 2-2 count on A-Rod.

Down to the last strike of still another painful loss, Rodriguez turned the game around with a prodigious three-run HR that put the Yanks ahead 4-3, and back ahead of the Rays by half a game. Talk about a clutch hit. Mo had no trouble saving the game, breaking another bat, and completing another A performance.

New York 4, Baltimore 3

Winning Pitcher: Robertson (4-4)

Save: Rivera (31)

Bullpen diary: The vertical movement of Mo's cutter has lost a few inches and the swerve is likewise not as dependable as it has been for so long. But his command remained impeccable—only three balls and nine strikes.

Game Two @ Baltimore, September 18

Sabathia's curve was unmanageable, yet he battled through seven innings while yielding only three runs. Meanwhile, the lineup was apparently roused by A-Rod's latest heroics and relentlessly battered Baltimore pitchers, providing an 8-3 lead when Joba replaced C.C. in the bottom of the 8th. Joba's fastball was popping at 94–96 mph and a double play got him out of a mini jam, giving him an A-. Gaudin finished up in fine style and earned an A.

New York 11, Baltimore 3

Bullpen diary: The last out of the game was a flyball to Greg Golson in RF. The rookie was unaware that the out secured C.C.'s first-ever twenty-win season, and blithely flipped the ball to a fan in the stands.
Pennant race: Yanks stay a half game up on the Rays.
Around the league: The concern of maple bats, vs. the harder ash, was revived today when Tyler Colvin of the Cubs was hit in the chest by a broken-bat shard while standing on third. It actually stuck in his chest and punctured a lung.

Game Three @ Baltimore, September 19

Pettitte was in prime form in his return, giving up only three hits in six innings. With a 3-1 lead, Joba struck out the only batter he faced on a nasty slider; A. Logan came on to whiff LH Luke Scott on a 95-mph blazer and was fortunate when Wigginton lined to short to end the 7th. Logan was yanked after LH Corey Patterson beat out a drag bunt to lead off the 8th. Logan's grade: B-.

Next up was Kerry Wood. A pair of singles closed the O's deficit to 3-2, then a sac bunt put runners on 2B and 3B with one out—and that's when Wood showed his mettle, whiffing Robert Andino on a bender, intentionally walking the tough Nick Markakis, and then getting Adam Jones to pop up a cutter to Cano. A B+ for Wood.

Enter Mo to save another victory. Too bad Luke Scott drilled Rivera's second pitch into the RF stands to even the score at 3-3. Before Rivera got out of the inning, he was clipped for a hard single and a blistering line drive right at Granderson in CF. The blown save resulted in the second F in Rivera's last four appearances.

Robertson cruised through the 10th. In the top of the 11th, the Yankees could not plate a runner who had reached 3B with none out. In the bottom of the 11th, the O's made short work of Robertson—a leadoff double followed by a game-winning single by Wigginton. Robertson got the loss—plus an F.

Baltimore 4, New York 3 (11 innings)
Losing Pitcher: Robertson (4-5)
Bullpen diary: Wood made gutsy pitches in the clutch, belying the "choke" label that several scouts had hung on him before he joined the Yankees. Rivera's cutters showed only slight horizontal movement and almost no vertical drop.
Pennant race: Although they did pinch-hit, both A-Rod and Teixeira were out of the starting lineup. This move, along with his periodic red-starring of his relievers, indicated that Girardi is clearly looking past the regular season and into the playoffs. Yanks stay a half game up on the Rays.

September 20–23, Tampa Bay Rays @ Yankee Stadium

The start of the first game against the Rays at the Stadium was delayed for the ceremony marking the unveiling of a plaque in Monument Park honoring the late George Steinbrenner. The plaque measured seven by five feet, not counting the granite base, was set higher in the wall, and was also much larger than the three-by-two plaques honoring the likes of Babe Ruth, Lou Gehrig, Joe DiMaggio, Mickey Mantle, et al.

Young Nova was masterful through five innings, before suffering his habitual meltdown (albeit a relatively minor one) in the 6th. The Yanks led 4-2 when he departed and the runner on 2B was Nova's responsibility. Logan faced three LH hitters and they all reached base—one on a duck fart, one on a walk, and one on a dribbler down the 1B line that Teixeira failed to handle. Logan: D-.

Gaudin then walked in the tying run before getting a flyball to end the inning. Gaudin seemed wary of pitching to contact and received D+.

In the bottom of the 6th, the Yanks rallied for four runs, highlighted by the rejuvenated Granderson's three-run HR (his second round-tripper of the game).

Robertson then had his second-straight unsatisfactory outing, giving up two hits and a run while managing only two outs. Robertson's grade: D+. Kerry Wood to the rescue, getting out of the inning on a long drive that Swisher corralled in deep LF. The 8th was a breeze for Wood to complete his A-rated outing.

Rivera was touched for a double and a run-scoring single—in addition to another hit batsman—before getting a groundout to Tex to end the game. Rivera: C-.

New York 8, Tampa Bay 6

Winning Pitcher: Gaudin (1-4)

Save: Rivera (32)

Bullpen diary: Logan was getting behind the hitters and never really caught up. Gaudin didn't quite get the job done—walking in the tying run—in his most crucial appearance of the season, yet he lucked into getting credit for the win. Robertson had nothing and, like Logan, seemed to be spent. Where would the Yankees be without Wood?

Rivera's cutter was lifeless once more. He did break another bat but also hit another batter.

Pennant race: Yanks move 1½ up on the Rays.

Game Two vs. the Rays in the Bronx, September 21

Hughes couldn't tame his curveball and battled his way through 118 pitches and five walks over the course of 6⅓ innings. The Yankees led 5-2 and the Rays had a runner on 2B when Vazquez took the ball. After not having pitched since September 10, his command was surprisingly good at first. A bloop single tacked another run onto Hughes' ERA, but a flyball and an infield bouncer ended the inning.

By the time Vazquez toed the rubber in the top of the 8th, the Yanks had extended their lead to 7-3. Two line-drive singles were followed by a flyball to medium center, which was then followed by Girardi replacing Vazquez with Chamberlain. Vazquez left the game with a grade of D+.

Joba suffered the indignity of having a comebacker hit him in the ass. With the infield single loading the bases, Brad Hawpe represented the tying run. Chamberlain's handling of this critical at-bat was revelatory. Three fastballs produced a 1-2 count before Joba threw a fifty-five-foot slider. Several more fastballs brought the count to 3-2. A walk would obviously force in a run and put the tying run on base. Since his only slider to Hawpe was a dirtball, it was only natural for the hitter to gear up for still another fastball. So when Joba offered a slider, Hawpe swung and missed. A gutsy pitch. After that dramatic out, Chamberlain finished the game with four easy outs, earning an A.

New York 8, Tampa Bay 3
Save: Chamberlain (3)
Bullpen diary: Did Vazquez's uneven performance eliminate him from the long-relief role in the playoffs? And since Ivan Nova has proven to be virtually unhittable when going through a lineup twice, would he be under consideration for this role?
Pennant race: Yanks move back to 2½ up on the Rays.

Game Three vs. the Rays in the Bronx, September 22

A two-hour-plus rain delay washed out a short but effective start by Burnett. The Yankees trailed 1-0 when southpaw Royce Ring made his first appearance of the season to begin the 3rd inning.

Even though Royce couldn't get his fail-safe curve near the strike zone, he whiffed lefties Johnson and Joyce on nasty cutters. A tapper to Cano from RH Bartlett ended the inning. The top of the 5th began with Ring popping up LH Reid Brignac and RH Navarro grounding out to 3B. But Ring was lifted after issuing a five-pitch walk, taking an A with him to the shower.

Dustin Moseley allowed the game to get out of hand by giving up three singles, a double, and a homer through his 1⅓ innings of work. That earned an F. Gaudin added fuel to the conflagration when he was dinged for back-to-back HRs in the top of the 7th and couldn't get out of the 8th. An F for him, too. Albaladejo walked the first two men he faced—to load the bases and then force in another run—before a flyball temporarily ended his distress. However, another walk plus two singles resulted in the Rays recording another straight number in the top of the 9th. The third F of the day.

Tampa Bay 7, New York 2

Bullpen diary: Ring's delivery was a few degrees lower than it had been in spring training. Did his outstanding performance force Girardi to consider supplementing Logan with a second lefty in the bullpen for the playoffs? Look for Ring to get more opportunities to show his worth in the final eleven games of the regular season.

Albaladejo showed a remarkable absence of control. His pitches were rushed and his front shoulder was flying open. In so doing, he reinforced the view that he's strictly a Triple-A pitcher.

Once again, Girardi saved his core relievers.

Robertson's back was aching, but an MRI revealed no structural damage, only some minor muscle spasms.

Pennant race: Back down to 1½ up.

Game Four vs. the Rays in the Bronx, September 23

In the much anticipated rematch between Sabathia and Price, C.C. was downright awful. He needed 111 pitches to navigate his way through 5⅓ dismal innings. He left with the bases loaded and Tampa Bay ahead 4-3, but when Chamberlain allowed all three of the runners he inherited to cross the plate, Sabathia was charged with seven runs—his highest total of the season. Joba was putrid.

The score was 8-3 by the time he was finished, at which point so were the Yankees. Joba: F.

Vazquez took over in the top of the 7th and, after walking Zobrist, tied a major league record (held by seven others) by hitting three batters in a row. A sac fly then plated another run. During the 8th and 9th innings, however, Vazquez was masterful. Even so, his grade could only be lifted to D+.

Tampa Bay 10, New York 3

Bullpen diary: Vazquez's delivery was off—once he lifted his left leg his body leaned slightly toward 1B. This side-to-side movement was something new, causing his front shoulder to open, and explained his momentary loss of control.

After the game, Vazquez said this: "I thought I had good command." Maybe he was just talking about the 8th and 9th innings.

Pennant race: Down to just a half game up on the Rays. Next: three games in the Bronx vs. the Sox.

When questioned in a pregame interview by John Sterling, Girardi agreed that this particular contest was the most important of the season thus far, and it put Tampa Bay and the Yankees even in the loss column.

Despite Girardi's perpetual avowals that first place in the AL East is the only goal they're seeking, it could very well be that gaining the wildcard berth would be more advantageous. Instead of playing the always troublesome Rangers, the Yankees would face the Twins—a team still beset by key injuries, and a team against which New York has traditionally had great success.

September 24–26, Boston Red Sox @ Yankee Stadium

Burnett had nothing and was lifted after 3 ⅔ innings on the short end of a 7-1 count. Albie's task was to eat up some innings, which he did but only after giving up a three-run HR. Grade: F.

Sergio Mitre hadn't pitched in eleven days, but his sinker was moving both horizontally (left to right) and vertically. Plus, his extraneous body movement was not in evidence. That's why his two-hit, two-inning stint earned him an A-.

A barrage of home runs—two each by A-Rod and Teixeira, plus one each from Swisher and Granderson—tightened the score, and brought Wood into the game at the top of the 8th. Although the Sox didn't score a run, they cracked a pair of sizzling line-drive outs. Wood was gone when two LH hitters were due up, after he began the 9th with a walk and a strikeout. Wood's grade: B.

Logan came on to easily handle LH Ortiz and LH Lars Anderson, thereby earning an A. (Anderson played well in that Scranton-Pawtucket game. He'll stay up in the bigs.)

Boston 10, New York 8

Bullpen diary: Credit the lineup for not giving up. In fact, with two out in the 9th, Cano represented the tying run when he missed an in-the-dirt splitter from Papelbon to end the game.

Pennant race: Yanks fall a half game back.

Game Two vs. the Red Sox in the Bronx, September 25

Ultimately another disappointing outing by Nova as the Yankees continued to stagger toward the finish line. Nova left after 4 2/3 innings behind 3-0, reemphasizing his inability to maintain his concentration when pitching out of the stretch.

Ring was brought in to have a go at Ortiz and was spanked for an RBI groundball single. Ring: D+.

Gaudin was Boston's next victim, and he let the game get totally out of hand, giving up two singles, back-to-back HRs, and a HBP, and was lucky when three rockets were caught in the deep reaches of the outfield. Still another F for Gaudin. Romulo Sanchez walked the first two hitters he faced to load the bases. He recovered by resorting almost exclusively to sliders, cutters, and change-ups, closing the inning with a pair of strikeouts. Sanchez's grade: C+. With his two-seamer showing some life, Albaladejo gave up a solid double, and was hit hard, but managed to pitch a scoreless top of the 8th. Albie's grade: C.

Chamberlain's first pitch in the top of the 9th was belted for a solid double, as was his fourth pitch. Two strikeouts and a groundout couldn't save him from getting an F.

Boston 7, New York 2

Bullpen diary: Ring's second audition was ultimately a failure, yet certainly warranted another look-see. When Gaudin gets hit, he gets hit hard. Sanchez's delivery was even more effortful than Chamberlain's. Albaladejo seemed much more comfortable, especially since his two-seamer produced two routine groundballs.

With the notable exception of Joba, none of the other five pitchers appearing in this game is a probable for the playoff roster.

The Yankees' loss was their fourth straight at home, and their thirteenth in their last nineteen games. Not so suddenly, the Yankees' pitching has nosedived. Plus, in the last two games, home runs have provided the only runs they've scored.

Pennant race: Yanks fall 1½ behind the Rays.

Game Three vs. the Red Sox in the Bronx, September 26

Girardi had previously announced that Moseley would be the starter as he positioned his rotation for the playoffs. But with the Yankees still needing a combination of three wins and Red Sox losses to clinch a berth in the playoffs, he went with Hughes.

Girardi's vehement denial that this was a "panic" move indicates that it most certainly was.

In any event, Hughes was brilliant, allowing one run and three hits over six innings. He was relieved by Robertson when he opened the top of the 7th by walking the first two hitters he faced. Robertson managed to keep the Yankees' deficit to 1-0 and thereby earned himself an A.

A home run by A-Rod gave the Bombers a 2-1 edge, but Wood allowed a leadoff single and was shaky in the top of the 8th. After delivering an intentional pass to Ortiz, Wood was lifted with runners on 1B and 2B. Wood: C+.

Rivera hadn't pitched in five days, so a prospective four-out save was certainly in order. And Mo got off to a good start when he worked Beltre in and out and eventually ended the threat by inducing a harmless grounder.

However, Mo then fell apart in the top of the 9th. A hard-hit fly-ball was caught in deep RF to begin the inning. Then a single, two stolen bases, and another hit tied the game. Two more steals allowed a sacrifice fly to put the Red Sox ahead 3-2 before a flyball ended the disastrous inning. An F for Mo.

However, the Yanks tied the game at 3-all against Papelbon in the bottom of the 9th, and Joba came on to get a pair of uncomplicated outs to start the 10th. Chamberlain's grade: A. Logan then earned his keep by getting Ortiz on an easy bouncer. An A for Logan.

The Yanks prevailed in the bottom of the 10th, winning on a bases-loaded, two-out walk to Juan Miranda.

New York 4, Boston 3 (10 innings)

Winning Pitcher: Logan (2-0)

Bullpen diary: Up until this game, Yankee relievers had allowed only 29.8 percent of inherited runners to score—third best in the AL. Despite Wood's somewhat erratic performance, he had now made twenty-one appearances without allowing a run. Credit Eiland for instigating another mechanical tweak in Wood's delivery. Whereas Wood used to lean his body slightly toward first as he released the ball, now his moving parts were on a straight line pointing toward the plate.

Mo's dismal outing represented his fourth blown save in September.

Pennant race: The Yankees' magic number for making the playoffs is now only 1. Yet, to a man, they insist that their goal is to beat out the Rays. The Rays lost, so Yanks are just a half game back.

September 27–29 @ Rogers Centre

Just when Burnett needed to demonstrate that he should be numbered among the starters in the opening round of the playoffs, he got clobbered for seven hits and seven runs in only 2⅓ innings. Albaladejo took over and, with his four-seamer topping at 93 mph, he zipped through the rest of the inning. Albie: A. Moseley then finessed his way through two scoreless innings. A- for Dustin.

HRs by Granderson and Teixeira made the score 7-5.

Robertson hurled 1⅓ scoreless innings, getting touched for only a solitary base hit. In truth, two of his outs came on his outfielders running down long drives to the deepest reaches of fair territory. Another out came when Wells foolishly attempted to stretch his double into a triple. To begin the bottom of the 8th, Robertson retired John Buck when A-Rod made a nice catch and throw of a scorched grounder. Despite the harmless results, Robertson's grade: D+.

Logan used a whip-like slider to pop up LH Lind and earn his third consecutive A.

Gaudin was then brought in to pitch to the dangerous Eduardo Encarnacion, who just missed losing a one-and-one 93-mph fastball that Granderson ran down against the CF wall. Gaudin's grade: B.

Toronto 7, New York 5

Bullpen diary: Before the game, Mo had a rare bullpen session with Eiland. The astute coach had noticed that Mo's grip had slipped so that he was no longer on top of the ball when he released it. This caused his cutter to be flat and situated dangerously high in the K-zone. And that's why Rivera's ERA over his last six appearances had been an astronomical 9.63!

Pennant race: Yanks remain a half game back.

Game Two @ Toronto, September 28

Sabathia overwhelmed the Jays en route to clinching the wildcard spot with an 8⅓ inning, two-hit, one-run effort. The Yankees led 6-1 when he wearied in the bottom of the 9th and delivered two free passes, causing Rivera to be summoned to get the last two outs in a nonsave situation. Here's what resulted after six of Rivera's cutters: a smoking drive by Wells that was right at Gardner in LF, and a hard-hit grounder that needed a dive by A-Rod to make the grab and the off-balance throw that ended the game. Mo's grade: B-.

New York 6, Toronto 1

Bullpen diary: After two remedial sessions with Eiland, it sure didn't look as though Rivera was any sharper than he had been lately.
Pennant race: Yanks remain a half game back.

Game Three @ Toronto, September 29

This was Vazquez's turn to audition for a starting role or at least the long reliever's spot in the playoffs. Unfortunately, he failed as miserably as Burnett had done just two days before—getting pounded for ten hits (including three HRs) and seven runs in 4 2/3 innings.

Ring came on to retire Lind on a harmless grounder, thereby earning an A.

Next up was Robertson, who uncorked a 95-mph fastball that, albeit out of the K-zone, was his swiftest offering of the season. A solid single and a line-out to deep CF lowlighted Robertson's effort, earning him a B.

Chamberlain was nicked for an unearned run in the bottom of the 7th after Wells reached on a throwing error by A-Rod, stole 2B, advanced to 3B on a wild pitch, and scored on a two-out single smacked on a 95-mph fastball that would have missed Cervelli's target by at least eighteen inches. The whiffs registered by Joba failed to elevate his grade above B-.

Sergio Mitre's sinkers were darting as though they were electrified. His three strikeouts—all of them on swings and misses—constituted his best performance of the season. Mitre: A.

Toronto 8, New York 4

Bullpen diary: Ring's fastball sat at 85 mph, but because of his almost sidearm delivery, lefties had trouble picking up the ball. Mitre made an impressive bid to be the last man out of the bullpen when the extra games commence.

Pennant race: Yanks remain a half game back. Girardi's insistence that his aim is to win the division title was reinforced when he played his regular infield for the entire game. And first place remains extremely doable since the Rays were playing almost as poorly as the Yankees.

Around the league: The Rangers won in improbable fashion. Nelson Cruz swung at and missed a third strike in the dirt, the Mariners catcher threw the ball wild to first, and Mitch Moreland came around to score from first. A walk-off strikeout. We've seen it all this year.

October 1–3 @ Fenway

The opening game of the last regular season series was rained out, prompting a doubleheader on October 2, with the first game starting at 4:00 P.M. and the nightcap scheduled to commence at 9:00.

It would be a very, very, very long day and night.

Because the Rays were getting beaten up in Kansas City, a sweep of the series would have given the Yankees the AL East title, home field advantage throughout the AL playoffs, and the Rangers as their initial opponents.

However, Pettitte's performance in the first game was even more significant than the still scrambled postseason permutations. Although he couldn't quite get a handle on his cutter, he did a passable job through 4+ innings—9 hits, 3 runs, 8 Ks, and 88 pitches, with the Yankees up 5–3.

Dave Robertson likewise battled with his command, striking out the side, while walking two. After a spinning curve was smoked for a single to start the 6th, Martinez lifted a flyball to medium-deep RF, and Robertson got the hook. His grade: B.

Boone Logan's heater reached 96 mph, quick enough to overpower Ortiz and force an easy double play to end the inning. But he was lifted after delivering a walk to LH Lars Anderson to commence the bottom of the 7th. Logan: B

Even though Chamberlain's first pitch was clocked at 98 mph, Bill Hall banged it into CF for a solid single. A subsequent wild pitch scored the runner Joba had inherited from Logan, but three quick outs limited the damage and registered a B- in Joba's ledger.

In the bottom of the 8th, Wood endured his most unsuccessful outing in pinstripes. Three walks, two Ks, with one run plating on an infield grounder, and the third out only coming when a foolish runner tried to score after Posada made a wild throw to 3B and A-Rod made a quick recovery to nail the potential go-ahead run at the plate.

The gift out kept the score knotted at 5-all, but couldn't raise Wood's grade of F.

Hughes worked the 9th in easy fashion, going almost exclusively with a fastball that ranged from 93 to 94 mph. Hughes' grade: A.

The Yankees tallied the winning run in the top of the 10th, and Rivera's new/old-grip cutter was a blast from the past as he breezed through a 1-2-3 inning. A back-to-reality A for Mo.

New York 6, Boston 5 (10 innings)
Winning Pitcher: Hughes (18-8)
Save: Rivera (33)
Bullpen diary: Joba's erratic outing was symptomatic of his entire season. Wood couldn't find the strike zone with a GPS. Hughes was razor-sharp in his brief tune-up for whatever role he'll fulfill in the ALDS. Rivera's cutter had the old-time snap, as demonstrated by the requisite broken bat that resulted from a jammed cutter.

Game Two @ Boston, October 2

The second game began about forty-five minutes later, with Burnett being given one last chance to prove that he deserved a start in the ALDS. And he was better than he had been, although he did yield four runs (only two earned) in six innings. Burnett left with the game tied at 4, but the Yankees scored two in the top of the 7th.

Mitre took the ball in the bottom of the 7th and kept Burnett's erstwhile win intact with a strikeout and a groundout. Mitre's grade: A.

A well-placed 80-mph fastball from Royce Ring got J.D. Drew to end the inning with a groundout. Then he greatly reduced his chances of making the ALDS squad when he started the 8th with a walk and then was smacked for a solid single by LH Ryan Kalish. An F for Ring, with only one more game to make his case.

Nova pumped his fastballs at 95–97 mph, but walked a batter to fill the bases before allowing the tying run to score when he issued another free pass. Nova did show some mettle by escaping from a bases-loaded one-out dilemma with a strikeout and a comebacker. Nova returned to the mound in the bottom of the 9th and issued two more walks but stranded them both by producing three flyballs.

In the bottom of the 10th, though, a leadoff double, succeeded by a sacrifice bunt and a single, ended the game and gave Nova an F at around 2 A.M.

Boston 7, New York 6 (10 innings)

Losing Pitcher: Nova (1-2)

Bullpen diary: Girardi was understandably unwilling to use his A-1 relievers twice within eight hours. With another A-OK outing, Mitre has emerged as the hot arm in the bullpen. Ring didn't throw hard enough to make his sidewinding delivery effective. Nova lost his steam after finishing the bottom of the 8th. In the two succeeding stanzas, his fastball never got quicker than 93 and sat at 91 mph.

Pennant race: After this long night's journey into day, the Yanks and the Rays are tied for first in the AL East. Since Tampa Bay holds the tiebreaker (beating New York 10-8 in head-to-head confrontations), only a Yankee win and a Rays loss can put the Bronx Bombers at the top of the AL East standings.

⚾ LONGTIME NEW York baseball writer Maury Allen died of cancer today. He was one of the best, and his colleagues thought so, too. He was a Baseball Hall of Fame voter, was given a Lifetime Achievement Award by the Society of Silurians, a longtime journalism group, and was inducted into the City College Hall of Fame, the International Jewish Sports Hall of Fame, and others.

Game Three @ Boston, October 3—Game 162 of the regular season

By default, Moseley was the starter and was decidedly mediocre. Smacked for a pair of HRs, Moseley left after five innings with the Bosox ahead 4-2.

Ring's last chance came against Ortiz. But with the infield drastically shifted toward RF, and with A-Rod stationed where the SS would normally be, Ortiz bunted Ring's first pitch toward 3B and could have crawled to 1B (which wouldn't have been much faster than Big Papi at full gallop). Because of the highly unusual circumstance, Ring rated a gentleman's C.

Robertson suffered from a total lack of command of his fastball, and also from brain lock. After walking Hall, getting pinged for an RBI single, then whiffing Jason Varitek, Robertson failed to check the runner on 2B and was victimized by a double steal. Another walk and Robertson was hooked with another F on his résumé.

Logan gave up a sac fly to Anderson and, with runners on 1B and 2B, the Red Sox initiated another double steal. There were two out, a lefty was at the bat, the lead runner had the base stolen, yet Posada threw to 2B—a weak throw that bounced away from Jeter and allowed the Sox to extend their lead to 7-2. Logan finally ended the track meet–cum–circus with a K. Logan: A-.

Joba worked the bottom of the 7th and struck out the side—after the leadoff hitter had smacked a spinning slider into the RF stands. The one bad pitch gave Chamberlain a D+.

Mitre finished the game and the regular season by continuing his hot streak—two groundouts and a flyball, thereby earning his third consecutive A.

Boston 8, New York 4

Bullpen diary: Robertson had no command of his fastball, suggesting that his arm was tired. Would Girardi dare go with Mitre instead of

Robertson in the ALDS? Not likely. During Logan's stint, Posada demonstrated for the nth time that his fielding is way below par. Same-old same-old inconsistency for Joba.

Next up: The Twins in Minnesota three days hence.

AL EAST

TB 96–66

NY 95–67

September–October Bullpen Scorecard

Phil Hughes (2 appearances): 3.87 = A–
Sergio Mitre (5): 3.4 = B+
Kerry Wood (10): 3.25 = B+
Boone Logan (15): 2.7 = B–
Joba Chamberlain (14): 2.67 = B–
Mariano Rivera (10): 2.3 = C+
Royce Ring (4): 2.3 = C+
David Robertson (14): 2.26 = C+
Romulo Sanchez (1): 2.25 = C+
Jonathan Albaladejo (7): 1.96 = C–
Chad Gaudin (8): 1.75 = C–
Dustin Moseley (3): 1.25 = D+
Javier Vazquez (2): 1.25 = D+
Ivan Nova (1): 0 = F
TOTAL: 2.45 = C+

Subpar performances by such mainstays as Rivera and Robertson failed to rescue the team when the starting pitchers faltered down the stretch. Moreover, because Pettitte was shaky in his return to action, while Burnett, Vazquez, and Moseley were downright awful, it's no wonder that the Yankees split their final twenty-four games.

PART THREE

Meeting Don Larsen, final grades, the playoffs,
the Yankees' team-building philosophy, predictions
for 2011, and my stadium tryout

Memory Lane

An Imperfect Day, Don Larsen, and Me

The Yankees have all the hits.

—MEL ALLEN, DURING LARSEN'S PERFECT GAME

The significance of an individual's whereabouts on specific historical occasions varies according to generational interests. Where were you when you heard about Pearl Harbor and the A-bombing of Hiroshima? The assassinations of JFK, MLK, and RFK? 9/11?

In the much more innocent days of my childhood, the key events that evoked the same kind of interest had to do with Bobby

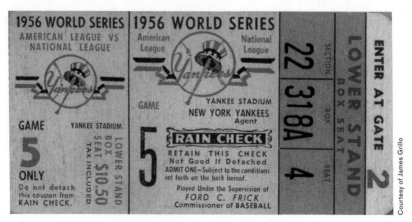

1956 World Series Game Five ticket

Courtesy of James Grillo

Thomson's Shot Heard 'Round the World. Being an ultra-orthodox Yankee fan then-now-and-always, the ten-year-old me ignored the Giant-Dodger playoff and was hitting fungos with two of my peers in Crotona Park.

"DiMaggio swings . . . And it's a long flyball to deep left field! It's going, going . . . Oh! . . . Nice catch, Jeff!"

Ah, but on October 8, 1956, I was fifteen and a senior at Theodore Roosevelt High School. And since some of our more humane teachers had TV sets wheeled into their classrooms so we could watch the Bronx Bombers in their annual World Series appearances, I was well aware that Don Larsen was pitching a perfect game.

When school finally let out, the Yankees led 1-0 and were at bat in the bottom of the 5th inning, and I was faced with a difficult choice:

I could impatiently ride the Third Avenue El for three stops, then run the two blocks to my apartment and watch the rest of the game.

I could walk the four blocks to the Tremont Branch of the New York Public Library and diligently work my regularly scheduled Monday afternoon duties as a clerk.

As a shelver of returned books, I had mixed feelings about my job: the grown-ups' books were packed into stolid walnut bookcases and the head librarian, Miss Wheatley, always insisted that each binding be placed flush with the front edge of the shelf. Nearest the windows were long tables where old men came to read *The Forward* backward and scholars to do term papers.

Miss Wheatley habitually sat in her tailored suits behind a large semicircular desk. Inside a dark drawer, she kept the only key to the dirty-book cabinet—mostly James Joyce, Henry Miller, the Marquis de Sade, and Jack London's *The Iron Heel*. The silence in the Adult Section was a benediction, the books thick, meaningful, and easily stacked in their proper places.

Unfortunately, most of my assigned hours were spent working in the Children's Room.

Upstairs, the sun shone hotly through a battery of large windows.

The bookcases were lower to the floor level and the books thinner. Mrs. Glazer was in charge there, a middle-aged matron who shushed the kids but also let them buzz about the room.

"Charles," she always said to me, "the books must be replaced properly on the shelves or else the poor little dears will never find what they want."

The older kids wanted to read John Tunis' Blue Sox series, Joseph Altsheler's pioneer novels, encyclopedias, *Tom Swift and His Electric Grandmother*, *Nancy Drew and the Mayonnaise Murders*. But the little ones drove me nuts.

"Where's *Curious George Goes to the Hospital?*"

"I can't find *A Is for Apple.*"

"I want *The Little Engine That Could.*"

"Where's *Inside, Outside, Upside Down?*"

The kiddies would pull out an armful of books, then sprawl on the benches reading and laughing. "Hey, Junior," I'd say. "Have yourself a good time, but please put those books back when you're finished, okay?"

Scrabbling on my hands and knees, pulling B's out of G's, sorting alphas from omegas. "Hey, kid. That's not where you found those books, right?"

In a dusty shaft of sunlight, juggling books for a crowd of mindless midgets. "Hey. Didn't I just ask you nicely to put those books back?"

Every so often, Mrs. Glazer browsed through the bookshelves I'd just "tidied." Checking up on me while I tried to form perfect order from total chaos.

"Hey, bozo," I'd whisper harshly to a brawling little urchin. "It's a nice day outside. Why don't you go play in the park?"

But on that particular Monday I was scheduled to work downstairs in the cool, quiet Adult Section—a treat that was dispensed about once every two weeks.

After much internal debate, I dutifully went to work for several reasons: The money I'd be forfeiting if I failed to show—three hours at seventy-five cents per. And the odds were astronomical that Larsen would pitch a no-hitter, much less a perfect game, since neither of these feats of brilliance had ever been achieved in the previous fifty-two years of World Series competition.

Plus, I trusted that, whatever Larsen might accomplish, there was no way my hometown heroes would lose Game Five at Yankee Stadium and thereby gain a 3-2 edge in the series. I even thought about playing hooky to eyeball the clinching game on Tuesday afternoon.

In my journeys around through the stacks, I'd surreptitiously ask what seemed to be an occasional kindly adult male after the Yankees score. But the eggheads who were perusing the books instead of watching the game had no idea.

It was only when I dashed home at the end of my shift that my mother, who was a diehard Dodgers fan solely on the basis of the Bums' having signed Jackie Robinson, sadly informed me of Larsen's monumental achievement.

My heart ached for years afterward, with my only consolation being that Larsen would certainly have failed if I had chosen to watch the rest of the game.

⚾ FAST-FORWARD twenty-five years.

I was living in Woodstock, New York, and had stopped by a sporting goods store in nearby Kingston to replenish my supply of sweat socks. Imagine my surprise when a sign in the window announced that Don Larsen was on hand to personally autograph the famous photo of his delivering the called third strike to pinch hitter Dale Mitchell that would end the game and secure his baseball immortality. Since the cost was a mere ten dollars, I moved to the end of the surprisingly short line.

When I finally arrived face to face with Larsen, he looked weary and at least ten years older than his chronological age of sixty-seven. I handed my ten-spot to a clerk as Larsen sighed and, without glancing at me, said, "What's your name?"

After I supplied the information, I said this: "You know, one of the great tragedies of my youth was that I went to my after-school job instead of going home and watching the end of the game."

With that, he looked up and fully registered my presence.

"You know something?" he said. "I must've signed a million of these things over the years, and you're one of only a handful of guys who were old enough to've been around then that admit that they missed the game."

He told the attending clerk to return my money, and then he reached out to shake my hand.

Even all these years later, the picture is mounted in the place of honor above my computer, and whenever I look at the photo, my right hand still tingles from the living touch of one of the most revered gods in the Yankee pantheon.

Bullpen Grades for the Entire Regular Season

Mariano Rivera (61 appearances): 2.8 = B-
A's: 32 F's: 6

His age increasingly became a factor as the season wore on. He pitched A ball in April, and faded to a B- for the season. While Mo's velocity remained fairly constant (90–92 mph), both the movement and the command of his cutter noticeably diminished. In fact, Rivera became increasing mortal after pitching into his second inning in Texas on September 11—a game that he lost after hitting a batter with the bases loaded. Using Rivera at that time was ill-advised, primarily because Mo had made twenty-three pitches the night before.

Joba Chamberlain (73 appearances): 2.6 = C+
A's: 26 F's: 13

An unacceptable 2:1 ratio of brilliant outings to miserable ones. Failed to make the necessary adjustments to slow his delivery, and failed to keep his front shoulder closed and therefore get more life into his high-octane fastballs. Made too many mistakes with both his heaters and his sliders. His inconsistency made him too untrustworthy to fit into a consistent role. Once Wood arrived, Joba was strictly a utility guy.

Damaso Marte (30 appearances): 3.0 = B
A's: 20 F's: 5

Logan mostly compensated for Marte's season-ending injury, but imagine how much Girardi could have mixed and matched with two lights-out lefty specialists in the bullpen. Marte's absence might be especially costly when the Yankees face the LH-loaded Twins lineup (Mauer, Thome, Kubel, and Span) in the ALDS.

Sergio Mitre (24 appearances): 3.35 = B+

A's 11 F's: 2

Once Eiland soothed Mitre's jittery delivery, he was a monster. Mitre was held back by a lengthy midsummer's injury and also by his not being given sufficient work to stay sharp. Indeed, Mitre showed his new-true value in the stretch run, when too many of his relief mates were exhausted.

Dave Robertson (64 appearances): 2.5 = C+

A's: 24 F's: 10

A poor beginning and a poor ending, the former attributed to some flaws in his delivery, the latter to weariness. However, considering that in 2009, Robertson pitched $43\,2/3$ innings in 45 games with New York, and that he hurled $61\,1/3$ innings this season, the twenty-five-year-old simply wore down in the stretch. Proof of this was the back spasms that put him on the shelf for five games in late September.

Boone Logan (51 appearances): 2.4 = C+

A's: 15 F's: 2

Virtually all of Logan's poor outings occurred early in the season, before he had the opportunity to work on his mechanics in Scranton. As such, his slider became tighter, his fastball faster, and his command was greatly improved. After he was brought up for good on July 17, Logan's grade was 3.0 (B), while he accumulated fourteen of his A grades as against only a single F. Logan was one of the heroes of the bullpen through the last eleven weeks of the season. Who could have anticipated that while Logan was merely a throw-in in the Melky Cabrera–for–Vazquez deal?

Kerry Wood (22 appearances with New York): 3.1 = B+
A's: 6 F's: 1

Guaranteed, the Yanks would never have qualified for the playoffs without Wood. Credit Cashman for the move, credit Eiland for raising his release point, and credit Wood for taking full advantage of the opportunity. With his curveball able to confound LH hitters, his fastball topping at 95 mph, and his cutter alive and kicking, Wood will be an attractive free agent after the season.

Alfredo Aceves (10 appearances): 2.8 = B-
A's: 4 F's: 1

Ace's aching back caused the Yankees to suffer greatly because neither Moseley nor Gaudin could adequately replace him as the long reliever and spot starter.

Ivan Nova (3 appearances): 2.58 = C+
A's: 1 F's: 1

Had the stuff, but lacked consistency and durability. At age twenty-three, Nova was not yet ready for prime time.

Jonathan Albaladejo (10 appearances): 2.4 = C+
A's: 2 F's: 0

Poor control, command, and poise. Also, his slow delivery allows runners to run amok. Albie is an exceptional Triple-A closer but, at the relatively advanced age of twenty-seven, that may be his limit.

Royce Ring (5 appearances): 2.25 = C+
A's: 2 F's: 1

For a reputed curveball pitcher, Royce had immense difficulty getting his out-pitch even near the strike zone. Even against LH hitters, his virtual sidearm delivery wasn't tricky enough for his 81–85 mph fastball to be effective against anybody but the most overzealous rookies.

Chad Gaudin (42 appearances): 2.1 = C

A's: 8 F's: 7

Most of his mistakes were high in the strike zone—and wound up high in the grandstand seats. Gaudin's slightly above-average stuff necessitated exceptional control for him to succeed on a regular basis.

Dustin Moseley (7 relief appearances): 2.1 = C

A's: 2 F's: 3

Needed to have pinpoint command to get anybody out. His cutter frequently moved nicely but too often was a dead fish. Gone and quickly forgotten.

Chan Ho Park (27 appearances): 2.2 = C+

A's: 8 F's: 4

Lost his outstanding fastball and couldn't get by on a consistent basis with his mediocre cutters, sliders, curves, and changes. One of Cashman's major off-season boo-boos.

Javier Vazquez (5 relief appearances): 2.1 = C

A's: 3 F's: 0

Like Park, Vazquez lost his fastball while transitioning from the NL to the AL. His three A's came on isolated (and brief) outings in midseason. In September, his auditioning for a long-relief role in the ALDS (or even in the future) was profoundly unsuccessful.

Phil Hughes (2 relief appearances): 3.87 = A-

A's: 1 F's: 0

Briefly reprising his 2009 role as a reliever, Hughes excelled in both emergency situations. Clearly, though, he's much more valuable as a starter.

Romulo Sanchez (2 appearances): 3.0 = B

Electric stuff. So-so command. At twenty-six, he should be much more seasoned than he is. Can't be trusted in anything but mop-up tours in the big leagues.

Mark Melancon (2 appearances): 1.5 = D+

His sinker was too light to be effective in the bigs.

Season Total: 2.59 = C+

A's: 148   F's: 54

A high-average collective performance by the gentlemen of the Yankees bullpen. Good enough to help boost the Yankees into a wildcard berth.

The starters carried them early in the season, while they returned the favor later on. Only Logan and Wood were reliable from late August through game 162.

But that was then, and the playoffs are now. Which, if any, of the relievers will emerge as heroes? And which might make their marks as goats?

The Playoffs

- How all eight teams' bullpens performed.
- More insight into the Yanks' pen of the future.

Good pitching will beat good hitting anytime, and vice versa.
—CREDITED TO SEVERAL PEOPLE

A few surprises in the roster Girardi and Eiland brainstormed for the Minnesota series. Rivera, Robertson, Logan, Wood, and Chamberlain were automatics for the bullpen. Since the Yankees will go with a three-man starting rotation—Sabathia, Pettitte, and Hughes—Burnett was included for possible use in long relief, or if a strikeout was needed very early in the proceedings to keep a man on 3B with less than two outs. The prospect of Burnett's going all-out to face one hitter was certainly appealing. Or else as another alternative in extended extra innings.

Mitre was among the chosen, an alert selection. Would he be the primary long guy?

The only reliever who didn't seem to belong was Moseley. If Burnett and Mitre were available to finish up short appearances by any of the starters (heaven forbid), then why pick Moseley? Since the Twins lineup is loaded with lefties, why not take a chance on Ring? The thinking must have been along these lines: Since Sabathia and Pettitte will each go twice if the series lasts the full five games, and since both can be presumed to throw at least 100+ pitches, then Logan will suffice. Another factor had to be the realization that Wood's curves and cutters have virtually nullified lefties.

In any case, the less work that the relievers get (with the exception of Mo), the better the chances of the Yankees surviving the ALDS.

ALDS Game One @ Minnesota, October 6

Not having worked in seven days, it was understandable that Sabathia was less than razor-sharp. After walking in the tying run, his stat line included 6 innings, 4 runs, and 111 pitches. However, Teixeira smacked a super-clutch two-run HR in the top of the 7th to put NY up 6-4 and make Sabathia the pitcher of record.

Logan was the first candidate to keep Sabathia's potential win viable, and he began the bottom of the 7th by getting LH Denard Span to loft a wicked slider to CF. Then Orlando Hudson bounced a 94-mph fastball to Cano for the second out. But Logan couldn't put away Joe Mauer when five consecutive 1-2 offerings were fouled off. Mauer finally lashed a slider for a base hit through the right side of the infield. Logan's grade: C+.

(Note: During the playoffs, grades will be influenced more by a pitcher's being able to get key outs than by his overall performance.)

Dave Robertson reported for duty and his first obstacle was RH Delmon Young. Since Young is notorious for swinging at the first pitch he sees, Robertson began the sequence with a bouncing curve. Unfortunately, the two subsequent 94-mph fastballs likewise missed the strike zone, and Young was the beneficiary of a six-pitch walk.

However, in a most crucial situation, Robertson disposed of Thome, who fruitlessly waved at a 1-2 curve in the dirt. The big-time out earned Robertson an A.

In the bottom of the 8th, Wood punched out Cuddyer with a 95-mph heater before walking LH Kubel. Then Danny Valencia was fooled on a cutter but hit a perfectly placed nubber that went for an infield single. Some of the pressure was alleviated when J.J.

Hardy bounced out, recording the second out but moving both runners into scoring position.

Wood wasn't hit hard, but his walking Kubel reduced his grade to C-.

Then came Mo-time. Rivera sought to jam Span with cutters, but went to 3-0 before he found the range. Eventually, Span smacked a sharp grounder to Jeter and the potential tying run was stranded.

In the bottom of the 9th, Rivera went in and out against Hudson and got him on a weak grounder. Mauer was easy pickings, hitting a comebacker on a cutter. Then came Young, who cracked a 93-mph sinker to short RF. Golson charged the ball and made a shoestring catch, but the six blind mice huddled and decided that Golson had trapped the ball. Replays clearly demonstrated their collective miscall.

Up stepped the mighty Thome, whose HR bat represented the tying run. The suspense was short-lived, though, when he popped a cutter to A-Rod to preserve the win for the Yankees and Sabathia. Mo registered his fortieth career save in postseason play, and reverted to his standard A form.

New York 6, Minnesota 4

Save: Rivera (1)

New York leads best-of–5 series 1-0

Bullpen diary: During the course of his four-out save, Rivera broke four bats! Also, his cutter was simply alive, and the new Mo looked like the Mo of old.

Of note: Roy Halladay threw a no-hitter today against the Reds, just two days shy of the anniversary of Don Larsen's October 8, 1956, game for the ages.

Game Two @ Minnesota, October 7

Pettitte's strong performance was another blast from the past. He was replaced by Wood after pitching seven innings with the Yankees up 4-2.

Wood was simply sensational. Only one of his nine offerings missed the K-zone. Showing all the weapons in his arsenal, he struck out two and was credited with an A.

The Yanks tacked on another run before Rivera climbed the hill. The Twins' best batter, Mauer, managed a handle-hit to LF before he was erased on a quick twin-killing. Thome then skied to LF to put a lock on the game. Mo needed only thirteen pitches to gain his latest A.

New York 5, Minnesota 2

Save: Rivera (2)

New York leads 2-0

Bullpen diary: Today's biggest hits were provided by Lance Berkman: a long HR plus a two-bagger that drove in what proved to be the winning run. And this latter hit was illuminating:

Game one had been extended when Golson's shoestring catch of a liner had been erroneously ruled a base hit. Rivera was then faced with the prospect of Thome representing the tying run—but one more pitch produced a simple flyball and the game was history.

In a crucial at-bat in game two, the home plate ump blew what should have been a third-strike call against Berkman. But where Mo simply persevered and got the job done the day before, Carl Pavano was shaken by the miscall. Berkman then blasted Pavano's very next pitch for his RBI double.

Stuff and command are vital aspects of a pitcher's repertoire, but nothing trumps poise.

Game Three vs. Twins in the Bronx, October 9

Relying on his bull's-eye fastballs, Hughes dominated through seven shutout innings, leaving on the long end of a 6-0 score.

Wood succeeded Hughes and got thumped. The specifics: a double, a flyball that was tracked down in deep RF, a single on a rolling curve, an RBI single, and a walk. The score was 6-1, with the bases loaded and one out, when Kerry took his F to the showers and was relieved by Logan.

One pitch—a 94-mph fastball—to Kubel resulted in a pop-up that froze the runners and gave Logan an A. Robertson was then called upon to squash the threat. Which he did by dispatching Delmon Young on a flyball. Robertson's grade: A.

Rivera breezed through the 9th, thereby earning his third A in three games.

New York 6, Minnesota 1
New York wins series 3-0
Bullpen diary: Wood's only curve was a spinner that was lashed for two bases; his two cutters were both strikes, but his fastballs (eighteen of them) were routinely off-target. Logan didn't work up a sweat, and Robertson's heaters clocked at 93 mph and were perfectly situated. Mo was Mo.

⚾ WELL, THAT was easy. The Yankees played better than their late-season swoon indicated, and where the Bronx Bombers came up with several clutch hits, the Twins were always a base hit short in every game.

The cumulative grades of the Yankees' relievers came out to B+ (3.2), including seven A's and one F.

Joba never got any game-burn and has been totally supplanted by the combination of Wood and Robertson. Undoubtedly, Chamberlain will see action, since the ALCS is a seven-game set.

⚾ MIKE LOPRESTI noted in *USA Today* that the Twins were the thirteenth team to get into the postseason in the first year of a new park. The previous teams, the Yanks and Cards, went on to win the World Series. Not this time.

Other Games, Other Pens

While the Yankees were uncoupling the Twins, three other play-off series were being contested. Here's how the bullpens of the teams involved fared under the pressure:

Philadelphia

With Roy Halladay hurling a no-hitter in game one and Cole Hamels going the route in game three, the relievers only appeared in the middle game of the series.

J.C. Romero, Chad Durbin, Jose Contreras, Ryan Madson, and Brad Lidge combined to pitch four shutout innings, allowing one hit and two walks, while whiffing a pair.

Lidge, Philly's closer, got the save. And the win was credited to ex-Yankee Contreras.

Cincinnati

The Reds got good production from their bullpen. Travis Wood, Logan Ondrusek, and Bill Bray pitched a total of 6 1/3 shutout innings in the opener.

Art Rhodes, Ondrusek, and Chapman combined for 1 1/3 innings in game two, but phenom Chapman was the victim of three unearned runs and was tagged with the loss.

In the finale, Homer Bailey, Bray, Nick Masset, and Aroldis Chapman came up with four shutout innings.

Texas

Alexi Ogando, Darren Oliver, Neftali Feliz, and Darren O'Day did the job as the Rangers won the two opening games. Together they allowed zilch in 4 2/3 innings. Ogando and O'Day continued their lockdown performances in game three with two-thirds of a scoreless inning.

But the Rangers' firemen were instrumental in igniting conflagrations in games three and four. Derek Holland was the loser in the former, while Feliz and Dustin Nippert combined to yield 8 hits and 5 runs in 3 2/3 innings.

O'Day continued his flawless work with a shutout frame in game four, but Holland was pounded for 5 hits and 2 runs in 4 innings.

Atlanta

Good jobs in games one through three by Jonny Venters, Peter Moylan, Mike Dunn, Craig Kimbrel, Billy Wagner, and Kyle Farnsworth, to the tune of ten scoreless innings.

In fact, Farnsworth (another ex-Yankee) was credited with the win in game two.

But Kimbrel broke the streak by yielding two runs in two-thirds of an inning in game three, and getting tagged with the loss.

In manager Bobby Cox's swan song, Moylan, Venters, and Kimbrel held the Giants at bay for 2 ⅔ innings, but the lineup couldn't muster enough offense to prevail.

San Francisco

Tim Lincecum went the distance in game one, but Sergio Romo, Brian Wilson, and Ramon Ramirez were smoked for four hits and four runs in four innings as Ramirez took the loss in game two.

Even though Romo gave up a late-game HR that tied game three (and was therefore discredited with a blown save), he got the win when the Giants won the game in the bottom of the 8th. Wilson earned the save with a one-hit 9th.

Javier Lopez, Santiago Casilla, and Wilson secured the series, clinching game four by combining for three shutout innings, with Wilson getting his second save of the series.

Tampa Bay

Randy Choate, Grant Balfour, Jeff Nieman, Dan Wheeler, and Joaquin Benoit all pitched well (and often) vs. the Rangers. Only Chad Qualls and closer Rafael Soriano were routinely smacked around.

🔵 HOWEVER, THE relievers that most immediately concerned the Yankees were the Rangers' bullpen staff. Here's how a scout analyzed them:

Alexi Ogando: "Has great pure stuff featuring a 94–98 mph fastball, a power slider and a splitter. If he gets ahead in the count, he's dangerous. So strike one will be an issue. Look for the Yankees to jump on his first-pitch fastballs."

Neftali Feliz: "Another power arm who can get up into the high 90s. Not a command-command guy, so he makes occasional mistakes up in the strike zone." (He would go on to win the AL Rookie of the Year award.)

Darren O'Day: "A flip-flop, underhand situational righty. He'll throw his Frisbees up there and get double-plays if guys try to pull him. RH hitters have to lay off the marginal low pitches and force him to elevate."

Darren Oliver: "He's a crafty bastard who knows how to pitch and is the primary LH out of the 'pen. His velo is nothing terrific—87–89, but he'll throw breaking stuff on fastball counts and use his change-up against RH hitters."

Derek Holland: "A power lefty with a 93–95 mph fastball and not much else. He'll be used sporadically because Granderson and Cano are terrific fastball hitters."

Dustin Nippert: "He's the long guy and the Yankees will be happy to see him."

"Overall, the Rangers have a bunch of relatively inexperienced power pitchers. But good hitters don't mind facing guys who can throw 95-plus, as long as they don't have another out-out pitch. The Yanks lineup should do pretty well against these guys."

ALCS Game One @ Texas, October 15

Not having pitched in nine days, Sabathia was more of a joker than an ace. His back leg was collapsing, his left shoulder was flying open, and he had trouble locating all of his pitches. The most egregious example being a 1st-inning three-run HR to Josh Hamilton on an 0-2 count when C.C. tossed a cookie down the middle instead of the change-up off the plate that he intended. Sabathia lasted only four innings, getting smacked for six hits and five runs.

With the Yanks trailing 5-0, Chamberlain took the ball in the bottom of the 5th. Joba last pitched eleven days ago and required several pitches to get command of his fastballs. But his slider was functioning from the get-go as he completed a three-up, three-down inning for his A.

Next up was Dustin Moseley, who hadn't pitched in nineteen days. But Moseley was in tip-top form. Surprisingly, his sinkers not only had serious dip but also broke smartly (and late) from left to right. Moseley complemented his bread-and-butter pitch with a change-up. Through two innings, the only blemish on his record was a runner who reached on an error. Otherwise, the six outs Moseley achieved included four whiffs. Moseley's grade: A.

In the top of the 7th, Cano blasted a solo HR to make the score 5-1.

The Yankees mounted a stirring rally in the top of the 8th against a variety of ineffective Rangers relievers who succeeded C.J. Wilson with the score now 5-2. The key hits: a two-RBI single by Rodriguez to pull the Yanks within 5-4, a game-tying single bashed by Cano, and a single to Marcus Thames that produced the go-ahead run.

With the Yanks now up 6-5, Wood took over the pitching chores in the bottom of the 8th. Wood had difficulty controlling his fastball and walked Kinsler on four pitches. However, Kinsler then committed a major faux pas when he was picked off.

Wood then gained command of his fastball, but had difficulty taming his cutter—until, that is, LH David Murphy grounded a surprise 3-2 cutter to Teixeira. To finish the inning, Julio Borbon flailed at a 93-mph fastball. Wood's grade: A.

Mo entered the fray looking for the forty-third postseason save of his career. The start of the inning was ominous when Moreland bounced a grounder through the middle and Andrus sacrificed him to 2B. But Michael Young struck out and the extremely dangerous Hamilton nubbed a lively cutter to A-Rod for the easy out.

Thus far, Mo had pitched the final outs in all of the Yankees' four 2010 postseason games, thereby earning his fourth consecutive A.

New York 6, Texas 5
Winning Pitcher: Moseley (1-0)
Save: Rivera (3)
New York leads series 1-0

Bullpen diary: For the first time all season, Chamberlain sported a small, scrabbly soul patch. Moseley was the bullpen's unlikely hero for keeping Texas from breaking the game open. Kinsler's baserunning mistake gave Wood a free out and greatly reduced his anxiety. Mo's cutters had great life and at 92 mph had much more zip than in recent outings.

New York's bullpen accounted for five scoreless innings, while the Rangers relievers suffered a disastrous meltdown.

Game Two @ Texas, October 16

Hughes threw what amounted to four-plus innings of batting practice—getting socked for ten hits (seven for extra bases) and seven runs.

Chamberlain was called upon to work the bottom of the 5th, and with his fastball topping at 95 and his slider dying as it neared the plate he had a relatively easy time, earning an A-.

Robertson followed with a productive $1\frac{1}{3}$ innings appearance. Still relying more on his curve than his heater, he was awarded an A.

Logan finished the 7th by getting RH pinch hitter Francoeur on a long flyball to deep CF and then throwing a nasty slider that RH Bengie Molina couldn't catch up with. But when Logan was worked for a nine-pitch walk by Moreland, he was lifted with a grade of B. Mitre cleaned up the mini mess by inducing a double play from Young and then whiffing Guerrero. Mitre's grade: A.

Texas 7, New York 2

Series tied 1-1

Bullpen diary: Chamberlain looked comfortable and confident. Guerrero got his base hit off Robertson on a pitcher's pitch that broke out of the K-zone. Guerrero is, of course, the best bad-ball hitter since Yogi Berra. Oddly enough, Logan had Moreland 0-2 but couldn't put him away. That's because Moreland fouled off five pitches to extend his at-bat long enough for Logan to miss the target with four fastballs. Mitre's sinkers were bottom-heavy and he got Guerrero on a disappearing slider.

🔵 THERE WAS no miracle comeback this time. Indeed, throughout the contest the lineup repeatedly failed to produce with runners in scoring position.

The pattern in game one was repeated—a poor start followed by five scoreless frames from the relievers.

With the series moving to the Bronx, the Yankees have to hope that their big-game pitcher (Pettitte) has a bigger game than the Rangers' big-game pitcher (Cliff Lee).

Game Three vs. the Rangers in the Bronx, October 18

Pettitte was brilliant, but he made one fatal mistake: an errant slider that Hamilton flicked into the RF stands to account for the only two runs Andy yielded. Meanwhile, Lee was awesome, allowing two hits and no runs, and striking out thirteen in eight innings.

Wood did keep the score close by shutting down Texas in the top of the 8th. Wood's grade: A. Logan was asked to start the top of the 9th by handling Hamilton, but a 93-mph fastball was lined into left-center for a leadoff 2B. Logan subsequently exited with a grade of F.

Robertson followed with his worst outing of the entire season: five hits and six runs in a third of an inning. What Robertson accomplished was to terminate any possibility of another Yankees rally, and also to empty the stands. Robertson: F.

After unloosing a wild pitch that plated the Rangers' 8th run, Mitre stanched the bleeding with a groundout and a flyout. Mitre's grade: B+.

Texas 8, New York 0
Texas leads series 2-1
Bullpen diary: Wood's heater topped at 95 mph and set up his other pitches. For some reason, Logan declined to throw a slider to Hamilton.

⚫ WITH GAME four imminent, Girardi and Eiland have to make a momentous decision. They had previously committed to starting Burnett, but might they go with Sabathia on three days' rest (something that C.C. has done with brilliant results in the past) to avoid getting in a 3-1 hole? That would make Sabathia available to pitch a possible game seven, also on short rest.

But assuming that Sabathia does the job tomorrow, Burnett would then have to go in game five, or else Hughes and then possibly Pettitte would have to go on three days' rest. Something that Hughes has never done, and that would also be extremely risky given Pettitte's recent injury.

It seems that Burnett is the best choice. Although he's been cuffed around for lo these many weeks (months?), A.J. has been a money pitcher in the past. Plus, with Joba, Wood, Logan, and Mo, the Yanks could piece together five or six innings if necessary.

Also, if the Yanks can't triumph in a critical matchup of Burnett and Tommy Hunter, then they don't deserve to have championship pretensions.

Game Four vs. the Rangers in the Bronx, October 19
Burnett was okay through 5 ⅔ innings. In the top of the 2nd, he walked a man, hit another, and they both scored—via a sac bunt,

a sac fly, and an infield hit. The Yankees were nursing a 3-2 lead when A.J. climbed the hill in the top of the 6th. In short order, he registered two outs and had two on with Molina due up.

However, even though he got ahead of Molina 0-2, there were red flags flying throughout the inning. Previous to the Yankees' lengthy at-bat in the bottom of the 5th, Burnett's fastball was regularly clocked at 95 mph. Throughout the top of the 6th, though, the reading was down to 90–91 mph.

Although Chamberlain was warmed in the pen and ready to go, Girardi stuck with Burnett. Unfortunately, Molina blasted a room-service 90-mph fastball for a three-run HR that put the Rangers up 5-3, and put the game in the bag.

To start the 7th, Robertson whiffed Andrus and got Young to hit a humpbacked liner to Swisher at 1B (Teixeira having left the game with a strained hamstring in the bottom of the 6th). An A for Robertson in this foreshortened stint.

Logan likewise didn't last long. Called in to deal with Hamilton, he threw a 93-mph fastball that was blasted over the friendly RF fence. Logan: F.

Chamberlain was next in line, but was unable to stem the tide. A double, a walk, and a run-producing blooper added another run before Joba struck out Murphy. After getting stung for a sharp single, Joba set down the Rangers without any further damage in the top of the 8th. Grade: C-.

The score was 7-3 when Mitre commenced the 9th by yielding a HR, a single, and another HR before retiring the side. Mitre's grade: F.

Texas 10, New York 3

Rangers lead series 3-1

Bullpen diary: Robertson's fastball showed effective cutting action— a fine comeback from his bummer the night before. Logan's initial pitch to Hamilton was a fastball that would have been a strike—if the plate were ten feet wide. Chamberlain's arm angle was slightly lower than usual, so his slider lacked bite. Mitre had nothing.

⚾ SINCE GAME one, the marshmallow-soft Yankee bats have gone 3-33 with runners in scoring position. Their bullpen was outstanding in the games in Texas, and horrible at home. And except for Pettitte's gutty performance against Lee in game three, all of the starters were ineffective.

With Teixeira now out for the duration, Swisher will play 1B. Even though Tex was hitless in the series (0-12), he was always a threat to break his mini slump in dramatic fashion, and his glove was always a factor.

Sabathia vs. Wilson in game five.

Game Five vs. Rangers in the Bronx, October 20

Sabathia didn't have his top-of-the line stuff, but there was nothing amiss with his courage. In allowing only two runs on eleven hits in six innings, C.C. made numerous clutch pitches. Meanwhile, the Yankee bats came alive, and when Wood took the ball in the top of the 7th, the hometown heroes led 6-2.

Throwing mostly 90-mph cutters to Andrus, Wood was victimized by a dribbler that went for an infield single. However, after Andrus advanced to 2B on a wild pitch, Wood picked him off, then ended the mild threat with a pair of strikeouts.

Next, Wood cruised through the top of the 8th, getting two groundouts and another K on seven pitches—all of them strikes. Wood's A was his third of the series.

The Yanks were up 7-2 when Rivera made his first appearance since game one and was at the top of his game. The only damage done was Moreland's concluding a nine-pitch battle by lacing an opposite-field single. With every at-bat, Moreland has demonstrated that he's a professional hitter. Mo's grade: A.

New York 7, Texas 2

Rangers lead series 3-2

Bullpen diary: Excepting his wild pitch, Wood's curve was sharp. Equipped with a hopping fastball, a snapping curve, a late-breaking cutter, and a slider, Wood is the rare late-inning reliever who can precisely locate four pitches.

Mo's cutter was alive and well, and he also employed a late-dipping two-seamer to effectively jam RHs Francoeur, Matt Treanor, and Andrus.

WHENEVER A key player is down and out, teammates routinely circle the wagons and play with increased focus and animation. With Teixeira's big bat absent for the duration, critical HRs were struck by Cano, Swisher, and Granderson.

Later that night the ghost of Gene Woodling appeared to me in a dream, saying that should the Yankees win game six in Texas— Hughes vs. Colby Lewis—then Pettitte will outduel Lee in game seven.

Game Six @ Texas, October 22

Hughes was jittery under pressure as the Rangers constantly had men on base and runners in scoring position. His shaky nerves were demonstrated when he uncorked a wild pitch while issuing an intentional walk to Hamilton. Still, Hughes managed to escape disaster by making several clutch pitches.

However, he was late covering 1B, thereby allowing Andrus to beat out an infield single to start the bottom of the 5th. Incidentally, while Berkman foolishly tried to make a play on the clearly out-of-reach grounder (to Cano), Teixeira would undoubtedly have stayed home and Cano's ensuing throw would easily have nipped Andrus.

In any event, the game came down to this: two on, two out, and a 1-2 count on Guerrero. That's when Hughes—finally cracking under the pressure—hung a curve that Guerrero smacked into left-center for a two-run double that put Texas up 3-1.

Robertson was called upon to keep the Yankees only a bloop-and-a-bang from tying the score. His first five offerings to Cruz were curves—a ball, two strikes, and a pair that were fouled off. Robertson's reluctance to throw Cruz a fastball was justified when he finally did unleash a 91-mph heater that Cruz blasted for a two-run HR.

Game, set, and match.

After Ian Kinsler straightened out another curve and turned it into a two-bagger, Robertson finally got David Murphy on a grounder. Robertson ended his season with another F.

Wood breezed through the bottom of the 6th but, after yielding a leadoff 2B to Young, resorted to a pair of intentional walks (the third of the game to Hamilton, and one to Cruz) before escaping at the cost of only one run scored.

The Rangers now led 6-1, giving Wood a grade of C.

Rivera mopped up the game and the season with a 1-2-3 8th inning. However, two of the outs were at-'em balls lined directly into waiting gloves.

Mo's last appearance rated a B+.

Texas 6, New York 1

Rangers win series 4-2

Bullpen diary: Robertson looked scared, and Wood was unable to command his curve. With the game out of reach, Mo didn't have his heart in his pitches.

And so, to paraphrase T.S. Eliot, the season ended not with a bang but with a whimper.

ALCS Grades

Moseley (1 appearance): 4.0 = A
Rivera (3): 3.9 = A-

Wood (4): 3.5 = B+
Chamberlain (3): 3.10 = B+
Robertson (4): 2.0 = C
Logan (3): 1.0 = D
TOTAL: 2.98 = B–; 9 A's, 5 F's

Not nearly good enough against the Rangers' aggressive, confident, fleet-footed, clutch-hitting lineup.

⚾ PITCHERS AND catchers report to Tampa in 113 days, but planning for 2011 starts tomorrow. What is the Yankees' strategy?

The Yankees' Winning Formula

Past

I don't know. I never see him. I room with a suitcase.
—PING BODIE, BABE RUTH'S ROOMMATE

When the original Yankee Stadium opened for business in 1923, it was dubbed the House That Ruth Built—because so many fans flocked to witness the Bambino hitting home runs at a record pace.

In truth, though, the Stadium should have been called the House Built for Ruth.

The contours of the playing field were explicitly fashioned to maximize the home-run power of the lefty-swinging Ruth, as well as his lefty sidekick, Lou Gehrig. The RF foul pole was situated just 295 feet from home plate. (This was changed to 296 feet in 1939.) The right-CF wall was 370 feet distant (altered to 344 in 1937).

In contrast, the LF stands were 281 feet away, but were adjusted to 301 in 1928. In left-CF, a prodigious 460-foot clout was necessary to clear the fence (reduced through the years to 457, 430, and 411). And CF was a full 461 feet away.

If the real estate encompassed by left-center and straightaway center was referred to as Death Valley, the short porch in left was enhanced by a prevailing wind tunnel, courtesy of the Harlem River, that turned flyballs pulled by lefty hitters into round-trippers.

Ruth's special gifts, and the environment that was fashioned to maximize the same, have always exerted a tremendous influence on the Yankees' game plan. To wit, lefty power hitters have always been the keystones of the Bronx Bombers' lineups.

Lefty Sluggers

Here's an alphabetical list of lefty sluggers who blasted more than 30 HRs while wearing pinstripes before 2009 and the change of venues. Included are their respective tenures with the Yanks, the number of times they equaled or exceeded 30 HRs, and their peak HR seasons.

Yogi Berra: 1939–49, exceeded 30 3X, 33 in 1941
Lou Gehrig: 1923–39, 10X, 49 in 1934 and 1936
Jason Giambi: 2002–08, 5X, 41 in 2002 and 2003
Tommy Henrich: 1937–50, once, 31 in 1941
Charlie Keller: 1939–49, 3X, 33 in 1941
Reggie Jackson: 1977–81, twice, 41 in 1980
Mickey Mantle (switch-hitter): 1951–68, 9X, 54 in 1961
Roger Maris: 1960–66, 3X, 61 in 1961
Tino Martinez: 1996–2001, 2005; 5X; 44 in 1997
Don Mattingly: 1982–95, 3X, 35 in 1985
Bobby Murcer: 1965–74, 1979–83; once; 33 in 1972
Graig Nettles: 1973–83, twice, 37 in 1978
Joe Pepitone: 1962–69, once, 31 in 1967
Babe Ruth: 1920–34, 13X, 60 in 1927

Lefty Starting Pitching

In order to *minimize* the home-run capabilities of opponents' lefty sluggers, the Yankees' tradition also included outstanding lefty starting pitchers. Here are the left-handed starters who have won 15 or more games in a season during their tenure in the old stadium, and their peak season(s):

Tommy Byrne: 1943–51, twice, 15 in 1949 and 1950
Whitey Ford: 1950–67, 10X, 25 in 1961
Lefty Gomez: 1930–42, 7X, 26 in 1934
Ron Guidry: 1975–88, 6X, 25 in 1978
Tommy John: 1979–82, 1986–89; twice; 22 in 1980
Jimmy Key: 1993–96, twice, 18 in 1993
Eddie Lopat: 1948–55, 5X, 21 in 1951
Rudy May: 1974–76, 1980–83; once; 15 in 1980
Herb Pennock: 1923–33, 6X, 23 in 1926
Fritz Peterson: 1966–74, 4X, 20 in 1970
Andy Pettitte: 1995–2003, 2007–10; 6X; 21 in 1996 and 2003
Dennis Rasmussen: 1984–87, once, 18 in 1986
David Wells: 1997–98, 2002–03; 4X; 19 in 2002

Lefty Relievers

To supplement these lefty starters, the Yankees routinely had an outstanding left reliever on call. Here are the left-handed bullpen men who compiled a 15-save season or more as Yankees:

Luis Arroyo: 1960–63, 3X, 44 in 1961
Steve Howe: 1991–96, once, 15 in 1994
Sparky Lyle: 1972–78, 5X, 35 in 1972
Joe Page: 1944–50, 3X, 27 in 1949
Dave Righetti: 1979–90, 7X, 46 in 1965

Honorable Mention: Steve Hamilton, a 6'8" one-batter specialist who featured a roundhouse curve and Folly Floater, but he rarely finished games. Mike Stanton, a versatile middle reliever and setup man, who usually gave way to either John Wetteland or Mariano Rivera to lock up the save.

Righty Relievers

The success of righty relievers like John Wetteland, Goose Gossage, and Mariano Rivera is not a contradiction of the necessity for LH relievers in the Bronx. As closers vs. situational pitchers, these guys had to face batters on both sides of the plate. The first two were just overpowering pitchers, and Mo can move his cutter in and out on both sides so beautifully.

A Word About Defense

In addition to lefty sluggers, starters, and relievers, the Yanks have traditionally sought to field exceptional defensive players. So, since the Gold Glove awards were instituted in 1957, sixty Yankees have been honored (a number that includes multiple awards and also Cano's being so honored for the first time after the 2010 season) as the best fielders at their respective positions. Interestingly, forty-six of the sixty were won by position players up the middle.

The only team with more Gold Gloves in the history of the award? The Cardinals, who are second behind the Yanks in number of World Series titles. Defense matters, clearly, and the Yanks are wise to stay focused on that.

⚾ ENOUGH ABOUT what's gone by.

What's the New York Yankees' plan for 2011 and beyond?

The Yankees' Winning Formula

Future

*Sympathy is something that shouldn't be bestowed on the Yankees.
Apparently it angers them.*

—BOB FELLER

The dimensions of the new Stadium have been made more symmetrical. From LF to RF: 318, 399, 408, 385, and 314. But most professional Yankee watchers agree that the jet stream blowing toward left is even more forceful now.

As expected, the current roster is well fortified with lefty blasters: Mark Teixeira, Robinson Cano, Curtis Granderson, and Nick Swisher. Perhaps Jorge Posada's power numbers can be revived as a DH in 2011. (To date, 189 of Posada's lifetime total of 261 HRs have been hit from the left side of the plate.)

The Yanks lack the kind of LH sluggers in the upper reaches of their farm system who could hopefully develop into big-league boppers. Of these, Juan Miranda, with his long swing, was traded. Leaving only Neil Medchill, who's still developing in the lower minors.

For the next two to three years, these traditional spots-for-success in the roster must therefore be filled via trades or free agent signings.

◗ ON THE field, Jeter, Cano, A-Rod, and Teixeira are certified Gold Glovers. Otherwise, Granderson and Gardner are also outstanding defenders among the regular players. Scranton call-up Ramiro Peña provided sure-handed defense at 3B, 2B, and SS off the bench. If he can stay healthy, Eric Chavez is a lefty power hitter who can spell A-Rod at 3B, Tex at 1B, and Posada at DH.

◗ FOR SURE, many slots in the lineup will be occupied by elderly players. However, Posada (who will turn forty in 2011) can still flourish as a mostly full-time DH and only part-time receiver. Look for Triple-A star Jesus Montero to get a shot at back-up catcher in spring training.

Jeter (thirty-seven) brings so much savvy, discipline, and Yankee pride to the mix that he's always a plus, even though his batting average went south of .300.

A-Rod's power stroke is already diminished by injuries at thirty-six, yet he remains a top-notch fielder and a dependable 35-HR, 125-RBI cleanup hitter.

Cano, Swisher, Granderson, Teixeira, and Gardner are star-quality performers. Also, sooner rather than later, Eduardo Nuñez will be ready for prime-time competition.

◗ EARLY ON, the starting pitchers were sensational while the bullpen was awful. This situation was reversed as the season progressed. That's precisely why refurbishing the entire pitching staff must be Brian Cashman's primary concern for the 2011 season.

By Christmas 2010, there were strong indications that Pettitte would retire (and he did), leaving a huge hole in the starting rotation. The Yankees offered Cliff Lee the moon, the sun, and most of the Milky Way, but the crafty lefty opted to sign with the Phillies for a couple of million hoagies.

Vazquez signed a one-year, $7 million deal with the Florida Marlins. Good riddance and caveat emptor.

After blitzing the hitters in the Dominican winter league—allowing only one run in eleven-plus innings—Ivan Nova was penciled in at the bottom end of the rotation.

Sabathia's surprise postseason knee surgery went a long ways to explain his subpar performances against the Rangers. Is the three-hundred-plus pounds that Sabathia has been carrying for lo these many seasons causing his body to break down? Or will he be pain-free and even more effective in 2011? The latter possibility seems the most reasonable.

Although Hughes' regular-season record of 18-8 was impressive, he was mostly ineffective during the second half of the regular season while getting unmercifully pounded in the ALCS. So what will be what with him?

The Yankees are thoroughly invested in developing LH starters, although for the time being youngsters like Manuel Banuelos, Jeremy Bleich, Jose Quintana, Francisco Rondon, Juan Heredia, and Juan Marcano are strictly spring-training fodder.

The Yankees' fallback plan was to ink a number of post-surgical pitchers who had once enjoyed various degrees of success: RH Buddy Carlyle, who last season pitched to a 3.59 ERA and averaged 8.5 strikeouts per nine innings in Japan; and Freddie Garcia, who went 12-6 with the Chisox with a 4-plus ERA that's the norm these days. Another low-risk guy who can hopefully finesse his way through six innings.

But the most interesting of these maimed signees was Mark Prior, who suffered a sore arm despite being celebrated for his perfect delivery. Prior to his recent Tommy John surgery, Prior was an eighteen-game winner for the Cubs in 2003. After not pitching in the bigs since 2006, Prior's latest comeback featured a 2010 stint in the independent Golden Baseball League, where he pitched a total of nine innings in relief, striking out twenty-two of the fourty-four hitters he faced, plus five scoreless innings for the Texas Rangers' Triple-A team.

Prior reported that his fastball was back up to 92 mph, but he doubted that he had the endurance to return as a starter. With Kerry Wood signing with the Cubs, Prior could have conceivably mounted a serious challenge to both Chamberlain and Robertson to become Mo's setup man.

Until, that is, the Yanks signed Rafael Soriano to both set-up and eventually replace Mo. This particular move makes the Yankees' bullpen the strongest in the league.

A.J. Burnett is an expensive albatross. Scouts claim that Burnett's problems can be rectified if his release point is altered: "With his slightly lower than three-quarters delivery, Burnett's fastball too often leaks back over the plate when he pitches to right-handed hitters. Elevating his delivery would provide more hop on his pitches and solve the problem. But, can Burnett make such a drastic alteration?" Let's see what Larry Rothschild can do.

IT SHOULD be noted that Girardi had been a catcher for the Cubs when Rothschild was Chicago's pitching coach. Clearly, Rothschild—whose MLB career included seven games with the Tigers in 1981 and 1982—is the Skipper's man. To further demonstrate his qualifications, Rothschild also aced a "test" that Cashman gave to him, Harkey, and Triple-A pitching coach Scott Aldred; Rothschild, like the others, broke down eight hours of film on the Yankee pitchers and, unlike the others, had the most to offer by way of the things he'd do with their techniques. And he lives in Tampa.

A QUICK look at some interesting developments in Arizona late in 2010:

Baseball fans are familiar with the Caribbean, Venezuelan, and Mexican winter leagues, but since 1992, MLB has organized the Arizona Fall League, where two or three prospects per major league team go to refine their skills and play in front of scouts. Thirty games are played in a packed schedule between mid-October and mid-November.

Since '92, the likes of Derek Jeter, Roy Halladay, Todd Helton, Jimmy Rollins, Albert Pujols, Torii Hunter, Alfonso Soriano, David Wright, and two dozen other future MLB stars came through this fall league.

Six teams are formed from the various player pools, and Don Mattingly coached the Phoenix Desert Dogs against the Mesa Solar Sox, Scottsdale Scorpions, Surprise (formerly Grand Canyon) Rafters, Peoria Javelinas, and Peoria Saguaros. This year, the Desert Dogs drew from the rosters of the Yanks, Braves, Marlins, Dodgers, and A's.

The Yankees sent catcher Austin Romine, third baseman Brandon Laird (looking to add outfield skills to his résumé), and pitcher Manny Banuelos, and the talk of fall 2010's games were the Nats' top draft choice, Bryce Harper—and Banuelos.

Manny is a 5'10" (short by Yankee standards) left-handed pitcher from Mexico and, according to *Baseball America*, is the sixth highest-rated prospect in the entire Yankee minor league system. He missed time early in 2010 due to an appendectomy, but he's bounced back with a mid-90s fastball and decent curve and change. He'll start the 2011 season with the Trenton Thunder.

A NOTE about the outlook for other teams in 2011:

Within the division, the Red Sox have reloaded, as always, but their starting pitching is suspect. Papelbon had a bummer season and, since he was often superseded by Daniel Bard, he could be traded. The Rays lost key players to free agency. The O's could continue to improve under Showalter, and the Jays got Boston's pitching coach, John Farrell, as their new manager.

Elsewhere in the AL, the Twins are scary if all healthy, at bat and in the bullpen. And the Rangers, the Rangers . . . they lost out on Cliff Lee, too.

NL-wise, it looks like the Phils and Giants are the most balanced, talented teams. The Phils are fast and strong, and Lidge seems to be back to form. The Giants are clutch at the plate and have great starting pitching, and we all saw Brian Wilson close it out, he of the oddly fake-looking beard and the fifth-fastest recorded pitch in MLB history.

⚾ HERE'S WHAT a scout believes to be the best way for the Yankees to reclaim the championship in 2011 and beyond:

> Posada has one more year on his contract. Make him the DH [done!] and let him loose after the 2011 season. To replace Posada behind the plate, sign free agent John Buck. [In mid-November he agreed to a free agent contract with Milwaukee, but then the Yanks went out and got Russell Martin.] Cervelli is a third-string catcher, and Montero can hit but is incapable of handling a big-time pitching staff. Use Austin Romine as backup with the plan of eventually having Romine take over.
>
> After Posada is gone, make A-Rod the full-time DH, move Jeter to third, and install Nuñez at short.
>
> As far as their pitching staff is concerned, I'd go hard after Rafael Soriano, make him the setup guy and sometimes closer, with the understanding that he'd succeed Rivera. [Done!]
>
> I'd trade Chamberlain and Swisher for a backend starter and a long reliever. To replace Swisher, I'd then break the bank to sign Carl Crawford [who opted for the Bosox]. Here's the lineup I'd want for 2011—Crawford, Granderson, and Gardner in the outfield. The infield would be the same as in 2010. Martin behind the plate and Posada and Thames splitting the DH slot.
>
> With an augmented pitching staff that includes at least another top-notch starter and Soriano, the Yankees would totally dominate baseball for the foreseeable future. All it

would take is guts and money, something the Yankees have always been famous for having.

Bullpen Diary

Here's what the Yankee bullpen might look like in 2011.

Mariano Rivera will be forty-one and, whereas he usually suffers through one bad stretch during the season, he underwent two of these periods in 2010. Somehow Mo will continue to perform at a Hall of Fame level for at least two more years.

The Yankees refused to pick up Kerry Wood's $11 million team option for 2011 as being too high a price for a bridge man. Added to the mix is Wood's desire to be a closer, an option effectively off the table with Mo's return. Soriano is a huge improvement over Wood.

Although he wore down in the latter part of the season, Boone Logan is another keeper. However, it was imperative that another lefty be added to the relief corps. Cashman came through, getting Pedro Feliciano, a durable curveballer from the Mets.

Contrary to what Damaso Marte and the Yankee organization have repeatedly insisted, throwing across his body does—and did—cause Marte's arm problems. After postseason surgery, Marte was not expected to return to action any time during the 2011 campaign.

When Royce Ring was optioned to Scranton after the ALCS, he refused to report and thereby became a free agent. Jonathan Albaladejo was granted his release so that he could sign with the Yomiuri Giants of Japan—for $1.9 million!

Mark Melancon was traded to Houston and Dustin Moseley to San Diego.

In a sad development, Alfredo "Ace" Aceves broke his collarbone in a motorcycle accident in Mexico and was not offered a new contract by the Yanks, but the Bosox did.

Despite Chad Gaudin's lowball contract, he did next to nothing to prove that he can be counted on and has no chance of wearing the pinstripes again.

Among the other 2010 survivors, Sergio Mitre was re-signed for the year at $900,000 plus incentives. He's the prime candidate for the fifth starting slot if, as is expected, Pettitte stays retired, and if the resurrection of another late signee, Bartolo Colon, fails. The off-season plan also included giving Ivan Nova a full shot at a starting role.

Joba Chamberlain was plagued by the same old bugaboos that have cropped up since his sensational rookie season (2008): profound inconsistency, laborious delivery, and a propensity for making mistakes up in the strike zone. The fact that he was a spare part during the playoffs indicated just how unreliable the Yankees deemed him to be.

Since Chamberlain could still command a worthy return, the Yankees should seek to trade him.

The Yanks will also give righties Ivan Nova and Romulo Sanchez another good look this spring. The only lefty minor league relievers considered to be live prospects are Gavin Brooks and Melvin Crousett.

The case of David Robertson is also a tricky one. Except for a lengthy period in midseason (along with a few grade-A appearances in the playoffs), Robertson was rarely the dominant force he was expected to be. However, he's still young (twenty-five) and highly coachable, and his delivery is smooth enough for Rothschild to successfully tinker with.

⚾ So, AS the pain of the 2010 ALCS erases the joy of the 2009 championship, the Yankees' mantra might be a variation of the old Brooklyn Dodgers' annual lament, "Wait till this year."

My Stadium Misadventure

Stickball, basketball, and avoiding getting beat up were my preoccupations growing up on Fulton Avenue in the Bronx in the sixties. Even so, after the conclusion of my sophomore season playing hoops for Hunter College, I still had a jones for some organized athletic competition, and I needed an excuse to avoid studying. So I tried out for the baseball team.

Up to this point, the closest I'd come to throwing a baseball in competition was to fire a Spaldeen in hopes of hitting the rectangular strike zone chalked onto a handball court wall in Crotona Park. For sure, I was fast and I was wild, but I was also fearless. There were no store-bought stickball bats available back then; we used broomsticks that we'd steal from wherever we could. These ersatz bats were thinner than the modern mass-produced versions—and the smaller hitting surface made any kind of solid connection with my blazers a rarity.

I soon discovered that I was just as fast—and just as wild—when throwing a real baseball off a mound. Hunter College's coach was Charlie Irace, a wonderful guy who had hit .325 during his one season with the Toledo Mud Hens in the Red Sox farm system. Unfortunately, his chances to ever become a major leaguer were dashed when he enlisted in the army immediately after Pearl Harbor.

But Coach Irace still loved to hit. He'd take batting practice along with the rest of the team, wowing us with his ability to spray line drives all over the field. And I made the final cut after I struck him out during an intrasquad game.

My first appearance in a ball game occurred at home against St. Francis of Brooklyn. I was sent to the mound to start the 7th inning with Hunter theoretically safely ahead by a score of 18-1. I went to a full count on the leadoff batter before he whiffed on a fastball that cut the heart of the plate. I was pumped! *Yes!* I was unhittable! Faster than Bob Feller, Bob Turley, Herb Score. Save some wall space for me in Cooperstown, gang.

Then as now, the standard procedure after a bases-empty strike-out that didn't end an inning was for the catcher to throw the ball to the third baseman to be whipped around the infield before being returned to the pitcher. Instead, the catcher pegged the ball back at me. Taken completely by surprise, I had to make a ducking, twisting catch to avoid getting hit in the face. I'll claim now that this threw my composure completely off.

After walking the next two hitters, I induced a right-handed batter to hit a meek groundball right at first baseman Ollie Mc-Donald. Even though he fielded the ball a mere two steps from the bag, even though there was one out and we were ahead by seventeen runs, Ollie decided to try for the double play—and wound up throwing the ball over the shortstop's head and into left field.

Not only did I fail to finish the game, I didn't finish the inning. In fact, I never got another out. My procession of walks was interrupted only by two hit batsmen.

Finally, with the score 18-10, Coach Irace told me, "You're gonna hurt somebody," as he mercifully pulled me from the game. I was so disheartened that I quit the team.

I stuck to basketball my junior year, but I gave the baseball team another try my senior year. I hadn't picked up a ball since the St. Francis debacle, but for some mysterious reason my control was slightly better. Very slightly, but sufficiently improved for Coach Irace to use me in relief against Fordham.

We had a 2-0 lead, the bases were loaded, and there was one out. I struck out the first batter with a lightning bolt of a fastball, but that was followed by a wild pitch that brought a run home and made the score 2-1. Then came a walk, and finally an infield pop-up to end (and save) the game.

I made one more appearance that year, a start against C. W. Post, where I notched two shutout innings—the highlight being striking out Richie Scheinblum (who would go on to an eight-year career in the bigs, hitting exactly .300 for the Royals in 1972). But the weather forecast was for rain and the sky was getting darker with every pitch. So when I walked the first two batters I faced in the bottom of the 3rd, I was yanked from the game. Our reliever proceeded to walk the next four batters, it never rained, and we lost by 6-1.

My college career ended with my registering a total record of 0-1, one save, and an ERA that approached infinity.

⚾ So, IMAGINE my surprise when a year later I received an invitation in the mail to attend a tryout at Yankee Stadium.

The tryout invitation was also a surprise to Coach Irace, but he helped get me ready. The Hunter College equipment room was locked for the summer, so Coach lent me his own minor league uniform, and I borrowed a pair of size-13 spikes from a teammate.

"You can't go there wearing dungarees and sneakers," he said. "You have to look like a player or they won't take you seriously."

I may have looked like a ballplayer when I arrived at the Stadium, but barely. I was six inches taller than Coach and my own pedal extremities were size 15. I used several large safety pins to secure my shirttails to my pants and I walked as if my feet were broken. Fortunately, only the nonpitchers were forced to run timed sprints.

Ah, the hallowed ground of the old Yankee Stadium, with its expanse of fair territory shaped like a slice of Wonder Bread. The flagpole straightaway in Death Valley. The immortals' plaques at the base of the bleacher wall. The grandstand roof overhung with a cold iron bunting. And the folded seats resembling rows and rows of blue tombstones.

After the pitching prospects warmed up by playing catch with one another, we took turns throwing to a battery of barrel-bellied coaches in Yankee uniforms. The coach who caught me wore number 89 and he crouched behind a portable home plate situated in foul territory about fifteen feet from where the real home plate was. As always, I was as wild as a hurricane, but he caught everything I threw. And I sure was fast that day. My best pitches hit his glove with good, loud thumps.

Most of the other pitching hopefuls threw for about ten minutes, but my inspection lasted nearly a half hour. I was pumped. I didn't care that all of my toenails were bleeding. I almost didn't feel the opened safety pins piercing my skin.

"You got a good arm, kid," the coach said. "Just wait there a minute."

He conferred with several colleagues and presently an old man in a stiff blue suit stepped gingerly out of the Yankees dugout. Being a loyal citizen of the Bronx, I recognized him as Johnny Johnston, head of the Yanks' farm system. Johnston assumed a front-row seat in the grandstands behind and to the right of Coach 89. He folded his hands over the top rail and squinted at me from under his straw hat.

This was it! My chance for greatness.

By now, my shoulder was aching, so I wound up slowly, closed my eyes—and tried to throw a 200-mph fastball.

Before my eyes reopened, I heard the ricochets echoing throughout the majestic ballpark.

And there was Johnston, sprawled beneath his seat, his hat rolling toward first base. The coach looked at me and held his hands to show I had missed the old man by inches.

"That'll be all, son," the coach said. "We've seen enough."

Afterward, we were given free lunches: a pint-sized carton of milk and two slices of white bread wrapped around an official sliver of bologna. I'll never forget showering and dressing in the Yankee clubhouse. Where Babe Ruth soaped his belly. Where the Mick put his pants on one leg at a time.

I'd never make the bigs and I limped for a month. I still have several pinpoint scars on my waist to remind me of the last pitch that I ever threw.

Memory Lane

All the Way Home

Play it? Man, that was my game. I liked to play punchball
more than anything else.
—ROCKY COLAVITO

We always played punchball in the street, and because our field
was bounded on one side by Crotona Park, the ground rules were
explicit: Any balls punched into the right-field trees or the park
were out. Balls hit past the third-base lamppost and up against the
left-field line of buildings were in play. Any flyball caught off a
building or a parked car was out. Any ball coming to rest inside a
second-floor fire escape was a ground-rule double, a third-floor fire
escape was a triple, and any higher fire escape was a homer.

(A brief explanation for any non-city readers: punchball doesn't
require a pitcher or catcher, as the batter simply tosses the ball up in
front of himself and then swats it with his fist.)

We played with a first and third baseman who could practically
shake hands across the narrow two-lane infield. Since Fulton Avenue
was a one-way thoroughfare running from home plate toward
second base, the infielders were responsible for calling, "Time out!
Car!"

The second sacker straddled a sewer cover and the lone outfielder usually roamed the sidewalk. Most of the time, Scar was a brave-handed first baseman—and his offensive game plan was to angle hot grounders through the infield and under parked cars for extra bases.

But, in the absence of a catcher, the most important ground rule stipulated that should a thrown ball beat the runner home, the runner was out.

Weeli was a steadfast Yankee fan, whose favorite pinstriped player was Mickey Mantle. And like his hero, Weeli's plan of attack was to hit prodigious home runs.

"There it goes!" Weeli yelped as he blasted the Spaldeen high and far toward a home-run fire escape. "I'm the Mick!" he shouted, even as the ball bounced off the railing and was caught by Moe for a spectacular out.

In truth, Weeli was somewhat relieved that his clout was caught, only because any ball snagged in a fire escape required the puncher to retrieve the ball. This meant a dangerous climb on rickety ladders and stairs from the street up or the roof down.

Sometimes the designated retriever was saved when the ball landed in Dr. Klorman's second-story fire escape, where a window opened and a fat arm reached out and snatched the precious ball.

"Go play in the park!" Klorman would scream. "Look what I'm doing!" With a scalpel, he would slice the ball along the seam, then toss the useless halves back into the street. "I'll call the police! I'll throw hot water on you!"

"Go back to sleep!" was Weeli's clever rejoinder, and we each chipped in two cents for a new Spaldeen.

🏐 IT WAS the bottom of the ninth, the last game before supper. Scar was up with two outs and Weeli was the potential winning run on second base. Slowly, Scar bounced the ball, approaching his rhythm, studying the defense. Moe played a shallow outfield, daring Scar to hit one deep off the buildings. Scar finally rocked back and tossed the ball shoulder-high, then a sidewinding fist socked the ball on a line off the bottom edge of Klorman's fire escape. The ball ricocheted sharply off an old Ford, then bounced high over Moe's head for a base hit.

Meanwhile, Weeli was chugging toward third base with his elbows held slightly behind his ribs and pumping in short high strokes just the way his hero ran the bases. "I'm even faster than the Mick!" Weeli shouted as he rounded third. But Moe made a quick recovery and fired the ball toward home plate.

Just then, a green Buick zoomed up Devil's Hill and turned too swiftly up Fulton Avenue. Moe's throw, the winning run, and the Buick converged on home plate.

"Time out!" somebody yelled. "Car!" But in the excitement of the play, his dire warning was ignored.

For an instant, Weeli flashed into the driver's eyes, but the poor guy was too astounded to hit the brakes. With the ball gaining on him, Weeli dove for home, hoping to roll on his right shoulder and so avoid the oncoming car.

Crunch!

The collision was noisy and messy. The blood came from several relatively minor gashes on Weeli's side, and the acute angle of his right forearm clearly indicated a nasty fracture. Indeed, as was the periodic fate of his hero, Weeli would wind up on the injured list for several weeks.

But meanwhile, the outcome of the game was still in doubt.

"He's out!"

"You're crazy! He's safe!"

Acknowledgments

There are so many to thank. I'll start with Jason Zillo, the Yankees public relations director, for his professionalism and invaluable assistance.

Others in the Yankee organization to whom I owe a large debt of gratitude include Mark Newman, Nardi Contreras, Dave Eiland, Roman Rodriguez, and Mike Harkey. Also David Robertson, Alfredo Aceves, Boone Logan, Joba Chamberlain, and Chan Ho Park.

In Scranton, my thanks are extended to PR director Mike Vander Woude and to Josh Horton, his invaluable intern. Plus Jason Hirsh, Jonathan Albaladejo, Ivan Nova, and Rumulo Sanchez for their interesting and illuminating testimonies.

Thanks also to Joe Ausanio and Tom House.

As a stranger to the inside delights of pitching, I can't express sufficient appreciation for the numerous current and onetime major league pitching coaches, as well as the legion of veteran advance scouts, who spoke to me trusting that I would protect their identities. Thanks, guys.

Still another perpetual debt goes to Helen Zimmermann, agent extraordinaire.

And a year of extra-inning thanks to my editor, Carl Lennertz, a lapsed Mets and Sox fan with a heart as big as old Yankee Stadium's centerfield.

Back to Scranton, the following employees of HarperCollins' distribution center participated in a *Bullpen Diaries* contest and the winners went to the Scranton game that I wrote about: Mark Harchar, Joe Warrick, Candee Zippi, Sarah Corey, Laura Battle (who also knew about the "secret" baseball mud), Laura Hughes, Marcy Stanton, Sharon Magnotta, David Walline, Olga Nolan, Bud Zondervan, Barbara Judge, Lucy Lapczynski, and Judith Maier.

Thanks to Martin Abramowitz of Jewish Major Leaguers, Inc., a baseball history organization documenting American Jews in America's Game; see cool sets of baseball cards at jewishmajorleaguers.org. And to John Zeck, for reminding me that Larry Sherry also pitched to his brother Norm, as did Koufax.

In addition, several printed sources were consulted and quoted, including:

Red Christian, "From Humble Beginnings Mariano Rivera Becomes the Greatest Closer in MLB History," New York *Daily News*, March 13, 2010. This was my primary source for Rivera's biographical material.

A quote on Rivera's hand position as he releases his cutter comes from "Mariano Saves," *Sports Illustrated*, October 5, 2009.

Some pertinent anecdotes came from Bob Cairns' *Pen Men* (St. Martin's Press, NY, 1992).

I found some wonderful quotes in Paul Dickson's *Baseball's Greatest Quotations* (Collins, NY, 2008).

To supplement Bob Feller's remembrance of the motorcycle event, I consulted his *Little Black Book of Baseball Wisdom* (McGraw-Hill, NY, 2001).

Historical stats came from John Thorn, Pete Palmer, Michael Gershman, and David Pietrusza's *Total Baseball*, Sixth Edition (Total Sports, NY, 1999).

Many thanks for the player photos from fresh new perspectives taken by Rachel Hood, Amanda Rykoff, Michael Baron, T.J. Perreira, Wally Gobetz, Keith Allison, and the Game Five Larsen ticket photo from James Grillo.

And to Marcus Opsal, for building BullpenDiaries.com, where I'll be posting more about Bronx dreams and pinstripe legends.